PERSPECTIVES ON

INDIA'S INTERNATIONAL RELATIONS

PERSPECTIVES ON
INDIA'S INTERNATIONAL RELATIONS

Kedar S. Arya

AKANSHA PUBLISHING HOUSE
NEW DELHI - 110 002 (INDIA)

AKANSHA PUBLISHING HOUSE
4649/21-B, Ansari Road
Daryaganj, New Delhi - 110 002
Phones: 23263193, 9811582579
E-mail: ektabooks@yahoo.com

Perspectives on India's International Relations

First Published, 2006

ISBN 81-8370-071-3

PRINTED IN INDIA

Published by M.P. Misra for Akansha Publishing House, New Delhi - 110 002 and Printed at Capital Offset Press, Delhi

To

All Freedom Fighters,

Statesmen & Architects of

India's Foreign Policy

this book is humbly dedicated.

Contents

Preface

> Nationalism is an infantile disease. It is the measles of mankind.
>
> —*Dr. Albert Einstein*

> The difference between a river and a swamp is that a river is confined within banks, while a swamp is not . . . Because a river is confined, and channeled, it has life. It is a mighty, moving, living thing. Because a swamp has no restrictions, it becomes thin and stagnant. ... In our modern life we boast of freedom. We want life without restrictions and without confinement. Only we forget that such living becomes stagnant.
>
> —*Leonard Cochran*

In case of India's foreign policy, sometimes it is said that it has baffled many people, irritated an even greater number and left a trail of confusion among her immediate well-wishers. No doubt, the policy pursued during the last few decades has contributed in some measure to the strengthening of international cooperation and maintenance of regional as well as world peace but it has proved fatal in some respects.

In fact, the formulation of foreign policy is inconceivable without giving a predominant role to the interplay of national interests. The foreign policy of a nation is a complex and dynamic political course which it adopts in relation to other States which must include the prevailing pattern of its interests as well as principles and ideals in its conduct towards other States. However, factors governing the formulation of foreign policy are not similar to those precise, well-out stones which can be handled like single bricks in the construction of an edifice.

The basic constituents of national interest, however, remain more or less constant and these would include security against aggression, the desirability of increasing the level of living standards of masses and the maintenance of stable conditions around the periphery of its borders. The achieving of these objectives cannot be accomplished without the driving force of ideas and thus every foreign policy inevitably contains traces of ideology though the task of statesmanship lies in arriving at a balanced integration between idealism and practical considerations as represented by strategic and geo-political considerations, the necessity of attracting economic aid as well as in scanning the prevailing alignment of political force on the international horizon. There need be no conflict between such general objects as world peace, abolition of racial discrimination, disarmament and the specific national interests. In fact the two may have complimentary role to play. Idealism without the kernel of self-interest may sound hypocritical and hallow, whereas total concentration on self-interest may result in the loss of wider avenues of support from the international community. For example, our national security is better served by maintaining cooperative links with our immediate neighbours. Clearly then the national interests of India should take into account the interests of these nations. By narrowing the concept of national interest to its own country, a government may lose friends and possible allies in strategic areas in times of crisis. The concept of national interest has to be continuously broadened since a narrower interpretation is likely to harm than help the achievement of the objectives.

Again, injection of ideological fervour in the conduct of

foreign relations also help in galvanizing an apathetic nation to greater and more sustained endeavours to achieve a faster rate of socio-economic progress. In analyzing the role of ideas Professor Cantwell Smith has said that ideology must precede technology to accelerate the process of modernizing and he quotes the example of the Soviet Union grasping the importance of ideology and using it to reap full advantage of technological inventions. However, in blending ideas with a policy care should be taken to avoid dogmatism or fanaticism because fanatics are more interested in imposing solutions than in illuminating choices. Speaking in 1949 Nehru counselled: "The world is a very diverse place and I see no reason why we should regiment it along one line......We have no particular despire to convert other people to any view or thought". In consonance with this trend of thinking of Nehru, India while trying to judge each vexatious international issue on its merits, has invariably avoided legalistic-moralistic approach in her relations with other nations.

As in the context of current time i.e., the 21st century, diplomatic international relations are determined on the counts of: economic interests, national security and terrorism.

Remarkably at global level, the priorities may be different tan in the case of neighbouring countries. India's relations with Pakistan and China are well known and have attracted worldwide discussion and debate. We have chosen here only rather small neighbours like Afghanistan, Nepal, Bangladesh, Bhutan and Sri Lanka. No doubt, the small issues become bigger and if peace and regional stability is disturbed the progress and development process will be hampered.

In the context of international relations, this book

specifically focuses on the following: Dynamics of Indian Foreign Policy; India and Nepal; India and Bhutan; India and Afghanistan; India and Sri Lanka; and India and Bangladesh etc. A glossary of relevant terms is added feature.

The readings, contained in this volume are substantially derived from the writings and views of many eminent diplomats, policy makers, politicians and statesmen. We are deeply beholden to them all. Our intention being to disseminate widely through this organ the well-publicised views of our veterans in the field. We equally owe a deep sense of gratitude to various magazines, newspapers, editors and their copyright holders for drawing upon them. Finally, we are grateful to our publishers for undertaking the publication of this work.

—K.S.A.

CHAPTER 1

Dynamics of Indian Foreign Policy

> Next to knowing when to seize an opportunity, the most important thing in life is to know when to forego an advantage.
>
> —*Benjamin Disraeli*

In fact, immediately after Independence India has a difficult task to shape the foreign policy. NAM, encompasses the soul of our international relations. Changing world order brought many changes in our diplomacy and foreign relations. From Nehru to Manmohan Singh, we have traversed a long path.

In fact, the collapse of USSR changed the world scenario and consequent American domination on World politics changed all equations. Sometme pro-Russia, we are gradually leaning to the US. Globalisation, liberalization and economic reforms have paved the way of India's becoming an economic giant. Gradually priorities on diplomatic front are changing.

The present chapter gives a vivid account of dynamics of Indian foreign policy in post-cold war era. Though equations change now and then frequently, here we come across various crucial determining factors before us. The views expressed hereinafter are substantially based on one of India's renowned diplomat and politician.

India has every reason to feel proud of the way Indian democracy has consolidated itself in this half a century and the way our system is prospering. At the same time, in these years, we have also built some legacies, and the legacies are the foreign policies which were started by the great Nehru whose name we hold in great reverence. So far as the historical growth of this nation is concerned, the legacy was trying to correlate itself to what was going to happen in twenty-first century itself. In the post-Cold War era, several new challenges are emerging before the world. The world order, which some powers are trying to spell out after the Cold War, is posing challenges for us.

Hegemonism is once again confronting us. Those who think that they have the power to build the new order, have a great deal of disdain for all of us; they have disdain for the Developing World, they have disdain for those who were not there in their midst when they were trying to build their own nations and, therefore, they were trying to build up some exclusive system for themselves. There were several forums, several exclusive clubs. One exclusive club was the Club P-7, comprising those who were nuclear weapon powers. There was another exclusive club which went by the name G-7 and it was a club of those who wanted to dominate through economic strength. But these powers, who were trying to monopolise a new world order, were also seeing that there were differences amongst themselves.

For instance, the discussion that was going on in the European Security Conference in Lisbon, the unanimity that they were trying to present was no more available. We saw the Russian Prime Minister Viktor Chernomyrdin reject the view of the type of disarmament the others were spelling out. He said 'that enlargement of the North Atlantic

Treaty Organisation would create a new and dangerous faultline between East and West at a time when the Continent should be striving to heal the old breach'. He also added: 'It is not clear that the appearance of a new dividing line would not lead to the worsening of the whole geo-political situation'. All the same, in some areas we have noticed that when it came to us, they presented a different type of unity often at our cost.

Therefore, when we think in terms of nuclear powers, we should also think in terms of the attitude they have about the non-nuclear powers. They are powerful people; they wanted that all forums and all institutions which were built with effort ever since decolonization began, and ever since the new countries were becoming free, the platforms that they had built, should be demolished. One such platform was the NAM platform. Several people referred to NAM as being irrelevant. That was exactly what these powers wanted us to believe and we would be playing in their hands, if we start to feel that G-5 is relevant, G-7 is relevant or the P-5 is relevant but NAM is not. Often we have been exposed to the various types of theories which they were trying to present to us--I mean the powerful ones--which were actually the treaties which were taking the countries of the world in one direction. It was a charade. One such charade was the NPT. Another charade was what was called the CTBT. Who defined these treaties? The NPT was signed. We did not sign it. India refused for correct principled reasons. We felt it was an unequal treaty. We felt it was something which did not really mean to stop proliferation. Who defined it? Who performed the tests? Those very people who had signed the treaties started testing again almost the day after signing the treaty. The same was the case with CTBT. Who defined the CTBT? This had to be kept in mind all the time. Therefore, when we think in terms of a nuclear power, we should keep in mind this angle that the deception of CTBT and NPT was something which had been inflicted on us. Consider what is happening to our industrial economy. All those who were trying to give us a new economic order, were trying to spell it in the name of the Dunkel Award. We had discussed the Dunkel Award at length in our Parliament and also the WTO's new constitution. We had our doubts and our suspicions.

When we examined GATT, we said that though we were joining it, we would always be vigilant. The Government of India's Cabinet had taken a decision that so far as our vital interests were concerned, if any non-trade elements were being introduced, India would take a firm stand on that. When we talk in terms of the CTBT or when we talk in terms of the NPT or the economy or anything, the foremost interest that we have to safeguard is our own interest and that interest-- is an enlightened self-interest--we know, is our future and, therefore, when we take a stand we abide by it. It was in this context, therefore, that whenever the issue of the CTBT arose we tried to see the writing on the wall where our legacy beckons us to respond, to preserve our Independence, preserve the independence of the Indian foreign policy and face with courage and fortitude all those challenges we were faced with. We are not an arrogant nation. We have never wanted confrontation. In the last fifty years or so various Prime Ministers have occupied these benches from Jawaharlal Nehru onwards.

One of the things which is always evident is India's grit to stand up when challenges are posed before her. In this context, therefore, when we reacted to the CTBT we were reacting in the correct sense. When unitedly we refused to sign the CTBT, therein lay the power of India's glory. Yet many people told us that we would be isolated. Many pressures tried to influence us and yet we did not bend. At the same time, we kept in mind the fact that we all knew that there was a price for this defiance. Defiance was not going to be tolerated by those who had arrogance of power and wanted to spell out a new world order which was very different from our own vision. Therefore, they first tried to degrade us and then pressurise us. Pressures in the modern times, are never direct. There are a lot of hidden hands which are working all the time. These hidden hands have only one objective and that is to break the unity which the defiant nations exhibit. How did they do it? By sapping our morale first. The CTBT, as laid down in the United Nations, said that there was a three-year period in which we must sign before the 'Entry into Force' clause becomes operative. In these three years, several things could have happened. One of those things which was happening was dangling of carrots and also wielding of the rod and the rod also manifests itself in many forms. Why did we lose the Security Council seat? Was it not a 'punishment? Was it not a rod that was being shown to us? Ultimately, when we have made up our minds, when the nation has made up its mind that it is not going to compromise on such issues, then, whatever comes in our way, we will take and we will take it with dignity.

The media propaganda is coming from outside. And now, in the modern sense, when the electronic media has become so powerful, that is where the response cannot come from the Government alone. The response can come from all of us together that we would not let an atmosphere prevail in the country that the media, insider or outsider, can cause confusion in our minds.

A nation cannot be defended with weak nerves. The safeguarding of a nation's interest needs more courage. When we are fighting a battle, we cannot ensure that every victory will be ours. Basically, what was the mandate? The mandate was, to stand up with dignity. The mandate was to preserve the dignity of the Parliament and its legacy regardless of the fact whether we get a temporary seat or a permanent seat on the UN Security Council. Efforts were being made to see that India did not get a permanent seat. Several formulae were going around. One such formula was, while Japan and Germany would be admitted, the rest would be considered later. From the very beginning it was a fight against Japan. We knew that it was a powerful nation. From the very beginning we knew that Japan's resources were far larger than ours. The Government preceding our's decided to contest the decision. When we came into office, the preceding Government wrote to me and it is on record that we should not withdraw. We were often asked whether India should lead NAM or whether it should not do so. Leadership is not contesting elections alone; leadership is not asking for garlands.

Real leadership surfaces at the time of difficulty when you have to take a stand. It was a proud moment when instead of just three we had forty nations supporting our decision regarding the CTBT and our claim to be awarded a non-permanent seat on the Security Council. I would like to repeat that three of the five nuclear-power States saw it advantageous to support us. The nation's interest is above everything. Therefore, when we fought the election, we fought with open eyes. The option was not between winning and losing. The option was between either withdrawing or contesting. As far as foreign policy was concerned, we were trying to involve all the parties in every forum. To every forum we send a composite delegation. If we had started having a partisan attitude, it would not have sustained us. There was a shift in the policy of China. I was quite conscious of the fact that the situation was such that our territory was in their possession.

There was no doubt about that. That is what we were trying to discuss with them. There are always two options in the world--either go to war or discuss. And we had chosen for good reasons to discuss. Gradually, we were moving in one direction and that direction had not been built only by me; it had been built by several people. In 1976, when Atal Behari Vajpayee went to Beijing, he was building in that direction as well. In 1988, when Rajiv Gandhi went there, he made some inroads. Narasimha Rao did the same thing. And now we were trying to do the same and therein lies the real greatness of this country, that with the change of governments we do not change policies and directions of policies. That did not mean that we were rigid or stagnant; it did not mean that we did not take into account all the changes that were confronting us. Mr Jyoti Basu did not go to Bangladesh to negotiate a treaty. He had not finalized any arrangement. I think it is a great strength of India that in this democratic system, we use all parties, all our forces, whenever we need them in a particular given situation.

It is primarily because we feel that when the question of the nation comes, we are all one. If Jyoti Basu's going to Bangladesh could help us in smoothening differences, why not? We are all Indians. We are all patriots. We are all committed to India's interests and, therefore, we all have to act together. The Indian foreign policy was taken a step further when all the SAARC Foreign Ministers met in India to discuss as to how we could go further on South

Asian Preferential Trade Agreement (SAPTA) South Asian Free Trade Agreement (SAFTA) and on other political questions. The vision of SAFTA was before us. The credit of constructing SAFTA goes to the government in power before us.

It has been the good luck of India and again by the previous government's efforts, we were able to have the full dialogue partnership with the countries on the other side, i.e. the ASEAN countries. We were also trying to build our regional cooperation. We were trying to work closely with the ASEAN countries and the Asian Regional Forum (ARF). On the other side, we were constructing our relationship in the Indian Ocean region, fourteen countries of the Indian Ocean region, i.e. from Australia, Africa, including two countries of ASEAN were forming an association. These fourteen nations' combination were trying to build a common market. We have a number of reasons to be proud of our cooperation with South Africa. South Africa is also a part of the Indian Ocean Rim countries and a part of NAM. I have had the privilege of talking to the Deputy President of South Africa. He reiterated his firm faith in the NAM movement and he said that they wanted to host the next NAM summit in South Africa.

NAM must never be looked at, in those terms that the Western powers want us to look at it. In Afghanistan, the Taliban was reigning. We have to ask ourselves that who were helping the Taliban? Taliban did not drop from the sky. They were from some country. They were trained in some country. They acquired arms from some country. They had been sustained by some countries. And the identity of those countries are pretty obvious to all of us. We knew who was doing the damage. And India had to stand up. India's stand in this situation has been different, not due to a fault of ours but because of the nature of the events. The Minister of Agriculture came to my rescue when I was not well and he went to Teheran to attend the first conference held there regarding Afghanistan.

The role that he played was very commendable, he upheld India's tradition. That also helped to project that the foreign policy was not the monopoly of the Foreign Minister. All of us were a part of it. India's policy regarding Pakistan is not polemical. Pakistan has been trying to isolate us but contrarily, has been getting itself isolated. That is why when Benazir Bhutto, former Prime Minister of Pakistan spoke in the United Nations, I did not respond to her. I did not want to enter into polemical problems because that did not serve any purpose. It is only a sheer pretense. I was asked to snap diplomatic relations with Pakistan. It was not a correct approach.

Even in 1962, when we had that unfortunate incident in relation to China, we did not close our embassy. Embassies, basically, are our ears and eyes. They are more important in adverse circumstances than in helpful situations. It is very easy to withdraw and bring everyone back home and keep them at safe distances from very difficult spots. But it's important that when the circumstances are difficult, our missions should be there. We explained our position regarding CTBT repeatedly. I had written to every Foreign Minister of the world twice. We had also instructed our Ambassadors to go to their Foreign Offices and explain our stand in detail.

This campaign, which had to be sustained by India, did not end there because we still had three years within which to decide. Therefore, in those years in between, we had to sustain our campaign. We also wanted to redefine the role of NAM because in the post-Cold War era it would need to play a radically different role. No foreign policy or security policy of a country can be constructed without this institutional back-up from the Parliament. For quite a long time, we had depended either on the structured bureaucracy or on the whims, wills or faculties of one individual minister or the other.

Political leadership should have a vision; only then can it assert itself, political leadership has to have a commitment; only then can it assert itself and political leadership does not mean 'individuals,' it means, 'institutionalization' and that is why we were moving towards institutionalization so that we were able to project India's strength through the policies that we followed. We reserve our options regarding the nuclear issue. I think it means a lot. If it had not meant a lot, then the pressure to sign would not have been so strong. The decision whether to sign or not was not an individual one. This is something to be decided by those who have the responsibility in regard to the defense strategy of the country.

It should be decided by those who have been entrusted with the responsibility of assessing threats to our national security from time to time. Weapons of any type to be built or not built, to be acquired or not acquired--should be left to them. In regard to Bangladesh and the Chakma problem, I had visited Bangladesh and discussed it. The response was very positive and helpful. I think that was the real essence of our relationship with the government then in Bangladesh which was that, on issues of contention, we were trying to find areas of agreement and co-operation.

The Foreign Policy of every country is integrally linked with its history and its basic ethos. Our republic is now half a century old. Fifty years ago, the Indian Foreign Policy was perceived on the basis of our experiences and the promises made during the freedom struggle. A unique feature of the Gandhian struggle was its non-violent character and intimate linkage with the anti-Apartheid struggle of the African people. Gandhi himself had courageously resisted discrimination, which was one of the basic tenets of the foreign policy of free India. The freedom struggle not only spelt out the future of India but also visualized how India would cope with the international situation. India was, at that time, confronted with the reality of the Cold War between the blocs.

Today we might talk of Non-Alignment as a concept. In Nehru's vision--or call it the legacy of the freedom struggle--one thing was certain that no country could consider itself free till its foreign policy was liberated from any commitment to one or the other bloc. At the time of India's freedom—the Non-Aligned world came much later--India had stated that it was not going to be a part of any bloc. Both the blocs condemned us. Stalin called Nehru 'the running dog of imperialism' and what John Foster Dulles said about India can be read in books.

It is in that context, therefore, that Nehru as the first Foreign Minister of India said that we did not want to join any bloc. In a way he was not talking of any bloc but of India being free to make its choice. Non-alignment has only one meaning and that is the freedom of choice. Each country should judge its own national interest and then decide what it wants to do. Nehru did not want either Moscow or Washington to decide our Foreign Policy. Today, we may term the decision as good or bad but the basic point is that a free India or a Republic could not have any other Foreign Policy--even if it has to relive its past. This was a challenge which the mighty did not like. But gradually, as the decolonization process advanced and country after country became free they all shared this viewpoint. Nehru did not go around asking people to join the Non-Aligned Movement. The former colonies realized that when a country sheds off the yoke of colonialism it has to perceive the paradigms of its foreign policy, i.e. what kind of a relationship it would have with rest of the world.

A large number of countries, more than one hundred at that time which were independent, realised that if they remained under the thumb of one bloc or the other, their freedom, would be compromised. That is why the Non-Aligned Movement expanded. With the end of the Cold War, the animosities between the blocs ended. Suddenly, we saw the pendulum moving in another direction. The designs of established hegemonies, be they in the economic field, in politics or in foreign policy were exceedingly oppressive. Some countries would like to keep the world under their thumb. Certain associations were formed; calling themselves G-7 and P-5. They might have differences among themselves but so far as hegemony over the Third World was concerned, it was a shared objective.

That is why when we talk in terms of our own future, and when we talk in terms of what we have to do, we have to perceive it as a challenge, particularly our concepts of freedom of choice. It is important for us to keep in mind that in the economic sphere, we are confronted with the G-7 and the P-5 As far as the nuclear NPT or CTBT goes, we did not sign these because they were flawed. Who defied the agreements after signing the CTBT? Who did the test? Not those who did not sign it. France signed it, broke it; China signed it, broke it. Even the CTBT, was drafted with certain reservations that permitted certain type of tests. This was our basic objection. We were asking them to make it more candid. It was a matter of pride that in face of such challenges, the nation stood united. We all felt that India's freedom was at stake and we should safeguard our interests. We anticipated some punishments to follow.

All the same, we stood up and I am glad that we did so. But signing the CTBT or not signing it did not end the story in September, 1996. The first punishment that followed was our defeat in the Security Council. Was it ever perceived that we could abstain and we would defy them and yet we would get elected to the Security Council? It must be known clearly as to who decides which candidate is best suited for a permanent membership of the Security Council.

Not the common vote, definitely not by the vote of Africa or Asia. Basically, powers are centralised and they would not let us sit in the Security Council after our defiance. For every defiance, we have to pay a price and all those nations who want to stand on their own feet, must learn how to stand up and defy. Defiance is unavoidable if we are to assert our independence. Pressures in the modern world are never direct. Gunboat diplomacy has had its day.

Pressures are now applied through indirect methods, which are called lobbies. Lobbies are built for that purpose and lobbyists have their own methods of functioning. We must understand the operational skills of the lobbyists to fully comprehend the nature of the pressures being applied on us. Our morale must not get sapped at losing this seat. After it has happened in the past also. We were once defeated by Pakistan in 1975. President Clinton has on record said that India would sign. That India would come around. That was the challenge to us. Would India have come around? Did India want to come around? Was it in India's interest to come around? Was it consistent with our self-respect to come around? Was it consistent with our legacy to come around? If it was not, then let us make our position very clear.

All this is part and parcel of the same situation. A defeat is also a method of a well-orchestrated pressure and an inadequate resistance. China, Russia and France stood by us, despite the pressure. By the time, the question of the Security Council came in, we had forty supporters. How did that happen? After all, increasingly, it was realized that whether it was the issue of CTBT or anything else, pressure had to be resisted. When we had forty supporters, it was very interesting to note the fact that out of the five nuclear powers, three voted with us. Why did they vote with us? Each one of them had its own compulsions.

China had its own reasons; Russia had its own reasons; and France had its own reasons. Therefore, when we refer to the post-Cold War, the CTBT is only one of the major unresolved issues that continues to confront us. In the post-Cold War era, it is regional cooperation that is most important, because there is no country in the world which is not concentrating on regional cooperation.

Europe is talking of Europeans; America is talking in terms of Mexico and Canada; Latin Americans have their own regional cooperation, Africans have their own and so do we. In the area of regional cooperation, our concept was not confined only to South Asia. We were looking at a wider area-- a neighbourhood does not only mean geographical proximity. It pertains to interest proximity as well. Interest may not be 100 per cent similar, we need to work out the highest common factor which facilitated our joining the full dialogue partnership with the ASEAN. We could not join it earlier because of the compulsions of the Cold War, wherein every country of the ASEAN had one commitment or the other.

In the post-Cold War era, our joining as a full dialogue partner of ASEAN is of benefit to us. The other dimension of Indian foreign policy was Central Asia. With Central Asia, we have age old relations. In our history, we had good relations with the Buddhist, the Kushan and the Mughal Central Asia. We have been trying to reorient these relations. These countries are rich in petroleum. In the twenty-first century, 40 per cent of available energy is perceived to be consumed in Asia, more than half of it by China and India together. Naturally, all eyes are turning to Central Asia. The politics of the next few years is going to be the politics of gas pipelines and that is where India's relationship with these countries would matter. We have, to an extent, succeeded in restructuring our relations with Iran. In the previous era, we exported goods to Central Asia via Odessa in the Soviet era.

This is a very circuitous route. We look forward to facilitate trade and enhance our relations. Iran has also undergone a major change. In 1990, I recall when I was a Minister, I was to go to Iran for an official visit. One week before my visit, the visit was officially cancelled by Iran on the plea that they were in sympathy with the suffering Muslims in Kashmir.

The same Iran, the same Mr Velayati, has come twice to invite India to participate in the Afghanistan Conference in Iran despite Pakistan Minister's telling them that if India was invited they would not come. Iran did not care. India was there, India was present at the Afghanistan Conference in New York. This was a new orientation of the Indian Foreign Policy. We are a factor in the Afghanistan situation although we did not want to interfere. We do not want to enter into any arms race in Afghanistan. We want a peaceful Afghanistan. We are strongly averse to the growth of blatant fundamentalism in our close neighbourhood. That is one of the reasons why we had continued to recognize the Rabbani regime. We had good relations with Dostum and Masood.

This was a new type of Afghan policy that we sorted out and pursued. But the central point of the Indian Foreign Policy was SAARC. In 1996, India was the Chairman of SAARC. It was a good thing for us, a good feeling for us because SAARC was undergoing a postive change. The birth of Bangladesh was a remarkable achievement for India. It was not solely the Indian Government's achievement, but a combined effort of India and Bangladesh. We must look at it in terms of a wider framework. We also had very good relations with Nepal. We had agreed to give them access to Bangladesh through India and the Mahakali Treaty was signed between India and Nepal during my tenure. The Non-Aligned Movement was the major plank of Indian foreign policy. What could have been the alternative policy? What do we do if we do not want to stay with those who are like us, if we do not want to stay with those who have gone through the colonial era themselves, if we do not want to stay with those who are also against the hegemonism of some powers? Then who do we want to stay with? Do we want to stay with the hegemonists? Do we want to go to the doorsteps of those who want to exploit us, whose interests are known to us and which are not in our favour?

Nehru had always said that we were not a bloc. We were a movement. The difference between a bloc and a movement is that you have the freedom of choice, sometimes voluntary, sometimes, non-voluntary. Not only this, autonomy of choice, and freedom of action is a central point of NAM, it is also something on which, a position of strength can be built. And that is what we had been trying to do. The issue regarding our border with China has not been sorted out. We feel that through the proposed Confidence Building Measures (CBM), we could improve our relations. In 1993, Narasimha Rao went to Beijing, to tranquilize the border. We have taken that tranquility one step further. But their claims regarding the boundary remain unchanged.

The new Sino-Indian mode is that although contentious issues remain, we are trying to work out cooperation in various areas. We gave a shift to our policy towards a people-to-people relationship with Pakistan by issuing more visas--more visas were given to the divided families that had come to meet their family members here. Did India gain or lose? Most of these people come from Karachi. Why did Pakistan close down the consulate in Karachi?

It was primarily because they wanted to hinder them from visiting India. Prior to closing of the Consulate, we were issuing 750 visas a day from Karachi alone. We were exerting our best to give as many visas as we could but the number did not exceed 300 because we did not have adequate manpower in our mission at Islamabad. Sometimes many speculations are made regarding the Indo-Pak talks. But whenever we talk, I feel, we should talk on a strictly official level. The thrust of the foreign policy that we were trying to pursue, if I may say broadly, was not reactive; it was active; we took initiatives. We had taken major initiatives regarding Bangladesh. We had taken major initiatives regarding Afghanistan. We had taken another major initiative regarding the Comprehensive Test Ban Treaty. We took initiatives regarding the ASEAN and, also to an extent and within a limited sphere, new initiatives regarding making our borders peaceful.

Spirit of Non-alignment Movement

In this era of global change, old alignments are yielding to new arrangements that may not be always palatable but their appraisal and understanding has to be the first task before any foreign policy. The Cold War was fought by two mutually-antagonistic 'international cultures'. A systematic global change has ended these agonizing confrontations. With the receding of tension between the two mutually-antagonistic power blocks, we now witness an emerging pattern of cooperation-cum-competition between their individual members. If Non-Alignment looks like a scattered force during this transition, it is because it is yet to recast itself for a new international role. It was in this context that I had proposed to my Yugoslav counterpart, Mr Loncer, in 1990, to convene an informal meeting of international foreign officials to collectively apply their minds to emerging challenges.

The NAM has, often in the past, intervened to safeguard peace and push back the colonial and racially-biased regimes. Contemporary situation demands that we collectively work our regimes to release ourselves from debt traps and economic degenerations. The IMF and World Bank prescriptions are further tightening the noose. Breathers, if at all, provide only short-lived relief. The crisis in which we find ourselves entrapped is not inevitable. It is not a product of forces beyond our control. Faulty and gross mismanagement of economies on one hand and myopic security perceptions on the other have caused it.

The NAM--in spirit of trust and cooperation--should initiate a process of evolving systems and attitudes to end regional wars and tension amongst neighbours. This may seem a gigantic and impossible task but some countries of Europe have already shown the way by burying old hatchets. Why can't we do it? NAM should also address itself to the task of changing the role and structure of the UN, that is being increasingly used, or may one say, misused by the rich and the powerful to advance their own interests. Any 'New Vision of the Future' has to inevitably spell out, as done by Nehru in the 1950s, principles that would require democratisation of the World bodies: the UN; Security Council, World Bank, IMF, GATT, etc. Today, the security of all nations-- big or small--inevitably implies economic development of all nations. Two villains have entered the international scene: Terrorism and Drug trafficking. The two are acting in nexus and sometimes acquire state support and even sponsorship.

An open arms bazaar facilitates their activity. Unless these are curbed by collective action they are bound to destabilize all societies. Even those who may be deriving temporary benefit from their nefarious activities stand to lose eventually. The evolution of an equitable environmental regime is another issue of vital interest to all South Asian countries. At present, the dice is loaded in favour of powerful industrialized nations.

Unless we act in unison we may be denied access to the latest technology and left to languish in dungeons of backwardness. Isn't it time that we in the SAARC undertook such an exercise to collectively corelate ourselves with the changing world? 'No South Asian Country should allow the use of its territory against the interest of another.' As Foreign Minister, I had espoused this principle and further promised that India would abide by this and never commit its forces outside its territory except in self-defence. I view the principle of self-determination positively since in all developing countries, the polity is over centralized and there is a heavy deficit of self-determination even when political systems are democratic.

Self-determination or participation in Self-Government must begin at the grassroot level through democratically-elected village councils and cover the entire political society. Elections must, of course, be free and fair and to establish their credibility a team of eminent persons from SAARC should, as a practice, be invited to monitor the process. Self-determination, however, must not be perceived to disturb national boundaries, as doing so would engage neighbours in prolonged and agonizing mutual hostility, bloodshed and resource drainage. We see a mushrooming of regional, sub-national and even communal identities all over the world, including Europe.

This sometimes strains inter-state relations and inhibits regional cooperation for peace, security and development. It is time, I would suggest, that South Asian leaders and opinion makers engage themselves in free, open-minded discussions to build a regional consensus on a stated basic principle that must govern South Asian relationships. Any framework of such a consensus must keep in mind that South Asia has been slow in imbibing the post-Cold War chemistry of cooperation. Our outmoded mindsets and faulty security concepts do not permit us to take a holistic view of security. Deeply ingrained suspicions of the neighbours result in ever increasing expense on military hardware, that in turn, intensifies economic distress, internal disturbances and creates enhanced need for outside help and support.

The first priority of India's foreign policy should be to consolidate and update its cooperative relations with the neighbours, not only in South Asia but also in Central,

South East and West Asia. In all these regions, important changes are taking place, and that is where imaginative initiatives are called for. On a bilateral basis, India has been able to impressively upgrade its relations with its South Asian neighbours. Though Indo-Pak relations still remain acrimonious, India's relations with Nepal, Bangladesh and Sri Lanka have taken a turn for the positive. Credit for improvements in Indo-Nepal relations is largely due to the first democratic head of Nepal, Mr Bhattarai, who appreciated India's security sensitivities and saw the futility of acquiring mini-arms dumps when the world was moving in another direction and India, in no way, posed any threat to its neighbours. With the transfer of the Teen Bigha, an outstanding issue was sorted with Bangladesh, our thanks are mainly due to the then Chief Minister of West Bengal, Mr Jyoti Basu.

Another neighbourhood of this subcontinent is Central Asia, where pronounced uncertainties prevail. Unfortunately, thanks to our legacy of the past, our diplomacy has not devoted the needed time and attention to this large and diverse region that extends from Mongolia and Kazakistan to trans Caucasia. There is a sudden explosion of unfamiliar ideas, alliances and conflicts.

Almost every new state is embroiled in dispute with the neighbours or is busy writing secessionist eruptions. The idea of a Pan-Turkic block threatens territorial integrities of many countries ranging from the Arabic States to China. Azarbaijan is an example worth studying to understand as to what could happen elsewhere in Central Asia and Caucasia. Nationalist upsurges there poses very problematic implications. Ethnically Turkish, the Azarbaijanians do not accept the Iranian model of a fundamentalist state; while they prefer the Turkish secular model there is a movement to create a 'Greater Azarbaijan' by including 20 million Azeris living in North Iran.

Iran is countering the Armenian and Georgian States. The Azeris also fear that the USA at some stage might support Christian Armenia. Unless the Russian-led Commonwealth of Independent States (CIS) or Russia itself intervenes to end such mini wars, regional instability could flow out in several directions, including ours.

While talking of Central Asia, one cannot ignore the Uzbeki nationalism that is trying to have its way in Kirgzia. It has already fought a war with the Turks in Farghana and Tashkent. Conflict between various Turki sub-nationalities are destroying the pipe dream of a greater Turkistan. These events in the Northern neighbourhood of the South Asian subcontinent have serious implications for other countries in this region particularly when new types of regional groupings are being hawked around. During my tenure as Prime Minister, newly independent Central Asian States with the exception of Kazakistan that preferred an Observer status, joined ECO (Economic Cooperation Council) comprising Iran, Turkey and Pakistan. The ECO Summit promised to create a powerful Islamic Market and it hoped that Afghanistan and Bangladesh will soon join in. Some scribes then spoke of a 'powerful Islamic state', wherein two of its members, Pakistan and Kazakistan have nuclear weapons and several others possess tactical nuclear weapons of the former Soviet State.

It would be erroneous to go by all that is being claimed. All former members of the Soviet state are very much linked with the CIS and the economy of the Russian state. Their adverse economic situations make them vulnerable. Besides, none of the non-CIS members of ECO enjoy such affluence as to underwrite their needs for economic stablisation and development. Iran could help but only marginally. Iran and Turkey have their own rivalling regional interests. Teheran spearheads a Caspian Sea Cooperation Zone to entice Russia, Kazakistan and Turkmenistan.

Turkey, on the other hand, is launching a rival Black Sea Cooperation Council comprising Turkey, Azerbiajan, Bulgaria, Rumania, Ukraine, Georgia, Moldovia and Russia. Policy makers in Delhi have to keep in mind the future role of Russia in this region. The Communist regime of seventy years had succeeded in modernizing social outlooks and transformed institutions in the region. Even when religion comes back to them, hopefully, it will adopt a secular milieu. While reacting to these happenings, India should keep in mind the fact that it enjoys high prestige in the region. Its relationship with Russia will continue on a firm footing. It must be said to the credit of Indian diplomacy that it is not acting in haste nor trying to transplant the Indo-Pak acrimony in this area. Indian Foreign Policy cannot be and is not a captive of situations in the North. It has to pay due, and even slightly more than due, attention to the Indian Ocean Rim countries. That is where commonality of interest between India and Sri Lanka gets pronounced.

In saying this I do not mean, in any way, to understate interests of Maldives, Bangladesh and Pakistan and also the two landlocked members of SAARC, Nepal and Myanmar. In the Cold War era, all of us in the subcontinent along with several other nations in NAM had made gigantic but unsuccessful efforts to transform the Indian Ocean to a zone of peace. With the end of the Cold War, the superpower confrontation in these waters has ended. Then why these mounting expenses and ever increasing military presence?

As far as the countries of the Indian Ocean are concerned, they may sometime clash with neighbours. But neither individually nor jointly can they pose any threat to the US. Sustained, blocked and punitive actions against Iraq have unveiled a new US strategy. It is now evolving a security system in the North Western part of the Indian Ocean, by including the countries of the Gulf along with Syria and Egypt, to sign a treaty of some sort. Exorcising the haunting ghost of Saddam Hussein is very handy for the US strategists who benefit a great deal from regional rivalries and faulty security doctrines that invite extraterritorial presence and interventions. It is now clear, if there was any doubt, that a subtle US strategy first built Iraq's military machine and then destroyed it. A myopic Saddam facilitated this task.

The war aims of UN Security Council and the USA did not coincide. The US was more keen to destroy Iraq and eliminate the emergence of any autonomous power in the Gulf. The Secretary of State, Mr Baker (Jr) had reminded me in those tumultous days of the Gulf Crisis that sources of energy were of vital interest to their security and economy and the US would not permit anyone to control them exclusively. In strategic terms, the Russian threat has disappeared and may not come back for quite some time. But the US now apprehends threat to her interests from the Third World countries, particularly those which are rushing to develop nuclear weapons. This fear has been aggravated by the prevailing turmoil in ex-Soviet States and efforts on the parts of Iran and Pakistan to lay their hands on available fission materials. Indian diplomacy had its own dilemmas regarding the NPT. When we look at the contours of the Indo-US relations that are presently a primary focus of India's Foreign Policy, we will realize that complex strategic political and economic situations confront us. Dissolution of the Soviet Union has placed the Indo-US relationship in a new framework. In its contemporary phase, Washington's strategic needs and requirements in South Asia have undergone a change. It requires eclipsing the past to explore areas of fruitful cooperation.

The White House has appreciated Indian concerns and policies regarding Kashmir. It is an evidence of the changed times and relations that Washington appreciated India's policies during the Gulf crisis and did not press it to join the war even symbolically, despite the fact that Pakistan had lent its troops. The two countries have stepped up interaction between their armed forces, building a cooperative and mutually-beneficial relationship. Unilateral invocation of Super 301 and US reaction to the Indo-Russia Agreement for acquisition of cryogenic engines are two such examples that have caused deep concern to India. Research and Development of India's Space Programme occupies a position of importance in India's vision of future. In the overall context, it is important for both India and US to sustain an upswing in bilateral relations. Both must continue to discover wider pastures of cooperation while avoiding to tread on each other's sensitivities. This is a selective presentation of the issues and situations that face Indian diplomacy that is also, at the same time, confronted with militancies in some states that are aided and abetted from abroad, causing severe strains on foreign relationships.

Importance

The latter part of the twentieth century inducted new elements that have invariably influenced diplomacies of all nations. Terrorism, drug trafficking, conservation of environment and promotion of the human rights now occupy a central position on the world stage. Nations take their own time to respond and adjust to these challenges; India is no exception. We have our own views about the emerging world order that must be made socially just and equitable. At the same time, our legacy beckons us to preserve the Independence of our foreign policy, judging every issue on its merit and keeping in mind our national interests.

From the day of its birth as an independent Nation State, India was resolutely opposed to all alignments that divided the world into camps. The end of the Cold War has to a great extent reduced tensions and opened new vistas of cooperation. Despite all the dramatic changes, I am unable to say that a 'new dawn' of peace and cooperation has arrived. Aggressive and exclusivist sentiments continue to tear apart the social fabric with disastrous consequences for development, peace and stability. A loose political concert continues to exercise military, economic, technological hegemony, while the voice of the developing world is marginalized. In these circumstances, the Non-Aligned Movement (NAM) acquires added importance for collectively safeguarding interests of the Third World.

Widespread terrorism cum fundamentalism poses a major threat to stability. It deprives innocent citizens of their right to life. Built on narrow outlooks that are anathema to liberal and democratic values, they pose a formidable challenge to civil societies. While exploiting openness and the freedom offered by democratic societies, they exploit and undermine them. As the G-7's Lyon Declaration said, 'the terrorist does not respect any social order or civilizational heritage'.

Thanks to shortening of distances and instant communications, the world today is truly a global village. Keeping this in mind, my government accorded priority attention to her immediate neighbours to promote peace and stability in the region, and for development of stronger economic relations. I visited almost all the countries in our subcontinent, soon after assuming charge as Prime Minister. We wished Pakistan stability and prosperity and with this in mind, proposed the resumption of Foreign Secretary level dialogue to address all issues of mutual concern on the basis of the Simla Agreement.

We attached the greatest importance to our relations with our neighbours. I have already stated that five basic principles of the Gujral Doctrine, which guided our relations with our immediate neighbours. These principles were first, India does not seek reciprocity but gives all that it can in good faith and trust. Second, no South Asian country should allow the use of its territory against the interest of a fellow country in the region. Third, that none would interfere in the internal affairs of the other. Fourth, all of us in South Asia must respect each other's territorial integrity and sovereignty. And finally, we would settle all disputes through peaceful bilateral negotiations. These five principles or a new Panchsheel' or the Gujral Doctrine-- if scrupulously adhered, are bound to achieve a fundamental recasting of the regional relationships including, I venture to say, radical change in the tormented relationship between India and Pakistan, in a friendly, and cooperative mould.

China is our important and largest neighbour involving our economic and security interests. Both of us decided to delink the final settlement of the boundary issue from the need to reinforce friendly relations. A number of Confidence Building Measures are now in place along the Line of Control. Sustained friendship between India and China will lay a durable foundation for a peaceful and prosperous Asia.

Geography has determined our historic and close relations with the countries of the Association of South East Asian Nations (ASEAN). With Myanmar joining its membership, we now share a nearly 1600-mile long border with this Association of ten sovereign countries. As stated before, our 'Sectoral dialogue Partnership' of 1992 was upgraded to a 'Full dialogue partnership' with the ASEAN. India played a pioneering role in the consolidation of the 'Indian Ocean Rim Association' which includes countries of the three continents: Australia, Africa and Asia. When fully operationalized, this could become a very large common market in the world. Europe--both the East and the West--has been our traditional associates. We have supported the political and economic integration of Europe. The annual Troika meetings between the European Union (EU) and India have been very beneficial. We have also concluded the third generation agreement with the European Union.

At the same time, our bilateral commercial relations with all countries of Europe remains satisfactory. India's long and cherished relations with the Russian Federation bear a hallmark of beneficial friendship and cooperation, based on mutual trust and confidence. Both of us have adjusted with the changed circumstances in Russia and the countries comprising the Commonwealth of the erstwhile Soviet Union. Their market economies give a more independent role to private enterprise, making our commercial interactions smoother. India's economic reforms programmes had a positive impact on Indo-US economic relations. Our bilateral trade had increased by 19 per cent with a turnover of nearly US$ 9 billion. As of 1996, the US companies accounted for over one-third (38 per cent) of the foreign investment commitments in India, and almost 20 per cent of the actual direct investments. The positive economic trends were sometimes lost in the cacophony of occasional differences--such as over the Comprehensive Nuclear Test Ban Treaty, that got an inordinate amount of media attention. However, we hoped that with the goodwill and mutual respect that we shared, there was no reason why we should not be able to overcome any ephemeral differences.

As I have stated before, India continues to oppose discriminatory and partial measures of arms control such as the CTBT and the NPT. India joined 27 Non-Aligned and neutral countries, at the Conference on Disarmament, to present a phased programme for elimination of nuclear weapons by the year 2020. This still remains on the international agenda but without any promise from the five Nuclear Weapon Powers.

Another important element which has a bearing on our foreign policy is the Indian Diaspora, created out of both forced migration as indentured labour during the colonial era, and voluntary migration in the more recent times. Handsome contributions made by the Indian Diaspora to their adopted countries as also to India have been well documented. While involved in the economic growth and social development of their host countries, they retain their links with India. They can be an important source of technological know-how and investments. Their remittances, particularly of the short-term Indian workers in the Gulf and other countries are a significant source of foreign exchange for our country. Our foreign policy must strengthen these relations, while ensuring that our actions do not in any way impinge on the sovereignty of the host countries. We have to keep these governments informed about the role and propaganda by few misguided extremist elements in the Indian Diaspora.

In conclusion, I must say that India's foreign policy

represents continuity and faith in the moral principles. We have retained these paradigms while responding pragmatically to past and emerging challenges, and to the changing global scenario. The primary interest of our foreign policy has been to safeguard our national interests--but not in the narrow and selfish sense. We have unflinchingly supported causes that were dear to us ranging from elimination of Apartheid to supporting the Vietnamese struggle. Some might talk in loose terms of India being isolated on one particular issue or the other. India is a big country of over 96 crore people. We cannot be isolated. We firmly believe in the ideal of the world coming closer together and ultimately realizing the ideal of One World.

We are a fairly young independent Nation State, though a very ancient civilization. Therefore, our foreign policy has gradually evolved, acquiring greater substance while responding to various challenges. We are securely moored in the framework of an inalienable perspective, that of the Panchsheel, Non-Alignment, developing friendly relations with all, and retaining an enlightened self-interest.

India's Security and CTBT

The new External Affairs Minister, Mr Inder Kumar Gujral, is an old hand at his job, having been one of the country's senior most diplomats. He has moved into his job with relative ease. Indian Foreign Service officials are comfortable working with him, as he knows most of them from his earlier stint. Mr Gujral spoke to *The Telegraph* on a number of issues, expressing India's concerns and the task before the new government to improve relations with neighbours.

Thus to sum it up, the CTBT had always been visualized as the first definitivc and irreversible step along the road to nuclear disarmament. It should have done so in two ways. First, the CTBT should have prohibited the designing and development of newer generations of nuclear weapons. Secondly, such a CTBT should have also signalled a shift in the perception of the nuclear weapon states who have sought to ensure their security through their nuclear arsenals for the last fifty years.

When the negotiations began we thought, somewhat optimistically, that the nuclear weapon states were ready to take such a first step on the road to nuclear disarmament. The negotiations have shown otherwise. It was a sad fact that the nuclear weapon states showed no interest in giving up their nuclear hegemony. The negotiations have ended without consensus because the text does not reflect the aspirations of the vast majority of countries for a nuclear weapon-free world. India was not alone in voicing these concerns. Many other countries also shared this conviction. It was a matter of regret that the Conference on Disarmament stopped negotiations on the CTBT to put forward a flawed text, to meet artificial deadlines, instead of taking advantage of the current moratorium on testing to continue negotiations for a universal CTBT that would meet the terms of the mandate.

It was also a fact that we had certain national security concerns which made it impossible for us to subscribe to a draft CTBT that is merely an instrument for horizontal non-proliferation rather than disarmament. Our security concerns obliged us to maintain our nuclear option. Yet, it was a fact that since we demonstrated our capability in 1974, we have exercised unparalleled restraint. We have refrained from carrying out tests and from weaponizing our option. However, we could not accept constraints on our option as long as nuclear weapon states continued to rely on their nuclear arsenals for their security. Our position on the CTBT emerged out of an open and intense national debate that pointed out that the draft treaty would permit vertical proliferation by permitting tests by non-explosive means. Our policy reflected national consensus.

After we announced our decision that we could not subscribe to this draft Treaty, the Article on Entry into Force was modified suddenly with the clear aim of imposing obligations on India. This was at the insistence of a small number of countries. Such a provision was unprecedented in treaty negotiating practice and contrary to international legal norms. It denied India it's sovereign right to exercise of consent and contained an element of implied coercion. It placed us in a position that we did not wish to be in. We were told that the text could not be modified but as we have seen, the draft text has been modified to accommodate one country's concerns. If this change had not been introduced or the Entry into Force provisions amended to address our concerns, we could have stood aside and let the draft text be adopted by those who supported it. But this attempt at coercion left us with no choice but to indicate our opposition to the draft text. Some friendly countries approached us with proposals of bilateral assurances with regard to this article. While we appreciate the spirit in which these gestures were made, we believe that in a multilaterally negotiated treaty, such private assurances did not address our concerns.

We were aware that some countries with which we have traditionally enjoyed close and mutually beneficial relations have adopted a different approach on the CTBT issue. We had in keeping with our practice, continued our dialogue with these countries in order to sensitise them to our concerns. Mutual respect implies respecting the right of sovereign nations to pursue their national interests even if there are differences of view. We are committed to developing and maintaining good relations with all countries and are confident that our differences on this issue would not affect our bilateral ties and friendly relations.

India has had a long-standing commitment to multilateralism. This has further accentuated today with the growing integration of our economy into global structures. We are increasingly engaged in our region. The Indian Ocean Rim Initiative and our membership of the ARF are developments that reflect acknowledgement of our constructive approach. In SAARC, we are trying to promote effective structures to enhance prosperity which can ensure stability in the region. India remains engaged in pursuing her policies for promoting peace, prosperity and stability and enhancing security in our region. We also continue to work with other countries to strive for achieving a nuclear weapon-free world.

The End of the Cold War

India was one of the relatively small number of states that were present at the creation of the United Nations. The UN was born of a war-shattered world's hope that it would be the benign, sometime stern, guardian of a world, committed to peace and cooperation among nations. Unfortunately, the end of the Second World War did not bring peace; it brought a long, often icy, Cold War. Scores of new nations in Asia and Africa emerged as sovereign states from the crumbling empires of Europe. The Cold War had a negative impact on the life of these new nations. We in the so-called Third world remained firmly committed to the United Nations as the only organization that could usher in world peace and promote global well-being. The vicissitudes through which the UN passed did not diminish our faith in this august body. We, the nations of the South, had special reason to rejoice at the end of the Cold War. India was all the more happy because from the very moment of its Independence, it sought the termination of this power struggle. We joined other nations to enunciate the principle of Non-Alignment to protect the independence of the new nations and their right to choose for themselves the kind of international relations they wished to have and the models of development they wished to adopt. We welcomed the collapse of the Cold War divide.

The Cold War mindset, which took deep roots in our minds, would yield to a new mindset of global detente and cooperation. An event of special importance in this context was the German unification. This reflected the fulfillment of the deepest aspirations of the German people. In the new Europe which was emerging a united Germany--in the model foreseen by a great son of Germany, Thomas Mann--would be a powerful factor in favour of Stability and peaceful cooperation. India looked forward to working closely with united Germany in the cause of peace and progress around the world. India has always rejected the logic of the Cold War and the division of the international community into opposing blocs. In accordance with our policy of non-alignment, we sought to simultarieously build relations of trust and friendship with both the Soviet Union and the United States.

The replacement of East-West confrontation by a new cooperative approach greatly facilitated our task. The year 1989 saw a further strengthening of our ties with the great democracy of the United State. With our time-tested friend, the Soviet Union we added new dimensions to our friendly cooperation. We hailed the historic endeavours of the Soviet people to reshape their political and economic structures on the basis of democracy, unity and economic efficiency. The United Nations was a participant in many of the momentous changes during the year. Its work in Namibia and Nicaragua provided splendid examples of its role, testifying to its renewed relevance and effectiveness in international affairs. And a great deal of the credit should go to the then UN Secretary General, Mr Perez de Cuellar, for his patient, prudent, painstaking and imaginative management of the world body. These are truly wise words spoken at a critical turn of history. India was always among the many nations who wished to see the United Nations emerge as the pivot and fulcrum of international peace and security.

The new effectiveness of the United Nations owed a great deal to the fact that the earlier confrontational relationship between the great powers gave way to a detente which, in turn, led to a new collaborative relationship. A cooperative relationship among the major powers is a necessary, but not a sufficient, condition for true multilateralism. The latter requires full and equal participation of all nations--big and small--in the multilateral decision-making process. The great issues of the day can no longer be decided in the capitals of a few major powers. The voice of the majority must not only be heard but also respected. The democratic principle is an essential requirement of a genuinely multilateral system. Nor can the concerns of the deprived majority of the world's population be denied priority on the international agenda. Peace and development are closely Interrelated and deserve equal attention. In the final analysis, the success of the United Nations will be measured in terms of its ability to reflect and meet the concerns of the majority of humankind.

India was gravely concerned at the crisis in the Gulf.

India's position was, and remained, clear and consistent. We were against the use or threat of force in the settlement of differences in inter-state relations. We firmly opposed aggression. The crisis had arisen from the Iraqi invasion of Kuwait. It followed that Iraq must withdraw its forces from Kuwait, as demanded by the Security Council. India did not recognize Kuwait's annexation. India fully subscribed to and strictly abided by all the resolutions of the Security Council concerning this crisis. The crisis led to the induction of foreign forces into the Gulf region. In the changed world environment, permanent foreign military presence was not desired by any country, nor was it in anyone's interest.

Since ages India maintained the most cordial and friendly relations with Kuwait and Iraq. Almost 2,00,000 of our nationals, who were present in these countries when the crisis erupted, found themselves caught up in its coils. Provision of essential food supplies for them, and other innocent victims from Third World countries, was a matter of the highest importance, from the humanitarian point of view, to the entire world community. In West Asia, there can be no durable peace without a just and comprehensive settlement based on the inalienable rights of the Palestinian people to self-determination, as well as the right of all states in the region, including Palestine and Israel, to live in peace and security within internationally recognized borders, in accordance with UN Security Council Resolutions 242 and 338. Israel's attempts to suppress the *Intifadah* or to block progress towards a dialogue could not succeed.

India reaffirmed its solidarity with the people of Cyprus, which partly remained under foreign occupation. We fully supported the sovereignty, unity and territorial integrity of that country. Some of the most hopeful developments during the year were related to Southern Africa. We warmly welcomed independent Namibia into the community of nations. Developments in South Africa held promise of real progress. Nelson Mandela, freed after spending a quarter of a century behind bars, galvanized the currents of peaceful change. We welcomed the talks initiated between the African National Conference (ANC) and the South African Government to clear the way for negotiations on a new non-racial constitution. While racism was on the retreat in South Africa, in Fiji, a constitution had been imposed which institutionalized racial discrimination. The Suva regime flouted internationally accepted principles of democracy and human rights. Its undemocratic and racially discriminatory policies were unacceptable.

In the Korean peninsula, there were some encouraging signs of reconciliation and dialogue. We regarded the historic meetings between the Prime Ministers of the Democratic People's Republic of Korea and the Republic of Korea as a major step forward. We supported all efforts aimed at the peaceful reunification of these two nations. And in conformity with the principle of universality, we further supported the aspirations of the Korean people to be represented in the United Nations, so that they could actively contribute towards the realisation of the purposes and principles of the UN.

There had been encouraging progress towards a resolution of the Cambodian problem. The Djakarta Meeting and the decision of the Supreme National Council held the promise of an early return to normalcy. We hoped that a settlement of the problem would fully reflect Cambodia's sovereignty and independence and ensure that its people could exercise their democratic rights to determine their own destiny free from foreign interference and intervention.

Myanmar continued to be held in thrall by forces unwilling to accept the decision that its people took in the national elections. We called upon Yangon to accept the people's verdict and work with the latter to establish peace and democracy in the country. Relations with our northern neighbour, People's Republic of China, showed steady and welcome improvement. Both countries have expressed their determination to settle the boundary question through peaceful and friendly consultations and also to develop relations actively in a variety of other fields.

We believed that full and faithful implementation of the Geneva Agreements, so arduously architectured by the Secretary General of the UN, would restore normalcy, stabilize the life and security of the Afghan people and also help in furthering the cause of peace and good neighbourliness in South Asia. We warmly welcomed the return of democracy in neighbouring Nepal. Differences which had earlier crept into our relations were happily and speedily resolved after the transition in Nepal thus reflecting the deep aspirations for peace shared by the two neighbours.

Pakistan has been nursing and arming terrorist activities in Jammu and Kashmir, causing immense human suffering, extensive misery and loss of innocent lives. All efforts on bur part to persuade the Government of Pakistan to desist from these activities were first ignored and then rejected. Characteristically Pakistan denied responsibility and involvement in these acts The Indo-Pak Simla Agreement, signed in 1972, fully spelt out these principles and despite Pakistan's blatant violation, India continued its quest to consolidate a relationship of cordiality and friendship between the people of the two countries.

Arms race, support to terrorism and aggressive polemics only add to tensions and create a climate of instability--which is so much out of place in the contemporary global environment. We proposed to Pakistan a set of measures that would induce mutual confidence and cooperation. But unfortunately Pakistan chose to ignore them and to persist in its unacceptable activities.

India and Pakistan can have a great future if we respect each other's integrity and unity, and if Pakistan desists from the temptation of interfering in our internal affairs. It is in this spirit that I will not refer to the gross flouting of human rights in Pakistan, particularly in Sind and Baluchistan.

The North-South dialogue, once nurtured by the international community, had fallen into neglect. It deserved to be revived. When political cooperation was on the upswing, why should economic cooperation languish? The head and the limbs had to function together if the body was to be strong. India has traditionally had the privilege, in this context, of working with other countries to make a North-South compact real and forceful.

The South-South cooperation to build up collective self-reliance was an important aspect of international economic growth. The Summit in Kuala Lumpur of fifteen developing countries including India provided a significant impetus to this process.

We were also awaiting the conclusion of the Uruguay Round. A great deal of expectation had been aroused in these negotiations and we were participating with the hope that the conclusions of the Uruguay Round would assist developing countries. Despite very severe economic difficulties, many developing countries including India made offers to their utmost ability. These were, however, not reciprocated, particularly in areas to which developing countries have attached importance such as textile, agriculture, tropical products and safeguards. It was difficult to visualize a balanced outcome of the Uruguay Round without substantial progress in these and other areas of greatest concern to developing countries.

Environmental concerns rightly moved to a top position in the international agenda. The UN Conference on Environment focused on the inescapable fact that protection of the environment required acceleration of development in the poorer countries. At the heart of the environmental crisis lay the persistence of wide disparities in levels of production and consumption between the developed and the developing countries. The very high per capita consumption levels in the industrialized world imposed corresponding strain on global natural resources and thus on the environment. On the other hand, extreme poverty in the developing countries was itself a cause of environmental degradation. In order to simply survive, poverty-stricken people were forced, for example, to cut down forests for firewood or overgraze pastures. The environment could not be protected in the developing countries unless the root cause of its degradation, namely poverty, was eradicated. Thus, sustainable development called for curbs on extravagant lifestyles in affluent countries and promotion of economic development in less fortunate areas. Sustainable development can only be equitable development. The call for a change in life-styles in affluent societies does not imply a reduction in living standards; indeed, it envisages an improvement in the overall quality of life.

It is now accepted that environmental protection

required the provision of new and additional funds for developing countries as well as the transfer of an environmentally benign technology to these countries on a preferential basis. Any new environmental regulatory mechanisms should be accompanied from the outset by full and adequate provision for funding the technology transfer. This is an essential requirement for effective action on the environment.

In conclusion, 1990 marked the end of a long historical period and cross over to another epoch. We now have to put our heads and hearts together to design a world of peace and development. We have to fashion the United Nations to reflect the end of the Cold War, making it responsive to the diversity of the world community, and representative of world democracy and equality of sovereign nations. Let the new era usher in world peace and a global fabric of cooperation. Let us all work together towards that noble objective.

India and Gulf Crisis

The Gulf War threw the country in the midst of a very deep crisis. The crisis did not pertain to India alone ; the dangers were, in a way, affecting the entire world. It was very disappointing that this situation arose particularly when the cold War had ended only about two or three months ago and when we were envisioning the future of the human race from a different perspective. India's stand on this issue was in conformity with its policy postulates framed by leading personalities like Mahatma Gandhi, the Father of our nation, and Jawaharlal Nehru. India is a country of great traditions that unify the nation in the hour of crisis. During the Gulf War, every country was worried about the safety of its citizens and so our Embassy staff was supplemented to serve our people in distress.

The Indian Foreign Service alone could not cope with it, as the repatriation of such a large number was a huge problem. It was difficult even to send a large number of planes because of the war environment prevailing in Iraq. The Iraqis were not in a position to open their airfield because of the UN restrictions.

The air corridors were similarly closed and so the pilots were extra cautious. The UN restrictions allowed us to send our planes only up to Amman. We tried to persuade them to let some flights emanate from Baghdad and Basra but to no avail. The rehabilitation of such a large number of people posed a great challenge. It was not a question of a party or a particular government. The rehabilitation of a large number of people, who were used to a prosperous life and well paid jobs, was a difficult task. So, the rehabilitation of all sections of society needed both efforts and resources. We were trying to involve the public to mobilize funds on a volunteer basis. Fortunately, the people responded whole heartedly. Repatriation of such a large number is expensive, particularly because the planes go empty on outward journeys adding to the costs and burden on the exchequer. It is our great tradition that in an hour of crisis, we always do our best. We were hopeful that the situation would improve and the tension would end. Prior to the crisis, a meeting of leading members of the Non-Aligned countries was fixed. It was to meet in Yugoslavia. After Iraq's attack on Kuwait added to all round anxieties, many members wanted to know as to how the NAM would respond. As I have said, we were deeply concerned and keen to lend our hand to end the critical situation. My colleagues in the Non-Aligned countries had similar concerns. In order to be helpful and consistent with our traditions, we restrained our utterances. This was appreciated the world over. In this complex situation, we were keen to understand the situation before deciding what to do and how to achieve the desired goals. Some honourable friends wished to inquire about the assets left behind by our people. We worked out a scheme, whereby the customs would let people bring their jewellery and keep it in the safekeeping of bonded lockers at the airport and take it back when they return. We had to close our Embassy in Kuwait because of obvious circumstances. The local authorities had notified all missions that electricity and water supplies would be disconnected and the diplomats would be denied diplomatic immunities after the notified day. Under the circumstances, we moved all our diplomats to Basra and augmented the Basra Consulate. We asked voluntary organizations to help our people and retained some of the local staff to render assistance to our citizens.

The route via Shattul Arab in Iran was made available only to Iranian citizens and not to others. We requested the Iranian government to let our people also use the route but the response was unhelpful. As for the transfer of funds, the situation was such mat no practical way out was available. A large number of our citizens in Baghdad also needed help. We tried to organize airlifts from Baghdad but international insurance companies had stopped covering the risk. So sending flights of Air India into Iraq became difficult. We examined the possibility of using some other airports in addition to those already transporting people to Amman in Jordan but it did not seem feasible.

The safety and security of the large Indian community that was living and working not only in Kuwait and Iran but also in the adjoining areas of the United Arab Emirates and Saudi Arabia were our concern. We shared the agony of their families who were very worried. The agony of our people of Kerala where almost every home, every hearth was affected caused us deep sorrow. The wives and the mothers were worried about the bread-earners of their families who were far way. The possibility of a war breaking out caused anxiety to all of us. We arranged for transmission of information of the welfare of our people living in Kuwait to their near and dear ones in different parts of India. We also had to ensure inflow of petrol and petroleum products to keep the wheels of life moving.

About 6,000 people were in Amman while several thousands more were on their way while about ten thousand had already reached Baghdad from Kuwait. We were trying to engage ships to bring them home if the shipping companies would permit them to bypass the blockades. We fully adhered to the UN sanctions adopted by the Security Council (Resolution Number 661). We were able to carry approximately 1,600 passengers everyday by air. The Air Force planes could bring in approximately 300 persons in one sortie. But clearance for using its airspace was not forthcoming from Iran. It was the Indian Prime Minister who sent me to Kuwait and Iran to personally ensure the safety and security of our nationals. When the Non-Aligned Ministers met, the Gulf crisis was foremost on our minds. The Non-Aligned bureau in New York had been meeting and keeping in touch with the UN. We all know that if there was a food shortage in Kuwait and Iraq, the first to suffer would be Asians--Indians, Pakistanis, Bangladeshis.

That is why I tried to persuade the United States to let our food supplies through. We were trying to persuade the powers that were active in the blockade to understand our concerns. The Government of India was not trying to mediate since mediation was feasible only when either of the two sides involved would seek it. We were for diffusion of the war like situation and were anxious to avert a crisis.

Iraq's invasion of Kuwait was certainly not justified. This is not the way diplomacy should be conducted, particularly in the post-Cold War era. The issue at the moment was not to apportion blames, the issue was how to diffuse the situation. Some countries chose in favour of military intervention, while some sent their armed forces.

The *Times* of London described the international armada already deployed in or enroute to Gulf as 'one of the largest assemblies of naval power in modern history'. It had already exceeded the NATO exercises in size and complexity. It was taking the world to the brink of war. Such a prospect was unfortunate. We do wish that the issue be resolved peacefully. Here I must say that we have a long history of close friendship with Kuwait. We expressed sympathy with the state of the people of Kuwait who were victims of a wanton attack. We, therefore, supported the UN Resolutions that asked for immediate withdrawal of the Iraqi forces from Kuwait. Therefore, the Kuwait mission continued to enjoy all the privileges of a diplomatic mission in India. We continued to recognize the sovereignty of the Kuwaiti rulers over their territory.

Safety and Repatriation of Indian Nationals During the Gulf War

Indians were concerned about their fellow countrymen in Kuwait during the Gulf War. It was an issue which cut across parties. Our fellow citizens, our compatriots, who were approximately 2,00,000 in number, were living in Kuwait. They had made very remarkable contribution to the economy and life of that country. I think it was naturally the first duty of any government to look after and safeguard them and to see that the situation did not go to the extent that any one of them should get hurt. Our anxiety from the beginning had been roused and we had been trying to do whatever was humanly possible. But a few things may be kept in mind. The first thing was that there was a war-like situation. Therefore, all lines of communications had been snapped. There was no communication available; the airport had been closed; seaport had been closed; telephone lines had been disconnected and telegram facility had been withdrawn. Therefore, it was not possible to directly communicate with Kuwait.

All the same, we were constantly trying to get in touch with the situation of the country through indirect means. We had tried all methods and there were standing instructions to all the Embassies of India throughout the world to try to get in touch with the host countries there and check up if any line of communication was available or not. We were constantly in touch with Iraq. Our entire Embassy in Baghdad was devoted to this task of keeping in continuous touch with the Iraqi Government. We were getting reports quite a few times a day. Therefore, the cell that had been set up was not only looking after the reports, complaints and enquiries that were coming in but also, at the same time, was keeping in constant touch. Fortunately, our Ambassador in Kuwait did a very ingenious thing, he was able to contact Nicosia on an amateur frequency and give us the information that all Indians in Kuwait were safe. This, by itself, was a matter of great satisfaction. We were trying to use that frequency again in order to keep in touch with them. The Government of Iraq had given us an assurance that orders had been issued to the military of Iraq to see that Indians were safeguarded by all means. They assured us that Indians were safe. This was the position as it stood then. I had given standing instructions that we should not take up the matter with the Iraqi Government; We were trying to persuade them and trying to see whether we could evacuate some people or not.

There were several options available. One option was that we could possibly get the people out via Amman by road. But the only issue was whether or not their own security concerns would permit them to open the border of Amman. This was something on which our influence could not work. The people of Iraq, whether right or wrong, were trying to work out their own perception as to what would safeguard their interest.

Therefore, this difficulty was there. We were exploring the possibility of evacuating Indians by sea and my instructions were that not only should we evacuate them by sea, if possible, but we need not bring all of them straight to India, because that would take more time. Even if we could take them to one of the adjoining Gulf countries, they would be safe but everything depended upon at what stage Iraq felt safe enough to reopen its airport or its seaport or re-establish communication systems. Minefields had also been laid because it was a war-like situation. We spared no efforts, money, or means, which could possibly provide relief to our fellow citizens there. We were also trying various communication systems. Saudi Arabia had some sort of a wireless communication with Kuwait. The situation had taken a turn for the worse because the Americans had taken certain steps. As regards other aspects, the Security Council had passed a resolution for mandatory sanctions against Iraq. That concerned us also. Half of our oil was coming from Kuwait and Iraq put together and this had to be kept in mind when we took stock of the entire situation. As far as bank transfers were concerned, the question of Indian banks not accepting Dinars did not arise, since the banks were not operational in Kuwait, any transfer that originated there was honoured in India. Not only citizens of India but ethnic Indians who did not have Indian passports, were also our concern. We were doing everything humanly possible to see to it that their lives and interests were safeguarded. All of us had friends and relatives involved there. Though we had set up a cell, unfortunately, we were not in a position to give individual information. We had information that most Indians were safe, but it was not possible for me to get individual information. There were some cases which were of grave concern to us. For instance, one of the persons whom I knew very intimately was a lady who was in the advanced stages of pregnancy. All her relations and friends were worried about her. There were three sisters, young girls, of a family who were in the British Airways plane flying from London to Delhi which was detained in Kuwait.

The family was naturally worried. I shared these anxieties. It was not a question of the government and the opposition. It was one of all of us being involved and all of us being concerned. I assured the nation that the government would not leave any stone unturned to come to their rescue.

India's Concern

The deterioration of the situation in the Gulf was a cause of grave concern to all Indians cutting across party lines. I have already discussed how we sought the safety of Indians in Kuwait and the measures we took for their repatriation. We were also concerned that the situation be resolved in a peaceful manner. It was imperative in this situation that diplomatic initiative should be taken to resolve the crisis. The importance of the Non-Aligned Movement in taking an initiative in this regard was very evident. Mainly at our suggestion, Yugoslavia, the then Chairman of the Non-Aligned Movement, decided to establish a Group of three countries--Algeria, India and Yugoslavia--and convened a meeting of this group.

An important question discussed by me particularly during my visits to Moscow and Washington was that of the sale of oil supplies at a reasonable price. Over 40 per cent of our oil imports, including supplies from the former Soviet Union, originated in Iraq or Kuwait. The responses that I got during my discussions both in Moscow and Washington were generally encouraging. The American Foreign Secretary then Mr James Baker told me that the US supported the proposal for an increase of production by Gulf producers and others so that the overall shortfall, and its adverse effects on prices and availability, could be minimized. The Soviet Government immediately agreed to seek an alternative source for the supplies of oil which had hitherto originated in Iraq and said they would welcome a delegation from India to work out the details immediately. They also offered oil of Soviet origin, an offer which was examined to see if it could be availed.

There was also the overall question of the adverse effects on the economies of countries like India, due to the crisis in the Gulf, particularly of the application of the mandatory sanctions imposed by the Security Council. So far as the mandatory sanctions themselves were concerned, India naturally kept in step with the world community. However, in our inter-dependent world, severe or draconian measures applied in any part of the world cannot but have adverse effects on the rest of the world. The UN Charter had visualized this problem, though not to the extent that it was assuming and had provided for recourse to the Security Council with regard to the solution of any special problems that may arise. In my discussions in Moscow, the Soviet Government agreed that joint efforts were needed at the international level to ease the burden on countries like India which were severely affected by the Gulf Crisis.

The subject was also discussed in Washington where I was told that the US also believed in international cooperation to ease the burden on countries like India which were most adversely affected. We had commenced consultations in New York with several countries, similarly affected, to explore the possibility of taking action through the UN.

There were other problems which were our major concerns such as the future of the Indian community, oil supplies and prices and the burden of sanctions. At the same time, we also had to think of possibilities that might de-escalate the crisis. Any measure for de-escalation would be in keeping with the general trend of recent years towards global detente and strengthening of peace.

We were also equally concerned about the destabilising effect of this crisis on our region. The Gulf region is a neighbour of South Asia. Escalation of tension or conflict there would have serious repercussions on us. We had already seen that Pakistan and Bangladesh had decided to send troops to the area of tension in the Gulf. This could very well be used as an excuse for further militarization of these countries, thus posing a threat to the security of the whole region. This made it incumbent upon all of us to look for openings for de-escalating and diffusing the tension.

I did not propose to assume a mediatory or good officer's role. I made this clear to all the leaders I met. Nevertheless, one of the objectives of the discussions was to find whether there was any chance of reversing the ongoing escalation of warfare. We tried to explore this tentatively at this stage and though my discussions during the tour did not reveal much of a meeting ground, it was imperative that our efforts to this end continued.

Clearly, humanitarian considerations were uppermost

in our mind because of the large Indian community and people of other nationalities including Iraq and Kuwait who were adversely affected by the food shortages and other circumstances. As I had already stated, there was an agreement among all concerned that food supplies for humanitarian purposes could be sent. However, in the context of the interdiction policy, we were not sure whether it could really work. We were exploring the possibility of sending a shipload of food from India to alleviate the suffering of the people of all nationalities caught in the current crisis.

Immediately after the onset of the crisis, we expressed our regret that the differences between Iraq and Kuwait could not be settled peacefully and stated our well-known position against the use of force in any form in inter-State relations and called for the earliest possible withdrawal of Iraqi forces from Kuwait. At the same time, we expressed our disapproval of unilateral action outside the framework of United Nations by any country or group of countries to enforce the mandatory sanctions decided by the Security Council. We were also against the induction or presence of foreign military forces in this region.

It was our hope that the crisis in the Gulf would be reversed and the international community would see the wisdom of making a determined effort to diffuse the tension and restore peace and stability in the region. Both the Arab League and the Non-Aligned Movement had an important role to play in this regard.

India and Globalization

Globalization and India is a theme which is of vital significance for life in India in the 21st century. As globalization has become a buzzword in major commercial and financial centres of the world, its implications for India need an indepth analysis. Professor M.S. Rajan, Professor Emeritus at the Jawaharlal Nehru University, has made a profound observation recently about the behaviour pattern of countries during the past 350 years.

He said that despite many changes in the world, the continuing desire of a small number of powerful states to exercise hegemony over others remained central to their behaviour, although the actors kept changing in different epochs. The pattern remains unchanged even today. Globalization *per se* is not a bad idea. If pursued under the framework of international solidarity and cooperation. It can build a humane society based on the social democratic concept of 'One World'. Those who are familiar with the social democratic ideology will remember that along with freedom, equality, democracy and justice, international solidarity is also a cardinal principle of social democracy. Therefore, the social democrats, by and large, have shown a greater willingness to share resources and fruits of growth equitably among nations and peoples. In their perception, all achievements, discoveries and inventions and wealth of the world are the heritage of the whole of humanity. And, therefore, everyone, transcending cultures and continents, is entitled to a just share in the fruits of growth. Though in the face of it, it may sound a little idealistic, a framework based on international solidarity and cooperation will be the right approach for the world. But, that is not the framework that guides the ongoing globalization. Anchored on the bedrocks of free market, privatization, monetarism and business nationalism, as conceived and perfected by Thatcherism and Reaganomics in the 1980s the basic character of the ongoing globalization is coercive, exploitative and domination oriented.

Guided by an imperialist instinct to dominate the world economy and politics, a few centres of economic and technological power are trying to reorganize the world economy to their advantage on neo-colonialist lines. It is aimed at making encroachment on the sovereignty and autonomous development of the less powerful states and create helplessness in them, by putting them under a syndrome of negative dependence, and lead them to a phoney debt-based developmental process, which will not only destroy their self-reliance, but will also increase their dependence on international money-lenders. Therefore, essentially, the philosophical foundation of the present globalization is flawed, greed, based and detrimental to the development of the developing countries. It is attuned to maximisation of profit, capturing of third world markets, destruction of the domestic markets of indigenous producers, destruction of potential jobs in the host countries of the Transnational Corporations (TNCs), and widen the gap between the rich and the poor inside and between societies.

It is being imposed on the developing countries by a few developed countries in tandem with their TNCs, the IMF, the World Bank and the WTO. Every vulnerable point of the developing countries has been ruthlessly exploited for the purpose. With the help of modern technology, globalization is directed today towards the concentration of power, information, wealth and production and supply in the hands of a few rich countries and their TNCs, and towards the building up of a global capitalist structure of exploitation in an octopus fashion. It is also directed towards the creation of a world economic and free-market system where survival of the fittest becomes the law. Unlike in the old colonial system where the local agents of the imperial power were visible and physically present for everyone in the colony to see, today, thanks to the modern technology, remote control systems have been established to quietly apply effective pressures on the political leadership of the developing countries to comply with the dictates of the largely invisible masters. The IMF and the World Bank also do their share of arm twisting to force the developing countries to effect structural reforms and pave the way for globalization and free market. Of late, the WTO also has joined this coercive apparatus to advance the interests of the rich countries and their TNCs. Pertinently, the fact that the IMF has already obtained an effective say in the WTO dispute settlement system on matters pertaining to monetary reserves, balance of payments, and so on, shows clearly in whose favour the tilt will be.

Liberalization of the Third World economies is a pre-requisite for globalization. To attain the pre-requisite, the TNCs demand the reduction of customs tariffs for their export items so that they can compete freely with the domestic products of the host country and progressively ebb them out and capture those markets. Similarly, they also seek unfettered freedom to invest in any sector of the economies of the developing countries and seek national treatment from the host country so that the latter will have little say in the operations of the TNCs. In these efforts, the TNCs are actively aided by their home countries, the IMF, the World Bank and the WTO.

A methodology that has been employed to put many countries on the track of globalization was to drive them into a debt trap. Indeed, the lending policies pursued by the international money-lenders during the past two-and-a-half decades have landed many developing countries into debt traps. And this vulnerability of the debtor countries has been fully exploited to promote globalization and liberalization. It may be found that the debt trap for the developing countries was laid way back in the 1970s when, in order to save the western banking system from collapse following the flooding of the world currency market with petro-dollars, the IMF advised many developing countries to borrow. To encourage more borrowing, new ideas like 'debt is not a bad thing', 'safe borrowing', and so on have been floated to manipulate public opinion, and the 'safe level' of borrowing have constantly been revised upwards to load the poor countries with heavy debts. As a result, most of these countries have been virtually reduced to the level of bonded labours of international money-lenders and, therefore, remain weak and vulnerable. Their purchasing power has diminished progressively as they have to find every year additional resources for debt servicing. However, the pull of the debt is such that most of the IMF borrowers soon returned to it for more loans for repayment of earlier loans. Similarly, the weakness of the debt-based economy is that despite large repayments, the cost continued to grow. For the developing countries, foreign debt has proved debilitating.

In a number of developing countries it provided new opportunities for foreign investors to swap foreign currency debts with solid assets in the debtor country at low prices, which otherwise is called 'debt for equity swaps'. However, in this whole exercise, the role of the IMF and the World Bank appears sinister. Contrary to the purpose for which these Bretton Woods institutions have been created, in recent decades they have become political and ideologically partisan and have taken upon themselves the responsibility of pursuing the goals of Thatcherism and Reaganomics by sending liberalization packages to the developing countries. Their loaded stipulations like export orientation, import liberalization, privatization, foreign private investments, etc., and other packages appear to have been drawn in tandem with the G-7 countries and the TNCs and are aimed at the promotion of interests of the developed countries and their TNCs.

By using debt and loan and its strategic position as an international money-lender, the IMF even dictates national policies of many developing countries. Not satisfied with this, the IMF is now seeking more powers to force all nations to eliminate national and local restrictions on foreign investments and to remove all restrictions on TNC investments. Moreover, it has been found that in their pursuit of globalization in many countries of Asia, Africa and Latin America the IMF and the World Bank liberally used their former employees and pensioners, who still occupied key positions in their own countries, to effect major policy changes from the top on the lines prescribed by them. It is not difficult to spot such champions of globalization and liberalization in many developing countries, including in India. However, the fact remains that many developing countries which have unsuspectingly followed the advises of the IMF and the World Bank on structural adjustment programmes and other measures to harness globalization have come to grief, as has been experienced in Latin America and Southeast Asia. It is quite clear that a main purpose of this whole exercise of globalization is to facilitate the TNCs to capture the domestic markets of the developing countries and to systematically liquidate small and medium local enterprises through methods like collaborations, mergers and take-overs.

These borderless entities, which mostly belong to the rich countries of Europe and America, are spread in areas like oil industry, tyre industry, chemical industry, foodstuffs, electrical engineering, electronic industry, and so on, and have themselves become huge sovereign capitalist entities over which neither national governments nor inter-governmental organisations has any meaningful control. In many cases they have become *de facto* monopolies, dictating prices globally. They control about two-thirds of the world trade. Pertinently, of the largest 100 economies of the world, more than 50 are TNCs. The turnover of General Motors, for example, is larger than the GNP of Denmark, and Toyota's turnover is more than the GNP of Norway. Similarly, it has been found that the combined sales of the world's largest 200 TNCs is more than the total income of 132 countries, including India. A striking feature of globalization is the globalization of prices without globalization of incomes which hits directly the poor everywhere. What can be the impact of this lopsided feature of globalization? If we take, for example, the globalization of prices of life saving medicines by the pharmaceutical companies of affluent countries, accompanied by privatization of the health care, it would simply mean death for millions of people from the poorer sections of society everywhere in the world as they cannot afford to buy these medicines at a globalized price.

Children and the aged ones from the these strata of the society will be the worst victims as they will not have the means to buy the high cost medicines. Their mortality rate will inevitably rise as a result. Therefore, we have to look at the impact of globalization from the angle of the poor people as well. We must not forget the fact that there already exists tremendous inequality in the consumption pattern of resources in the world. While Europe and the United States, with their 20 per cent of the world population together consume 80 per cent of the world resources,' 50 per cent of the world population, which live in the poorest of the developing countries, accounts only for 5.6 per cent of the world income. Moreover, the gap in the average per capita income between the rich and the poor countries remains at 58:1. Globalization will only further aggravate this existing inequality. That trend does not deserve encouragement or support. Another notable characteristic of the current globalization is that it is not attuned to humanitarian goals and is devoid of ethics or compassion. As Pierre Schori, a leading social democrat and Sweden's Deputy Foreign Minister, rightly observed recently, 'globalization without a global political and ethical framework cannot be a driving force for combating poverty and creating peace, democracy and development'.

Indeed, if globalization is expected to promote a balanced global interdependency, a globalized social standard should also be part of that agenda. But, there is no such social agenda which is aimed at overcoming the problems of poverty and hunger in the developing countries. The human welfare is left at the mercy of the market forces which does not augur well for the poorest sections of society. The poor everywhere gets marginalized under the impact of globalization. Since globalization is pursued through liberalization and deregulation strategies, its main concern is how to promote the interests of the export-oriented industries or of the TNCs rather than the betterment of the standard of living of the people. Therefore, if one looks at the ongoing globalization from a wider angle, one is struck by the fact that the whole programme is attuned to weaken the economies of the developing countries and preserve the dominance of a few rich countries. What is in progress, in the name of globalization and liberalization, today is the preparation of the layout and fixing of the conduits for smooth net resource transfer from the poorer countries to the rich countries on a permanent basis in the 21st century.

The IMF, the World Bank, the WTO and the G-7 are all partners in this project. Already billions of dollars (one estimate say $500 billion) are flowing every year from the South to the North in the form of trade advantages, debt servicing, royalties, profits on foreign investments and capital flights which has crippling effects on the South. There should be no doubt that a globalized world, as it is moulded today, will belong to the dominant and powerful countries and their TNCs in which the TNCs will play a pivotal role in every area of economic activity, with adverse social impact.

Therefore, this globalization is a euphemism for recolonization of the developing countries. As a great Indian socialist leader and humanist (Late) Jayaprakash Narayan said, the time to defend a structure is not when it totters on its slender pillars, but when someone begins to chip away parts from it. This valid advice we have to keep in mind when we formulate our response to the challenges of globalization. It is against this background that India has to chalk out its response to globalization and liberalization. I am not sure whether the Indian votaries of globalization and liberalization had carefully weighed the pros and cons or long-term implications of globalization before they launched economic reforms and structural adjustment in 1991 and tuned India's policies towards globalization and liberalization. When Manmohan Singh was India's Finance Minister, at the behest of the IMF India devalued the rupee, lifted many restrictions on imports, initiated privatization of Public Sector Undertakings, reduced allocations for Research and Development and slowed down technology development, and took measures to pass on a substantial portion of our domestic market to the TNCs, which are nothing but new East India Companies.

In India, instead of following a consensual approach on the basis of a wide ranging public debate, globalization and liberalization have been imposed from the top, like a palace coup. Indeed, the country was driven into it by a few enthusiasts who were then occupying key positions in India's Finance and Commerce ministries and who had a reverential approach to the IMF-World Bank prescriptions. Since 1991 they sincerely tried to implement the structural adjustment programmes stipulated by the IMF and the World Bank which contained loaded prescriptions like export orientation, import liberalization, privatization, foreign private investments, and so on which are all attuned to systematise a steady flow of net resources from India to the West. However, the fact that India's official approach in this regard was not based on any hard-headed assessment or foresight is clear from a remarkable letter which K.P. Geethakrishnan, India's former Finance Secretary and an initial supporter of liberalization when it was introduced in 1991, sent to his successor Montek Singh Ahluwalia, present Finance Secretary and an enthusiast of liberalization, in January 1995. In his letter, which he wrote in the wake of the economic crisis in Mexico, Geethakrishnan said that 'in free-market politics, there is no place for compassion or sympathy' for the poor, while there might be much at stake for the western countries pushing these policies. He made it clear that globalization-liberalization is not the right course for India.

It may be recalled that Mexico, under the leadership of President Carlos Salinas, had reoriented its economic policy under the guidance of the IMF, the World Bank, and the United States. And in the end, the whole economy got derailed. The free market approach led to the impoverishment of the Mexican people. Their anger against those who put Mexico on such a disastrous track reached the crescendo when the opposition leaders demanded that leaders like President Carlos Salinas should be tried for treason. Let us hope that such a situation will not arise in India. However, India has to draw lessons from the Latin American experience and also from the recent crises that swept through Southeast Asia and the tiger economies of East Asia. Ever since India decided to liberalize, the TNCs and their home country governments have mounted enormous pressure on the Government of India to reduce customs and excise duties and increase their market access. They wanted equal opportunities in the Indian market for several products where India has achieved high quality production. The IMF and the World Bank have also put pressure on India to reduce tariffs.

The enthusiasm shown by the Government of India to favour foreign manufacturers at the cost of India's domestic enterprises was criticized in the Indian manufacturing circles. India's steel producers like SAIL and TISCO had complained against the government's decision to reduce duty on some rolled steel products. I would like to underline, in this context, that neither the Government of India nor the Indian entrepreneurs, including Tatas and Birlas, should overestimate their positions and entertain an illusion that in a free market jungle their enterprises can successfully compete with the TNCs and survive in the country's domestic market. If they still entertain such fancy thoughts, they should check their facts and come to a realistic assessment of their position *vis-a-vis* the TNCs and the forces behind them. In fact, in front of the TNCs, India's national 'giants', like the Tatas and Birlas, are just small entities. As far as other small and medium enterprises are concerned, less said the better. Therefore, realistically, all our enterprises--big, medium and small--need protection in our domestic market. Otherwise, in a jungle of free-market they will get liquidated in no time. It must also be borne in mind that for the developed West, India is a targeted country in a mixed sense. Being the second largest country in the world with more than 900 million consumers, of which today at least 170 million could be categorised affluent, India's huge market potential is a big and enduring attraction for the West. Therefore, capturing this big potential market by hook or by crook is high on the agenda of the developed West.

India is a targeted country in another sense also. In the West, it is viewed as a potential major power and a potential competitor in many areas including technology, missile technology for example, trade and services. Therefore, preventing India from acquiring such competitiveness is also an unstated objective of some interested big powers. Such approaches are discernible in certain actions like the US application of export controls to prevent technology transfer to India and the American action to stifle US civilian space cooperation with India. Similarly, the United States is known to have used its diplomatic influence to prevent other countries from providing specific technologies to India, as in the case of the Russian action in 1993 not to honour a binding contract to supply India with cryogenic engine technology, although it had no relevance to missile development. More recently, the United States has imposed stringent safeguards and reporting requirements, in a new set up of high performance computer export rules, which will deny India access to even low-grade super computers. Under the new rules, its users in India will have to agree for on-site American inspection if they imported such computers for civilian use. Therefore, India will have to rely largely upon its own R&D for its critical technology requirements. However, what is important to note is the psyche which governs the attitudes of big powers towards

India, while they push hard to get the Indian markets opened for them.

If globalization and liberalization is about market access, India's market access in the West has not improved in any significant way. India has not found much additional space in the Western market for its manufactures. On the other hand, India is faced with a shrinking market access in the West. In recent years the Western countries have erected many new non-tariff barriers or imposed *de facto* trade sanctions against Indian exports under the pretexts of labour standards (child labour), technical standards, sanitary standard, or by using patenting instruments, like the patenting of the Basmati rice to the Ricetech in the United States. The flimsy pretext on which the Indian rayon skirts, a very popular item in the United States, were pushed out of the US market to favour domestic producers, by saying that they are not fireproof, is also a case in point. Similarly, non-tariff barriers were raised in Europe and the United States against Indian exports like marine products, pharmaceutical items, milk and dairy products, agricultural products, processed food items, and so on. The European Union's new stipulation, effective from I April 1998, that the milk product should remain untouched by human beings from the stage of milching up to retailing is clearly directed against India's ambition to become a major exporter of dairy products. The hitherto used sterilization technology was suddenly found inadequate for European Union's health standards! Added to this is the steady declining trend in the European Union imports. The European Union figures show that between 1981 and 1990 the total share of imports of the European Community got shrunk from 52 per cent in 1981 to 40 per cent in 1990. Of this, the share of Class-2 imports, a category in which much of the Indian exports belong, has been reduced from 42 per cent in 1981 to 31 per cent in 1990. So, realistically speaking, the EU market for non-EU members is progressively shrinking. Globalization and liberalization will not change that trend in favour of India or other developing countries. Therefore, India's efforts to further expand its market in the West through unilateral actions like globalization and liberalization is unlikely to bear any fruit. It will end up only as an act of self-injury. For real market expansion India will have to seriously look elsewhere also—in the South itself.

The point is that a whole lot of non-tariff barriers are being raised in a concerted manner against India's potential export expansion. Strangely enough, while the West is pushing India to open up its domestic market for their exports through globalization and liberalization, the West is systematically closing down its market for Indian exports on one pretext or another through protectionist measures. India has to take note of this mind set and take appropriate defensive measures to protect its vital interests. How to meet the growing challenges of non-tariff barriers raised against Indian exports needs careful consideration of Indian experts.

Like with many other oil importing developing countries, the IMF and the World Bank have used India's weakness as a debtor country to dictate national policies to promote globalization and liberalization. This weakness stems from the fact that India's foreign debt stands today at $ 98 billion, and the country is spending 26.3 per cent of its export earnings every year for debt servicing which is on the high side. Making use of this weakness, the IMF and the World Bank dictated 'structural adjustment programme' to India to effect changes in the country's economic and monetary policies. The programme contained heavy dosages of domestic liberalization and import liberalization. In 1997, the IMF descended to lower levels and asked India to hike prices of petroleum products and phase out fertilizer subsidies. Also, it demanded reduction of civil service employment, cutting of subsidies, more privatization, a flexible approach to exchange rate management and more openings for the foreign banks and foreign insurance companies. It has also pressed for further trade liberalization through further tariff cuts, speedy elimination of quantitative restrictions (QRs) on consumer goods and phasing out of small scale sector reservations. The implications of these demands for India, if conceded, are anybody's guess. In recent years, the WTO has joined the IMF and the World Bank to assist the globalization-liberalization process in India.

The WTO, with the support of US, EU, Canada and Australia, is also putting pressure on India to lift quantitative restrictions and to phase out restrictions on agricultural imports. One implication of this liberalization of food imports would mean the loss of livelihood of millions of poor farmers. Its spillover effects for India will be disastrous. What does globalization mean in the lives of ordinary people of India is best illustrated by Anand Patwardhan's recent documentary film, *Fishing in the Sea of Greed*. The film depicts the hardships of Indian fishermen due to the induction of huge foreign ships of the transnational fishing companies, with their 15 km long nets and on-board processing plants, for fishing which destroys the livelihood of millions of fishermen in India's coastal belt. From a posse of mechanized trawlers of the 1970s, India's poor fishermen today are faced with a large number of huge foreign ships fishing around against their small catamarans.

According to Patwardhan, one such ship can scoop up more fish in one day than what a thousand catamarans can catch in a year. Similar situations exist in many other sectors of livelihood of ordinary Indians due to globalization and liberalization. The central issue in India's economy today is poverty eradication. An essential pre-requisite for achieving this goal is to provide productive jobs for every able bodied person in India and take the country towards a near full employment situation. That would require a more labour intensive economic reform. Globalization-liberalization runs counter to this imperative need of the country. Instead of releasing people from poverty, globalization will put more people into the poverty bracket. India need not rush into this globalization process, like moth's fatal attraction for the flame, and get hastily enmeshed into a globalized system where it would remain a victim of the situations of others' making. Therefore, it has to be extra cautious. I feel that until and unless it obtains an effective position in the global decision making process it will be disastrous for India to surrender its sovereign spaces of decision-making to foreign powers on the basis of illusory expectations. India can prosper only from domestic economic growth, for which we should find new resources through domestic savings, rather than collecting more and more crutches from abroad in the forms of loans, direct foreign investment (the annual inflow of which in any case is less than 0.25 per cent of India's GDP), and so on to ensure high rate of domestic investment.

INDIA WILL LOOK AFTER ITS OWN SECURITY

—*Sunday:* 7-13 July 1996

Mr Gujral is representative of a government which is made up of more than 20 different political parties. And with someone like Mulayam Singh Yadav making controversial statements--the last two were that India, Pakistan and Bangladesh should become a federation and that Pakistanis and Bangladesh is should be allowed to travel freely here--Mr Gujral has his job cut out for him.

Gujral has had a long diplomatic career. After a public spat with Sanjay Gandhi over a pro-Emergency broadcast over All India Radio, Gujral took up assignment as India's Ambassador to the Soviet Union at the height of the Cold War. At that time, world opinion was against Indira Gandhi's Emergency regime and it says something about Gujral's survivability that he remained at that job even after the Janata government came to power.

The Soviet experience gave him a sense of real politik. And being a Punjabi, he also has a special feeling for the Pakistani establishment and there was a little of the personal element in it when its Foreign Minister, Aseef Ahmad Ali praised Gujral as soon as he took over.

But he is still very pragmatic. Speaking to *Sunday,* Inder Kumar Gujral seemed undaunted by all this. Quietly forceful and completely comfortable with his assignment, he fielded a wide range of questions. Excerpts from the interview:

Sunday.- The first Janata government's relations with Pakistan were better than the second Janata regime's, Why?

I.K. Gujral: Pakistan's interference in India's internal affairs increased particularly in 1989. Prime Ministers in the past have tried their best to improve relations. We in India, irrespective of the government in office, have tried to keep the relations warm and cordial with the Pakistani people and the government.

The Prime Minister and I have responded to their letters (showing interest in bilateral talks to resolve problems). We await their response.

Q: Does that also indicate greater trade between the two countries?

A: The South Asian Association for Regional Cooperation (SAARC) countries got together to introduce the era of South Asian Preferential Trade Agreement (SAPTA). The trade agreement has to be approved and permitted by SAARC laws. India has already endorsed it and now it is for Pakistan to decide. That will surely widen the area of trade between the two countries.

Q: Why didn't you sign the Comprehensive Test Ban Treaty (CTBT)?

A: India's policy ever since (Jawaharlal) Nehru's time has been in favour of nuclear disarmament. We have consistently been projecting the idea of not only a test ban but a ban on all weapons of mass destruction. And the CTBT was initially meant to do that but now we feel that the draft does not help fulfil the purpose.

The five nuclear powers have not promised to ban the weapons of mass destruction. Thus for me to be associated with something that is a mere charade is out of the question. Those who have the arms are trying to sermonise those who do not have arms. The draft treaty does not take care of all these things.

Q: What could be the consequences of all this?

A: The consequences can't be any because we are not the ones who have the arms. Relations between two in any case are not unilinear but multi-dimensional and they will continue to prosper.

Q: On the one hand China is supplying M-11s to Pakistan and on the other, we want to have a good relationship with China. Don't you see a contradiction there?

A: That is a question that should be answered by all those who have signed the Non-Proliferation Treaty (NPT). The NPT norms are being flouted time and again. India will look after its own security. We have to periodically assess the threats and respond to them.

Q: Is there any need for India to declare itself as a nuclear power?

A: We have to settle everything according to our threat perceptions. When we say we preserve our options, it means we will respond to a situation as it develops. This is the ingredient of every country's foreign policy.

Q: What is the current position on India's efforts to become a member of the UN Security Council?

A: India is a contender for the South Asian seat. But Japan is also contending for that seat and that does not make sense. Japan should be considered for the Far Eastern seat.

Q: What is your position on the Burmese pro-democracy movement?

A: As a democracy we naturally have sympathy with all democracies. However, we do not believe in intervening from outside. We have sympathy with Myanmar as a country and hope that their problems will be sorted out democratically and peacefully. We are also keen on Myanmar becoming a part of SAARC, which can happen with the help of all SAARC nations.

Q: What is your view of the Tamil ethnic problem in Sri Lanka?

A: We respect the policies of President Chandrika Kumaratunga and have full faith in them. So far, she has been successful in sorting out the Tamil problems in Sri Lanka. We would definitely not like to interfere in their affairs. I only hope that the refugees can go back home with dignity and honour.

Q: Do you consider the infiltration of Bangladesh is into India to be as big a problem as the Bharatiya Janata Party (BJP) says it is?

A: Bangladesh has a new government. We would like to sort out all the existing problems with them.

Q: Do you intend to replace certain Ambassadors? Naresh Chandra, the Indian Ambassador to the US, was currently in the news.

A: I need not clarify that since there was no proposal to call Naresh Chandra back, postings will take place in the normal course.

INDIA HAS NO FEAR OF ISOLATION: GUJRAL

--*The Economic Times:* 5 July 1996

External Affairs Minister I.K. Gujral says India does not fear global isolation on the nuclear test ban issue and is not prepared to 'climb down' from the stand that it has taken on the Comprehensive test Ban Treaty (CTBT).

'National security interests are not safeguarded on the basis of votes taken or on the basis of how many supporters we have or how many we don't have,' Mr Gujral said, adding, 'no country in the world does it'.

'If there are some powers that think that they cannot go with us, I have nothing against them. But I would say:

India cannot compromise its own security interests,' he said.

Asked if India was prepared to climb down for the sake of a compromise on the stalled treaty, Mr Gujral shot back: 'On security issues, how does one climb down?

'We are saying, please promise at least, even if you don't implement, that you are one day going to abolish all nuclear weapons. We are also saying, please take into account the security environment around India,' Mr Gujral said.

He said India will not react after assessing the reaction from world capitals as to whether Indian interests have been accommodated or not, but security will remain the 'bottom line and the front line' in any negotiation.

Mr Gujral, who has come back to steer Indian diplomacy after a gap of six years, said the CTBT issues apart, the 'central point of our foreign policy has to be to renew friendship and cooperation with our neighbours'.

He said India had responded 'positively' to the Pakistani leadership's overtures soon after Prime Minister HD Deve Gowda's government took over and was awaiting its response.

He said India had not reacted even when it was noticed that some public speeches of the Pakistani Prime Minister and Foreign Minister were not in the same spirit as the letters, 'because we do not want the process or the possibility of our dialogue to get thwarted in any way'.

He said 'India had, in fact, taken some "unilateral steps" to encourage people-to-people contact because the basic posture of Indian foreign policy is that we want to have friendly relations'.

Asked if India would respond to Pakistan's demands on what it calls the 'core issue' of Kashmir, Mr Gujral said he would not like to prejudge or prejudice the discussions, but would reiterate that India was 'prepared to discuss all subjects without preconditions on either side'.

To reports about a Sri Lankan offer of mediation at the instance of Pakistan, Mr Gujral said there was no such proposal from Sri Lankan Foreign Minister Lakshman Kadirgamar when he came recently and Colombo appreciates the fact that 'it is the bilateral dialogue that we are trying to activate between us and Pakistan'.

He said India would build very friendly relations with the United States. There are some issues on which we do not agree. But there are several issues on which we agree. And I emphasize more the areas where we agree than the areas where we do not agree,' Mr Gujral said.

He said he had not yet planned any visit to Washington but would visit New York in September to attend the UN General Assembly session.

THE RIGHT TO TEST

--*Outlook:* 17 July 1996

Foreign Minister I.K. Gujral spoke to Sunil Narula on Indians retaining of the Nuclear option due to national security reasons and the country's threat perceptions. Excerpts:

India has always taken a moralistic stand on Nuclear disarmament. Why are we talking national security now?

I don't think we've ever taken any stand which didn't have the input of national security. It so happens that our national security and our moral posture coincided. Even today every country would be safe, including us, if there were no nuclear arms around. That's our general approach, and we continue to have it. In Geneva, we said that the treaty being drafted doesn't rid the world of nuclear arms. So when we say we are talking about security, it's not something new. Every country gives priority to its own security interests.

We never said it in so many words ...

I don't think so. Till now we'd been faced with one reality, that was the Cold War. Therefore, the articulation and the phraseology was different, our rhetoric was different. This conference is in a way a continuation of the NPT. Our policy regarding the NPT and this is consistent. We did not sign the NPT, we're not signing this. There is a clear linkage between our policy on the two.

In March, Salman Haider had said nuclear arms are not essential for our security. Isn't this contradictory?

When he said nuclear arms are not necessary for the world, he meant for everybody. He didn't mean everybody can have nuclear arms and India can feel secure. His statement has not been correctly understood.

What use is it to have an open nuclear option if we don't exercise it?

I've never said we won't exercise it. The question invariably asked is when? Now the 'when' is correlated with our assessment of threat. Whether it's a nuclear weapon or not, the weaponry is selected on the basis of threat perception. When we say our options are open, it means we'll act as per our threat perception.

It's thought if India conducts tests, the West will come down hard on us.

I'm not saying the world will come down hard on us or not, nor am I saying we should test or not. What I'm saying is, if at any stage our security planners come to the conclusion, which they have not now, that a test is called for, then whatever the world might say we may have to do it. Security decisions are not taken on the basis of referendum or popularity.

There's no transparency in our security policy.

Security policies are never transparent anywhere in the world. Do we know the security policy of all our neighbours? Do we know the weaponry they have?

India won't suffer if the Indian public is aware?

I'm all for open debate, but that doesn't mean you tell everyone, "I've got a knife in my pocket to defend myself.

Do we expect sanctions?

The issue is not sanctions. The point is, we've made it very clear that we're unable to sign the treaty as it is now drafted. We're meeting after a month, let's see if there's any change... if so, we'll act accordingly.

IN OUR NATIONAL INTERESTS

--*Frontline:* 12 July 1986

External Affairs Minister, Inder Kumar Gujral is one of the most experienced members of the United Front Cabinet. Besides holding important portfolios including External Affairs in past Ministries, the suave politician was India's Ambassador to the Soviet Union in the late 1970s. He spoke to John Cherian in New Delhi on a wide range of issues on 22 June, soon after India's decision on the CTBT. **Excerpts:**

Q: What are your comments on the reaction to India's decision not to sign the CTBT?

A: The reactions of some countries are on expected lines. The decision taken by India is in conformity with our national interests. That is where the line is drawn. All the same, we have never slammed the door. We will continue to participate in discussions relating to various dimensions of the issue. In Indian diplomacy we have never walked out or slammed the door.

Q: Is there scope for improvement in bilateral links with Pakistan?

A: We have welcomed the two letters, one from the Pakistan Prime Minister and the other from the Foreign Minister, as soon as our Prime Minister took office. We have responded to that with equal enthusiasm. We all feel that dialogue should continue so that it will lead to an environment of good neighbourliness. As we have said in our letter, we are prepared to discuss every issue without any preconditions on either side. Naturally the dialogue will have to begin at the level of officials but we will respond when we get an answer from the leadership of Pakistan to the Indian Prime Minister's letter.

Q: Is the focus of the new Government also going to be on economic diplomacy?

A: Economic diplomacy has come to occupy centrestage in the post-Cold War era the world over. That is the Indian perception too. Therefore we would like to cooperate with our near and distant neighbours to strengthen the Indian economy.

Q: What will be the foreign policy priorities?

A: We attach a great deal of importance to relations with neighbouring countries and also countries outside the region. For instance, India has become a dialogue partner with ASEAN (Association of South East Asian Nations). We have good relations with Central Asia and all the former Soviet states in the region. We would like to build on that. Our relations with the United States have been very cordial, of course; it has been our largest trade and economic partner. Sometimes there are different points of view but it goes to the credit of both countries that we have been able to work out amicable solutions. This will continue to be our approach. But we expect the United States to appreciate some of India's sensitivities.

Q: What about relations with Moscow?

A: Our relations with Russia have a long history which is very positive. Unfortunately, Russia had been going through a difficult phase but now its economy is slowly coming back to its original shape. There is hardly an area, be it cultural, political or economic, in which we have not been close.

Q: Has Sri Lanka expressed any misgivings about the composition of the Government? There have been some reports in the Indian media.

A: The coming of the Sri Lankan Foreign Minister as our first guest after the formation of the new Government was very much appreciated. We consider this as a gesture of great friendship. We had an exchange of views in an atmosphere of cordiality and friendship. We expressed the hope that the situation in their country will improve to such an extent that they would be able to repatriate the several thousand displaced Sri Lankan refugees in Tamil Nadu and elsewhere. We want people to go back of their own free will. Nor will we exert any pressure on the displaced persons. India has promised to give a helping hand to Sri Lanka for the rehabilitation of the displaced persons.

Q: In recent times the tendency of Washington to impose unilateral economic blockades and trade embargoes on countries it does not like is causing great concern to the international community. What are your Government's views on the issue?

A: As a matter of policy we are against blockades and economic sanctions by one country against another. International cooperation suffers because of such policies. We hope that differences will be sorted out through dialogue and discussions. No one country should assume that it has the policing responsibilities.

[We owe a deep sense of gratitude to the original contributors, newsppers/publications from where the basic information is reproduced here.—*Editor*]

CHAPTER 2

India and Nepal

India and Nepal are closely linked—historically, economically, and culturally. Both have common ethos and aspirations. Both inherit a legacy of mutual co-existence and faith. But in the era of globalisation, many changes are being felt. Emergence of muslim fundamentalists in Nepal, terrorists and other criminals are finding a safe hide in Nepal. Recent political upheavals in Nepal are also influencing mutual interests. Presence of Pakistani and Bangladeshi terrorists in Nepal is gradually deteriorating mutual amicable relations. In fact, a prosperous, strong and politically stable Nepal can only be the prime concern of Indian foreign policy. India always rendered and committed for this. A buffer state between China and India, Nepal should share India's agonies and concerns. This chapter puts light on India-Nepal foreign relations.

A landlocked country, Nepal was sandwiched between two giant neighbours—China and India. To the north, the Himalayas constituted a natural and mostly impassible frontier, and beyond that was the border with China. To the south, east, and west, Nepal was hemmed in by India. Without an outlet to the sea, Nepal was dependent on India for international trade and transit facilities.

During the British hegemony (1858-1947), Nepal sought

geostrategic isolation. This traditional isolationism partially was the product of the relative freedom the country enjoyed from external intervention and domination. From the mid-nineteenth century, when Britain emerged as the unchallenged power in India and the Qing Dynasty (1644-1911) in China was in decline, Nepal made accommodations with Britain on the best possible terms. Without surrendering autonomy on internal matters, Nepal received guarantees of protection from Britain against external aggression and interference. London also considered a steady flow of Gurkha recruits from Nepal as vital to support Britain's security in India and its other colonial territories.

In the 1950s, Nepal began a gradual opening up and a commitment to a policy of neutrality and nonalignment. At the 1973 summit of the Nonaligned Movement in Algiers, King Birendra proposed that "Nepal, situated between two of the most populous countries of the world, wishes her frontiers to be declared a zone of peace." In Birendra's 1975 coronation address, he formally asked other countries to endorse his proposal. Since then, the concept of Nepal as a zone of peace has become a main theme of Kathmandu's foreign policy.

As of mid-1991, Nepal had been endorsed as a zone of peace by more than 110 nations. Many of these countries also recommended a regional approach to peace as the goal. Without the endorsement of India and the former Soviet Union, however, the prospect of broader international acceptance was dim.

At the beginning of the 1990s, Nepal had established diplomatic relations with approximately 100 countries. Nepal was an active member of the United Nations (UN) and participated in a number of its specialized agencies. Nepal also was a founding member of the South Asian

Association for Regional Cooperation (SAARC) and had successfully negotiated several bilateral and multilateral economic, cultural, and technical assistance programs. Because of its geographical proximity to and historical links with China and India, Nepal's foreign policy was focused mainly on maintaining close and friendly relations with these two countries and on safeguarding its national security and independence. Nepal's relations with the United States, Europe, and the Soviet Union showed new signs of vitality in 1991.

Even after India had achieved independence from Britain in 1947, Nepalese-Indian relations continued to be based on the second Treaty of Sagauli, which had been signed with the government of British India in 1925. Beginning in 1950, however, relations were based on two treaties. Under the Treaty of Peace and Friendship, ratified in July 1950, each government agreed to acknowledge and respect the other's sovereignty, territorial integrity, and independence; to continue diplomatic relations; and, on matters pertaining to industrial and economic development, to grant rights equal to those of its own citizens to the nationals of the other residing in its territory. Agreements on all subjects in this treaty superseded those on similar matters dealt with in the previous treaties between Nepal and Britain. In the Treaty of Trade and Commerce, ratified in October 1950, India recognized Nepal's right to import and export commodities through Indian territory and ports. Customs could not be levied on commodities in transit through India.

India's influence over Nepal increased throughout the 1950s. The Citizenship Act of 1952 allowed Indians to immigrate to Nepal and acquire Nepalese citizenship with ease--a source of some resentment in Nepal. And, Nepalese were allowed to migrate freely to India--a source of resentment there. (This policy was not changed until 1962 when several restrictive clauses were added to the Nepalese constitution.) Also in 1952, an Indian military mission was established in Nepal. In 1954 a memorandum provided for the joint coordination of foreign policy, and Indian security posts were established in Nepal's northern frontier. At the same time, Nepal's dissatisfaction with India's growing influence began to emerge, and overtures to China were initiated as a counterweight to India.

King Mahendra continued to pursue a nonaligned policy begun during the reign of Prithvi Narayan Shah in the mid-eighteenth century. In the late 1950s and 1960s, Nepal voted differently from India in the UN unless India's basic interests were involved. The two countries consistently remained at odds over the rights of landlocked states to transit facilities and access to the sea.

Following the 1962 Sino-Indian border war, the relationship between Kathmandu and New Delhi thawed significantly. India suspended its support to India-based Nepalese opposition forces. Nepal extracted several concessions, including transit rights with other countries through India and access to Indian markets. In exchange, through a secret accord concluded in 1965, similar to an arrangement that had been suspended in 1963, India won a monopoly on arms sales to Nepal.

In 1969 relations again became stressful as Nepal challenged the existing mutual security arrangement and asked that the Indian security checkposts and liaison group be withdrawn. Resentment also was expressed against the Treaty of Peace and Friendship of 1950. India grudgingly withdrew its military checkposts and liaison group, although the treaty was not abrogated.

Further changes in Nepalese-Indian relations occurred in the 1970s. India's credibility as a regional power was increased--and Nepal's vulnerability was reinforced--by the 1971 Indo-Soviet Treaty of Peace, Friendship, and Cooperation; the 1971 Indo-Pakistani War, which led to the emergence of an independent Bangladesh; the absorption of Sikkim into India in 1974; increased unofficial support of the Nepali Congress Party leadership in India; rebellions fomented by pro-Beijing Naxalite elements in 1973-74 in West Bengal State bordering Nepal; and India's nuclear explosion in 1974. Nepal adopted a cautious policy of appeasement of India, and in his 1975 coronation address King Birendra called for the recognition of Nepal as a zone of peace where military competition would be off-limits. India showed some flexibility in placating Nepal by distancing, if not disassociating, itself from the Nepalese opposition forces based in India, agreeing to a favourable trade and transit arrangement in 1978, and entering into another agreement on joint industrial ventures between Indian and Nepalese firms. The latter agreement, by opening the possibilities of India's investment, indirectly furthered India's domination of Nepal's economy. India also continued to maintain a high level of economic assistance to Nepal.

In the mid-1970s, Nepal pressed for substantial amendments to the 1971 trade and transit treaty, which was due to expire in 1976. India ultimately backed down from its initial position to terminate the 1971 treaty even before a new treaty could be negotiated. The 1978 agreements incorporated Nepal's demand for separate treaties for trade and transit. The relationship between the two nations improved over the next decade, but not steadily.

India continued to support the Nepalese opposition and refused to endorse Nepal as a zone of peace. In 1987

India urged expulsion of Nepalese settlers from neighbouring Indian states, and Nepal retaliated by introducing a work permit system for Indians working in Nepal. That same year, the two countries signed an agreement setting up a joint commission to increase economic cooperation in trade and transit, industry, and water resources.

Relations between the two countries sank to a low point in 1988 when Kathmandu signed an agreement with Beijing to purchase weapons soon after a report that China had won a contract for constructing a road in the western sector to connect China with Nepal. India perceived these developments as deliberately jeopardizing its security. India also was annoyed with the high volume of unauthorized trade across the Nepalese border, the issuance of work permits to the estimated 150,000 Indians residing in Nepal, and the imposition of a 55 percent tariff on Indian goods entering Nepal.

In retaliation for these developments, India put Nepal under a virtual trade siege. In March 1989, upon the expiration of the 1978 treaties on trade and transit rights, India insisted on negotiating a single unified treaty in addition to an agreement on unauthorized trade, which Nepal saw as a flagrant attempt to strangle its economy. On March 23, 1989, India declared that both treaties had expired and closed all but two border entry points.

The economic consequences of the trade and transit deadlock were enormous. Shortages of Indian imports such as fuel, salt, cooking oil, food, and other essential commodities soon occurred. The lucrative tourist industry went into recession. Nepal also claimed that the blockade caused ecological havoc since people were compelled to use already dwindling forest resources for energy in lieu of gasoline and kerosene, which came mostly via India. To withstand the renewed Indian pressure, Nepal undertook a major diplomatic initiative to present its case on trade and transit matters to the world community.

The relationship with India was further strained in 1989 when Nepal decoupled its rupee from the Indian rupee which previously had circulated freely in Nepal. India retaliated by denying port facilities in Calcutta to Nepal, thereby preventing delivery of oil supplies from Singapore and other sources.

A swift turn in relations followed the success of the Movement for the Restoration of Democracy in early 1990. In June 1990, a joint Kathmandu-New Delhi communiqué was issued pending the finalization of a comprehensive arrangement covering all aspects of bilateral relations, restoring trade relations, reopening transit routes for Nepal's imports, and formalizing respect of each other's security concerns. Essentially, the communiqué announced the restoration of the status quo ante and the reopening of all border points, and Nepal agreed to various concessions regarding India's commercial privileges. Kathmandu also announced that lower cost was the decisive factor in its purchasing arms and personnel carriers from China and that Nepal was advising China to withhold delivery of the last shipment. The communiqué declared that Kathmandu and New Delhi would cooperate in industrial development, in harnessing the waters of their common rivers for mutual benefit, and in protecting and managing the environment.

Security Environment

Although landlocked Nepal was surrounded by both India and China, the kingdom's geographic, economic, and cultural orientation was more closely linked to India. Whereas many Nepalese stressed the differences that defined Nepal's national existence, India's policy makers tended to stress the similarities that bound the two countries together. According to New Delhi's perception, South Asia constituted an integral security unit in which India played the lead role. Many Nepalese resented this interpretation and accused India of being insensitive to Nepal's status as an independent nation.

Despite New Delhi's insistence that stable, independent neighbours were vital to India's security, many Nepalese regarded India as a regional bully. Because of these differing attitudes, Nepal's relations with India oscillated considerably over the years, particularly in matters relating to security.

In a speech before Parliament in 1950, the Indian prime minister, Jawaharlal Nehru, summed up India's security concerns vis-à-vis Nepal. He stated: "From time immemorial, the Himalayas have provided us with magnificent frontiers. . . . We cannot allow that barrier to be penetrated, because it is also the principal barrier to India. Therefore, as much as we appreciate the independence of Nepal, we cannot allow anything to go wrong in Nepal or permit that barrier to be crossed or weakened, because that would be a risk to our own security." Nehru and his successors subsequently stated that any Chinese attack on Nepal would be regarded as aggression against India.

In 1950 China forcibly annexed Tibet, which New Delhi regarded as a buffer zone shielding the subcontinent from real or potential Chinese incursions. Nepal thus came to play a much larger role in India's security calculations. Fearing that China might eventually subvert or invade Nepal, India signed a Treaty of Peace and Friendship with the Rana regime in 1950. Although not a formal military alliance, the treaty required both parties to consult and "devise effective countermeasures" in the event of a security threat to either country. Nepal's inclusion in the Indian defense perimeter was made explicit by an exchange of secret letters--later made public--that accompanied the treaty, stating inter alia that "neither government shall tolerate any threat to the security of the other by a foreign aggressor." To assuage Nepalese fears of Indian domination, the treaty also stipulated that Indian forces could be introduced into the country only at the invitation of the Nepalese government. The two sides simultaneously signed a trade and transit agreement that extended reciprocal rights with regard to bilateral trade and residential arrangements as well as transshipment of Nepalese goods through India.

In 1952 the Indian Military Mission arrived in Kathmandu to reorganize Nepal's armed forces and bring the kingdom's defenses more in line with India's security requirements. In implementing changes, Nepal drastically reduced the size of its postwar army and revamped its training and organization along Indian lines. Indian advisers also played key roles in training the civil service and police force. Many Nepalese--military officers and civil servants, in particular--were outraged by India's actions, which they saw as an insult to national self-respect. Indian influence was further strengthened, however, by the cooperation of both countries' militaries on several occasions in the 1950s, when at Nepal's request Indian troops helped quell disturbances near their common boundary. As Sino-Indian tensions mounted in the late 1950s, Indian soldiers and technicians assisted in staffing some of the checkposts on the frontier with Tibet. Despite close military ties, Nepal, however, has never allowed garrisoning of Indian troops or joint military exercises in the country.

In 1962 Indian and Chinese forces fought a brief but decisive war over desolate stretches of their disputed frontier.

India's unprepared forces suffered a humiliating defeat, despite the fact that China unilaterally withdrew its forces after several weeks of heavy fighting. Although Nepal did not become embroiled in the fighting and both belligerents respected the kingdom's territorial integrity, the war reinforced Nepalese perceptions of their country's perilous role as a Sino-Indian security buffer.

Because of India's growing influence and Nepal's corresponding dependence on India, international diplomacy has always been a vital element of Nepal's survival strategy. Nepal was an active participant and a voice of moderation in the United Nations (UN) and the Nonaligned Movement, although the viability of the latter organization was in doubt after the end of the Cold War. In addition, Nepal firmly supported the South Asian Association for Regional Cooperation headquartered in Kathmandu. SAARC eschewed any role in regional security because the threats perceived by Nepal and the other small states of the region were often at variance with those perceived by India.

In 1975 King Birendra proposed that the UN declare Nepal a zone of peace, where military competition would be off-limits. In Birendra's view, the proposal symbolized Nepal's desire to maintain cordial relations with both its neighbours by placing internationally sanctioned restrictions on the use of military force.

Nepalese-Indian relations underwent major jolts over a protracted period starting in 1988. In June of that year, Birendra concluded a secret arms purchase with China, whereby Beijing would supply obsolescent air defense artillery at bargain prices. India probably learned of the deal within days or weeks of the agreement and protested vigorously that Birendra's action had violated the spirit, if not the letter, of the 1950 treaty. Although the appearance of a limited number of vintage air defense weapons hardly represented a threat to Indian Air Force contingency plans, India interpreted the sale as a dangerous precedent that could not go unchallenged. As bilateral tensions mounted, India added other complaints regarding Nepal's supposed insensitivity to India's vital interests. Birendra, capitalizing on nationalistic fervor, was intransigent and insisted that Nepal had the sovereign right to determine its own defense requirements. He also pointed out that Nepal's use of air defense assets against India would never arise as long as Indian fighters respected Nepalese air space; New Delhi countered that the only plausible use for the weapons was against India.

In March 1989, the Nepal-India trade and transit agreement came up for renewal. India's prime minister, Rajiv Gandhi, refused to extend the agreement unless Nepal agreed to meet India's commercial and defense concerns. After both sides refused to back down, India allowed the agreement to lapse and closed thirteen of the fifteen border checkposts that regulated most of Nepal's trade with the outside world. The blackade was a severe blow to Nepal because there were no other reliable transit routes. The Chinese rail line in Tibet ended 800 kilometers short of the Nepalese border, and the road linking Kathmandu and Tibet was closed much of the year by avalanches and monsoon landslides. Although the Nepalese army was pressed into action to keep Nepal's section of the road open to the extent possible, it could improve the situation only to a limited extent. Pakistan and Bangladesh were hardly in a position to supply major assistance because their only land routes to Nepal traversed India. The Soviet Union, the United States, and other Western powers quietly declined to take sides and urged India and Nepal to return to the bargaining table.

In the final analysis, the dispute underscored a central geopolitical reality: landlocked Nepal did not have the military, diplomatic, or economic clout to withstand an Indian blockade as long as the government in New Delhi was willing to risk international opprobrium and press its case against the kingdom. Many Nepalese saw New Delhi's actions as "punishment" for Birendra's show of independence and as a manifestation of India's supposed policy of isolating and subjugating its smaller neighbours. Some Nepalese observers, however, criticized Birendra's handling of the dispute, arguing that the king harnessed popular fervor against India to rally patriotic support behind the palace.

Some fifteen months of economic dislocations and diplomatic recriminations placed heavy pressure on both sides to halt the slide in relations. Finally, both sides reaffirmed the 1950 treaty, and Kathmandu agreed not to purchase defense items abroad without consulting New Delhi. Birendra requested that China stop delivery of a final shipment of air defense equipment. Relations gradually returned to normal and improved significantly after Nepal's democratically elected government assumed office in May 1991. The dispute convinced many Nepalese, however, that India had the capacity and will to pressure small neighbours in pursuit of its foreign policy objectives--a message that New Delhi clearly intended to convey to Beijing.

The recent Maoist insurgence and disturbances in Nepal as led to near ousting of Monarchy in partial way, in this wake India-Nepal relations became tense. Let us march ahead optimistically.

CHAPTER 3

India and Bhutan

The Himalyan Kingdom of Bhutan, though a small country, occupies strategies position. A peace loving nation, Bhutan has amicable relations with India. India also respects Bhutanese ethos on all counts. Here we have tried to illustrate dynamics of India-Bhutan relations in the present day context.

The present Indo-Bhutanese relations are governed by the treaty concluded between the two countries in August 1949. The treaty was largely based on the earlier treaty which Bhutan had signed with the British India Government in 1910. It was under Article VIII of this treaty that the Government of Bhutan agreed to be guided by the advice of the British Indian Government in regard to its external relations. The treaty was hailed "important as it put an effective stop to Chinese attempts at any further colonisation of Bhutan." Chinese interests and activities in Bhutan towards the close of the nineteenth century but particularly during and immediately after the Younghusband Expedition to Tibet had convinced the then policy makers in India that the only way to put a stop to all such Chinese claims and intrigues with regard to Bhutan was to sign a treaty with Bhutan on such lines as would entitle the British Indian Government to conduct all the bilateral relations of

Bhutan. Through such a treaty China, it was contended, will have no right to have any direct dealings with Bhutan. Indeed, by 1908-09 the idea that Bhutan might act as some kind of buffer state between India and China came to be accepted as the most rational policy as far as the British Indian interests in the Himalayan region were concerned.

China, it was further argued, "had made strenuous attempts at populating the inhospitable tracts around Batang in eastern Tibet, not far from the northern borders of Bhutan." China had also claimed to be the suzerain power of Bhutan. Even though all such claims had been rejected by the then Maharaja of Bhutan yet this was considered to be no guarantee that China would desist from repeating their claims in the future or, that Bhutan could be prevented from being lured into Chinese designs. Sir Charles A. Bell, the Political Officer in charge of Bhutan and Sikkim affairs therefore, while recommending the revision of the treaty of 1865 with Bhutan, observed in 1908. In view of the great importance of the interests at stake it is necessary for us to endeavour to obtain the assent of Bhutan to her placing her foreign relations under our Control, whenever opportunity for obtaining that assent may occur

This, he said, would counter all the Chinese advances in Bhutan in the recent years. A brief historical background of the circumstances which finally led to the signing of the treaty in 1910 will indicate as to how strong was the Chinese factor which urged upon the then policy makers in India the necessity of the conclusion of the treaty. As a matter of fact the strategic assessment of the region as made by them was such that they found no alternate arrangement more suitable than this. The need for the conclusion of the 1949 treaty with Bhutan was also conceived largely in the context of free India's strategic and security interests in the Himalayan region; the geo-political realities being such. Yet, what was equally important was that Bhutan, a small neighbour of India, must not have any such apprehensions and suspicions under which the treaty of 1949 and its necessary features may smack of any imperialistic designs on the part of India.

Shorn, therefore, of its imperialistic goals which was an added thrust, the treaty of 1949 is largely a continuation of the policy, the foundations of which were laid during Curzon's rule in India towards the beginning of the twentieth century. To a large extent the China factor in Indo-Bhutanese relations can be traced to the physical and geographical factors rather than purely to the perceptions of the policy makers. Situated between the two Asian giants, India in the south and China in the north, it is the strategic location of Bhutan, more than anything else, which makes it obligatory on the part of Indian leadership to have friendly and intimate relations with Bhutan.

It is also on account of its location that Bhutan has witnessed all the pulls and pressures that must characterize the mutual relations of two powerful neighbouring nations. The land-locked situation of Bhutan on the other hand is a permanent factor limiting Bhutan's role as an independent country. She is dependent upon her neighbours for an opening to the world at large. Known as "the World's last Shangri-la", Bhutan was a closed country till 1960. As in the case of other Himalayan countries including Nepal and Tibet, a deep sense of preservation of her identity made Bhutan also keep her doors shut to the entry of all foreigners particularly Europeans. Naturally, therefore, its contacts with the world at large, beyond its Himalayan neighbours were non-existent till about two decades back. Yet, within Hie Himalayan region and with her Himalayan neighbours Bhutan maintained fairly regular inter-relationships particularly in trade and religious matters. In the maintenance of intra-Himalayan contacts Tibet was the focal point. Her second closest neighbour was of course India. Bhutan was also the principal gateway for India to Tibet as much as Sikkim. But ever since the events in Tibet in the late lifties and sealing of the border with Tibet, Bhutan, for all her communication with the outside world, came to depend completely on India. In short, after the independence of India in 1947 and the birth of Communist China in 1949 the need for a buffer region between the two Asian giants led the Government of India to review, with certain adjustments, the treaty with Bhutan.

Treaties with identical objectives were also signed with the other two Himalayan kingdoms of Nepal and Sikkim in 1950. The occupation of Tibet by China during 1950-51 brought vital changes in the Himalayan region which called for certain adjustments in India's bilateral relations with the Himalayan states. New strains appeared in India's overall Himalayan policy. During the phase of *"Hindi-Chini-Bhai Bhai,"* India's attitude towards the developments in Tibet was more of complacency combined with a sense of resignation. This was despite the fact that in the Parliament in India the need to evolve "a more positive policy" in the Himalayan region was voiced. The policy of peaceful co-existence which China followed till about the close of the decade of 1950s was more a kind of strategy adopted by China to help her acquire necessary capability to influence and control the external environment, "which did prove successful for her as for as the Asian continent was concerned."

Once that capability was acquired the so-called policy of peaceful co-existence of China was abandoned for a more militant line in international as well as external affairs. So much so that by the end of 1959, it seemed as if "China had declared a virtual war against the outside world." With the occupation of Tibet and India's formal recognition of Tibet as a region of China in Sino-Indian agreement of 1954 a new phase of Sino-Indian relations began. But at the same time it brought certain vital changes in the geo-political conditions in the Himalayan region to which Indian leadership got awakened subsequently and belatedly. Ever since the opening of the present century, if not earlier the British had emphasised upon Tibet as a large frontier zone.

For Curzon, in particular, the most acceptable strategy in this respect was that Tibet and the entire Himalayan region should fall outside the sphere of interest of any other great power even though his dealings with Tibet had a "considerable bearing on both the Persian and the Afghan problems." Once Tibet became a part of China, its borders were stretched closer to those of India. The commanding position which China occupied in the Himalayan region posed new threats to the security of the entire east and north-east regions of India. Similarly the Himalayan kingdoms of Bhutan and Sikkim as much as Nepal now came to have a common border with China. Physically speaking therefore, China is now closer to Bhutan, with about 350 kms. long common border, than ever before. Moreover, the occupation of Tibet has enabled China to exploit the historic and centuries old intimate ties between the people of Bhutan and Tibet. The first known ruler of Bhutan who is credited with having, consolidated the present kingdom of Bhutan was Ngawang Namgyal. He was a Lama and came from Tibet towards the seventeenth century.

Ever since then Bhutan recognised Tibet as its spiritual home. That the people, through the mountain passes, maintained a fairly good deal of trade relationships is evident from the early travellers' accounts. A close ethnic similarity is also found between the people of Bhutan and Tibet.

The early settlers in the western region of Bhutan are believed to have descended from the Kham province in Tibet. A board similarity between the architectural forms and styles of the official buildings of Bhutan with those of Tibet also speaks of the intimate contacts between Bhutan and Tibet. Indeed Tibetan manuscripts designate the origin of Bhutan as a colony of Tibet. Yet irrespective of the exact origin of "Bhutan" and its long and very intimate contacts with Tibet and through Tibet with China, Bhutan throughout the centuries, "jealously guarded the sovereignty of her kingdom and repeatedly defied and spurned any suggestion which might be construed to mean that she was subordinate to either Tibet or China." One can, however, argue that there have always been two Tibets.

One, an ethnic and cultural Tibet which had a much bigger sway over a considerable part of the Himalaya extending from Ladakh to Sikkim and from Tibet proper to Nepal. Throughout this region, with by far the large majority of the people who were Northern Buddhists, the Dalai Lama was the one supreme spiritual head. Then there was the political Tibet the sway of which was relatively smaller and there the authority of the Dalai and Panchan Lamas was limited within the political boundaries of Tibet. Therefore, in spite of very strong ethnic and cultural ties "individualistic Bhutanese were hardly conducive to be servile to others... . Believing in and adhering to their own particular type of Lamaistic Bhuddhism they retained their freedom independent both of the Tibetan and the Chinese." Be that as it may, the tributary relationships which Bhutan maintained with Lhasa till recently and the strong cultural bonds with the people of Tibet enabled the Chinese to claim some special relationships with the people of all the Himalayan areas, even those in the north eastern parts of India. The old British Indian records dating back to 1907 also reveal as to how the Chinese tried to exploit these cultural and ethnic similarities.

Speaking of the closeness between Bhutan and Tibet the Amban was further reported to have said : "Tibet, Nepal and Druk Yul (Bhutan) are side by side like the molar teeth in a man's mouth, and the subjects of all three are those of one kingdom."

One could easily infer from all this that China interpreted her regisnal interests in the territories and kingdoms comprising Tibet, Nepal, Bhutan and Sikkim as both legitimate and historic. The great Chinese leader Sun Yat Sen had staked Chinese claims on these territories including Bhutan. So long as Bhutan is looked upon by China as one of his lost territories, the desire to "liberate" it will lurk very strongly in the minds of the Chinese leadership. Indeed these claims and expressions got strengthened after the occupation of Tibet by China, psychologically speaking. Chinese claims and appeal to the people of Bhutan were indirect before Tibet became a part of China. But ever since the occupation of Tibet they have a direct appeal to the sentiments and feelings of an average Bhutanese. Bhutan is looked upon as one of the five fingers of the palm of Tibet; if palm is now a part of China so should be the fingers. This is the logic on which China has been pursuing her policy towards the Himalayan territories ever since her successful suppression of the revolt in Tibet in 1959. In the realisation of these goals of her policy in the region a concerted and deliberate effort on the part of China to create some kind of estrangement between India and Bhutan has been the principal feature of her diplomatic strategy in the Himalayan region.

Any intimacy between Bhutan and India will be looked upon as a setback to her interests in the region. There is adequate historical evidence to establish that even during 1908-10, China tried to forestall the conclusion of the treaty between the British Indian Government and Bhutan by putting forward all kinds of claims as would have proved Bhutan's feudatory relationship with Peking. She even tried to ignore the treaty of 1910 by dealing directly with the Maharaja of Bhutan either through written communications or by sending presents to the rulers. Almost an identical diplomatic posture of China was witnessed in 1950s. The "special relations" which the treaty of 1949 established between Bhutan and India were not acceptable to China. The question of Sino-Bhutanese boundary, the Chinese leaders claimed, did not fall within the scope of Sino-Indian talks held in 1960-61. By treating Bhutan as an independent entity "beyond the framework of the treaty of 1949" Peking hoped to drive a wedge between India and Bhutan. Her attempts to send some gifts to the Maharaja of Bhutan in 1953 and two years later when the Chinese officials started issuing visas directly to the Bhutanese indicated the Chinese strategy followed even during the period of Sino-Indian friendship. But on all such moves and efforts the response of Bhutan towards Peking had always been unfavourable. Yet, it was the Tibet revolt in 1959 and its aftermath which opened "the eyes of the ruler of Bhutan to the realities of the Chinese menace." Realising that China might achieve through pressure diplomacy and infiltration from the side of Tibet what she had failed through peaceful diplomacy, Bhutan sealed its borders with Tibet in 1960.

As a consequence all trade contacts with Tibet came to an end putting serious economic strains on Bhutan. The occupation of about 300 square miles of Bhutan territory by China left no scope of any doubt in the mind of Bhutan ruler of the Chinese intentions. The opening of the decade of 1960 ushered in a new chapter in the history both of the internal development of Bhutan and her foreign relations. The then Maharaja, Jigme Dorji Wangchuk, under his imaginative and farsighted leadership, decided to open up Bhutan, which had been almost a closed country, to the outside world. Deciding to rely almost exclusively upon India's help and assistance, opening up of Bhutan was helpful for India also, politically speaking. A closed a Bhutan was only an invitation to subversion from the side of its northern borders and a gap in the defence of the eastern sector of India.

But China continued to follow its two pronged diplomacy in Bhutan with a view to bringing Bhutan out of this closeness and intimacy with India. In 1961 she made yet another offer of assistance to Bhutan for its economic development which was turned down by the then Maharaja of Bhutan. Side by side the reports of occasional intrusions into Bhutan territory were also received. This was being done presumably to pressarize Bhutan to open direct negotiations with the Chinese authorities. Yet China failed either to wean Bhutan away from India or to pressurize her into the establishment of any diplomatic or other communication with Peking. The new ruler of Bhutan, Jigme Singhye Wangchuk, in his Press Conference on 20 August 1972 stated very clearly that "there was no contact between the two countries except that Bhutan's envoy at the United Nations was often invited to parties thrown by the Chinese representatives and this in turn was reciprocated."

It was at the time of his coronation that a significant event took place. After a period of about a decade and a half, Bhutan not only sent an official invitation to China alongwith twenty other foreign countries but China also responded to the invitation by sending a delegation led by Ma Mu-Ming. The event was played up by China in its communication media and was interpreted as having opened a new page in the friendly contacts of Bhutan and China. The delegation according to the New China News Agency was accorded a "cordial and friendly hospitality by the Royal Government and people of Bhutan." It took special note of the desires of the Bhutan Government to rely on its own efforts in deveploping its economy and safeguarding its sovereignty and economic self-reliance.

Though officially there was no reaction to these reports in Chinese media and India maintained a stand of chosen silence but outside the Indian official circles the visit of Ma Mu-Ming was interpreted as a beginning of renewed efforts on the part of Peking "to cultivate its relationship with the Bhutanese Government and people." The event was also significant from another point of view. The Foreign Affairs Minister of Bhutan stated that Article 2 of the treaty of 1949 under which Bhutan was to seek the advice of the Government of India in the conduct of its foreign relations did not make it compulsory for Bhutan to accept that advice.

But, ever since then, till 1979, no serious demands or efforts were initiated by Bhutan as would have enabled her to have direct communication opened with Peking. Nevertheless South Block had come to realize the need to make some adjustments in India's bilateral relations with Bhutan within the overall framework of the treaty of 1949. The grant of some concessions to India's northern neighbour was found to be desirable since Bhutan was in search of a new identity in the wider international community With the admission of Bhutan as a member of the United Nations in 1971 and also of a few other international bodies as the Colombo Plan and that of the nonaligned movement, it was Bhutan's quest for a new role in the world community which got occasionally articulated in a demand for a change or revision in the treaty of 1949.

It was the imperative of diversification of Bhutan's foreign relations to which India rightfully and positively responded. India sponsored her membership to the United Nations and sought the support of the other member nations of the world body which led to her admission finally in 1971. To help her diversify her trade relations an agreement was signed between India and Bhutan in 1978. The same year India agreed to change the nomenclature of the Bhutanese mission in New Delhi; she now has a full fledged Embassy in the capital. In 1979 Bhutan set up an Embassy in Dacca, its second in the subcontinent.

It was towards 1978-79 that some members of the National Assembly of Bhutan again called for closer links with China. These members, it was reported earlier, had expressed certain reservations on the full implications of Article 2 of the treaty of 1949 under which Bhutan was only to seek the guidance of India in the conduct of her bilateral relations. Once again, as in 1973-74 it was felt in India that a section of the Bhutanese official circle was not satisfied with the working of the provisions of the treaty of 1949. Indeed no less a person than the Maharaja of Bhutan was reported to have said in an interview that "the treaty of friendship can certainly be brought up to date." But on the question whether Bhutan was aspiring to have close relations with China the Maharaja described it as "utter non-sense."

Nevertheless when for the first time in the meeting of the non-aligned summit in Havana in 1979 Bhutan took an independent stand on the Kampuchean issue different from that of India," it caused "a flutter in the dovecots of South Block." To many in India it appeared that Bhutan was not fully happy with the evolution of her relations with India. It was more disturbing since the dragon kingdom was found to be following a line of policy which China had adopted on this particular issue. Naturally, therefore, the incident had caused some anxiety to the decision makers in the South Block.

But Bhutan's stand on the Kampuchean issue at the Havana Summit can also be viewed in the context of a caretaker Government in New Delhi at that time and its concerted and chosen low profile role in foreign affairs combined at times with an attitude of indifference even. Bhutan also perceived India's role in the summit conference on these lines. The King, Jigme Singhye Wanghchuk had said that it was wrong to say that Bhutan had taken a position at Havana which was at variance with the stand taken by India. The King observed:

> India took no position at all : Can you blame us if we took one and can our stand be described as being in opposition to India's ? In any case only a couple of months after the Summit conference at Havana, Bhutan once again officially stated that they had decided to maintain a policy of not seeking diplomatic and trade ties with China. In February 1980 when King Jigme Singhye Wangchuk paid an official visit to Delhi he reaffirmed that Bhutan will continue with its traditional policy within the framework of the

treaty of 1949. It put to rest all such misgivings in Indian and foreign circles that almost three quarters of a century old Indo-Bhutanese ties were under any serious stress on account of the demand in some Bhutanese circle for opening of contacts with China. As a matter of fact the voicing of such aspirations and demand for the treaty of 1949 or entire review of the Indo-Bhutanese relations must be looked at from another prespective. That is the possibility of normalisation of Sino-Indian relations. To quote Tsering, Foreign Affairs Minister of Bhutan :

> Some National Assembly members felt that if China and India became friends Bhutan would lose all importance to Peking and New Delhi. They thought we should make our own efforts to develop ties with China or be left out in the cold.

It might sound unrealistic though, keeping in view its size and strength, but this aspect of her foreign policy Bhutan shares with Nepal which seeks to play the role of a balancing factor between India and China. *Detente* between India and China might lead to Bhutan losing much of her relevance to both the big neighbours of her : it is this feeling more than any other that might have led to the demand either for establishing ties with China or for revision of the Indo-Bhutanese treaty of 1949.

REFERENCES

Charles A. Bell, *Tibet: Past and Present,* London, 1924, p. 101.

Foreign Secret E. Cons., October 1908, No. 119, paragraph 7.

Foreign Secret, E. Cons., June 1907, No 638; Extract from a letter from the British representative in Nepal to India, 20 January 1907.

H.E. Richardson in his *A Short History of Tibet,* New York, 1962 and Charles A. Bell in his *Tibet : Past and Present,* Oxford, 1924.

Harish Kapur, *China in World Politics,* New Delhi, 1975, p. 21.

India, *Lok Sabha Debates,* Vol. 1,1954, Col. 320.

M.D. Dharmdasani, "Zone of Peace: Nepal's Quest for Identity," *China Report,* Vol. 15, No. 5, September-October 1979, p. 13.

Mao Tse-Tung, *Chinese Revolution and the Communist Party of China,* Bombay, 1951, p. 9.

Parshotam Mehra, *The Younghusband Expedition: An Interpretation,* Bombay, 1968, p. 359.

Pradyuman P. Karan & William M, Jenkins, Jr., *The Himalayan Kingdoms: Bhutan Sikkim, and Nepal,* Ne Jersey, 1963, p. 49.

R.K. Chatterjee, *Indicts Land Borders,* New Delhi, 1978, p. 181.

Ram Rahul, *The Himalaya as a Frontier,* New Delhi, 1978. p. 96.

Times of India, 22 August 1972.

V.H. Coelho, *Sikkim and Bhutan,* New Delhi, 1969, p. 76.

Chapter 4

India and Afghanistan

> Teach me to feel another's woe,
> To hide the fault I see;
> That mercy I to others show,
> That mercy show to me.
>
> —*Alexander Pope*

Afghanistan has had seen many turbulent incidents on all walks of national life. After withdrawal of USSR troops, Islamic fundamentalists snatched the reign. And thereafter Afghanistan has been undergoing devastating situations. US attack on Afghanistan to suppress the terrorist outfits of Al-Qaeda is still on. Though a democratic government is established there, yet situation of panic still prevails. India has contributed a lot in the development of Afghanistan. But after its becoming a harbour of terrorists, India suffered the pangs of terrorism in J&K and other places.

This chapter highlights some crucial issue pertaining to Indo-Afghanistan relations.

It looks as though the unhappy situation in Afghanistan is going to remain unchanged in the foreseeable future. The crisis has continued to escalate since April 1978 because on successive occasions, extraneous issues have intruded to the detriment of the prospects of a solution. By now a pattern seems to have emerged which, in all likelihood, will persist. The domestic and external components of the crisis have been interacting with each other, creating a cause-and-effect sequence.

A crucial question is: what prompted the Soviet Union to move her troops into Afghanistan? It seems entirely probable that the decision was taken in the light of the Soviet perception of the thrust of events in the Persian Gulf. Only a couple of months earlier, Iran had seized American hostages in Tehran. Perhaps the Soviet leaders concluded that the way the situation was developing, the U.S. might undertake a surgical strike in Iran to secure the release of the hostages in case no solution was forthcoming. The Russians possibly decided that they must be in a position to derive the optimum advantage whenever that scenario developed.

Clearly, the situation in Iran, with all its explosive potentialities and geo-strategic considerations of military presence in close proximity to the scene of action, was an important input. Equally, the United States' going slow on the ratification of the second agreement on the Strategic Arms Limitation Talks (SALT-II) was beginning to cause the Soviet leadership considerable anxiety. Many Soviet diplomats and academicians around this time spoke bitterly of the "unpredictability" of the Carter administration.

But what finally decided them must have been the falt that Hafizullah Amin had begun to act truant. Certain facets of the Soviet policy in Afghanistan can be comprehended only in the context of what may be described as the "Sadat syndrome". The manner in which President Anwar Sadat pulled the rug from under the Soviet feet in Egypt has left a permanent mark on their thinking.

The diplomatic grapevine had been buzzing with stories since September 1979 that the Soviets were seriously considering Amin's ouster. He had openly defied the Soviet Union by frustrating the efforts for Left unity in Afghanistan under the leadership of Noor Mohammed Taraki. Amin obviously had a pipeline to Taraki's establishment through the latter's aide-decamp, Major Daoud Taroon who later on was discovered to be a staunch Amin supporter. Amin was quick to precipitate a crisis by dropping Aslam Watanjar and Sherjan Mazdooryar from the Council of Ministers while Taraki was still in Moscow. On his return to Kabul, Taraki invited Amin for a meeting in the President's House in a bid to get him to agree to the Moscow formula, if need be at pistol point. Amin declined to attend but finally agreed to go on the personal assurances of Major Daoud Taroon. When shots were fired at Amin in the presidential palace, Major Taroon stepped forward to protect his friend. Amin rolled down the stairs and managed to escape in the jeep of his bodyguard escort. He returned a few hours later with troops loyal to him and took over the reins of power after taking Taraki into custody. Taraki's assassination followed, perhaps on the spot, or perhaps a few days later.

Not only was Taraki deposed within a couple of days of his return home from Havana via Moscow, but Amin demanded and secured the recall of the Soviet Ambassador to Kabul. Soon thereafter the official media in Kabul was putting out clear signals to Pakistan that Amin was willing to patch up with Islamabad. Amin said in October 1979: "We want peace with Pakistan and would certainly like to settle all bilateral differences." This was in answer to a question whether he would recognise the Durand Line as an international frontier to reduce tension with Pakistan. Earlier, in May 1979, he had stated that "any Afghan Government recognising the Durand Line cannot hope to survive". Pakistan was excruciatingly slow in taking the hint and by the time she got ready the fat was already in the fire.

In the wake of the Soviet troops moving into Afghanistan, *Pravda,* the Soviet daily, had argued that—"the Chinese, Egyptian and American intelligence service instructors trained the saboteurs against the Afghan Government at camps in Pakistan officially described as refugee facilities... Intrigues by counter-revolutionary gangs jeopardised the very existence of the Afghan Republic. The Soviet Union has never concealed that it would not permit the transformation of Afghanistan into a base for preparation of imperialist aggression against the Soviet Union.,Soviet aid and support to Afghanistan is not directed against any country neighbouring it or against any of our neighbours. Washington's goal is to make up for its loss of influence following the downfall of the Shah in neighbouring Iran."

Selig Harrison testifying before the U.S. Congress Committee on Foreign Affairs on September 23, 1981 said—"One of the arguments often advanced by Administration spokesmen behind closed doors is that Pakistan can only be induced to serve as a conduit for and to the Afghan resistance if the U.S. accedes to its arms requests. But evidence is multiplying that Islamabad has been quietly facilitating Sino-U.S.-Saudi-Egyptian inputs of aid to the resistance for more than a year. Pakistan's attitude to the Afghan issue has been and will continue to be governed primarily by pressures from other Islamic countries by its growing dependence on economic support from the U.S. and Saudi Arabia."

If the mere possibility of Sino-U.S. support for the low-profile insurgency operation based on Pakistani territory could impel the Soviets to march their troops into

Afghanistan, it would be naive to expect that the actual involvement of these two powers, with whom the Soviet Union has serious problems, will persuade the latter to abandon its position in Afghanistan. There has been considerable speculation on whether the Saur revolution was an indigenous uprising or the handiwork of the Soviet Union. The reunion of the Khalq and the Parcham groups, after prolonged estrangement, may not be fortuitous. The Soviet Union certainly had some cause for anxiety because of the major diplomatic initiative of the Shah of Iran for promoting regional co-operation and the elimination of disputes between Afghanistan and Pakistan on the one hand and Pakistan and India on the other.

Pakistan had been dragging its feet on the process of normalisation with India for some four years after the Simla Agreement. Then suddenly both Pakistan and India made quick work of concluding a series of agreements to resume diplomatic relations, restore postal, telecommunication and trade links and reopen road and rail travel for the nationals of one country to visit the other. Pakistan also negotiated with Afghanistan to resolve the political disputes plaguing the two countries since 1947. Both Zulfikar Ali Bhutto of Pakistan and Sardar Mohammed Daoud, the President of Afghanistan visited each other, and a draft agreement for Afghanistan proclaiming its acceptance of the Durand Line as the international border between the two countries had been worked out.

Another development around this time was that the Shah of Iran loaned to Sardar Daoud the services of his experts from the Iranian intelligence service SAVAK to streamline the security system of Afghanistan. Given the Shah's closeness with the USA and his distance from the

Soviet Union, it would not be surprising if the latter viewed these developments with some misgivings. It may also be mentioned that in 1973, India had declined to participate in the Asian Security Plan proposed by Leonid Brezhnev, the Soviet leader.

But there was no indication that the Soviets were getting restive and moving towards or getting ready for a pre-emptive strike. All the evidence shows that the Soviet Union was scrupulously correct in its dealings with Sardar Daoud. Nor has there been any suggestion that the Soviet advisers in the various organs of the Afghan Government had acted in a manner which could even retrospectively be linked to a Soviet involvement in what happened on April 27, 1978. As such there are valid grounds to discount the theory of the Soviet Union masterminding the Saur revolution. By all accounts it was an indigenous affair.

It may also be noted that the USA would not have taken the easy view that it did of the Soviet Union having masterminded the event. Until the tragic assassination of Ambassador Donald Dubs on February 14, 1979, the USA was quite content to carry on business as usual with the new Government. There was a regular exchange of contacts between the Afghan Foreign Office and the American diplomats, both in Kabul and elsewhere. There is, however, no doubt that within hours after the revolution commenced some Soviet advisers reached out to aid the new regime.

Taraki himself confirmed this while denying that the People's Democratic Party of Afghanistan (PDPA) had acted on instructions from Moscow. But even according to the USIS publication ("Chronology of Afghanistan Events--A Retrospective") the number of Soviet advisers in Kabul in April 1978 was no more than around 350. The precise consideration which induced the Soviet decision in December

1979 to move its troops into Afghanistan may be difficult to determine. It could be any one of the factors enumerated above either by itself or combining with a bit of everything towards that end. Some aspects of the domestic and diplomatic factors are relevant to what has happened in Afghanistan. The Saur revolution occurred as a consequence of the failure of the Afghan polity to provide for continuing adjustment to contain the hiatus arising out of the reluctance of the tribal power structure to accommodate the emerging urban middle class. As long as the spread of modern education and acquisition of technological skills was confined to the upper echelons of society, with their roots firmly embedded among the land-owning classes dominating the tribal power structure, their influence extending to the corridors of power in the national Government, the new forces did not have to contend with opposition.

However, when the pace of modernisation expanded to take in the urban lower middle classes which hitherto had been outside the pale of the feudal power structure, the process ran into a dead-end because the capacity of the national economy to absorb the new skills was extremely limited. Thus, by the turn of the decade in 1970, a new class endowed with modern education and technological skills had emerged without any avenues for its absorption. Its interests, were in direct clash with those of the ruling power. Simultaneously, the inherent contradictions of the feudal power structure were also creating a clash of ambition within its fold. Daoud's coup of 1973 was essentially a manifestation of the latter. The emergence of Daoud at the head of a Republican regime served as a catalyst in two ways. First, the feudal power structure was shown to be vulnerable and as a result suffered a diminution in its legitimacy.

The clash of ambition within the feudal aristocracy was sharpened and its capacity to put up a solid front against the winds of change stood seriously impaired. Second, the vast mass of urban lower middle classes looked expectantly for a release from the stifling suffocation of a primitive society in which its acquired, skills had no opportunity of gainful utilisation. When Daoud failed to provide for the rising expectations of this class he had explosive discontent on his hands. Even before this process began moving towards its logical culmination, two other factors had already developed. Afghanistan's status as a buffer between the British imperial power on the one hand and the Soviet Union on the other, lost its *raison d'etre* because of the unhappy state of relations between the two principal successor states of the Imperial Government of India, namely, India and Pakistan.

This became instrumental in forcing the Afghans into the Soviet arms by obstructing and frustrating the former's traditional inclination to seek economic, cultural and commercial links with the sub-continent. A situation was created in which Afghanistan had no other option but to look towards the Soviet Union for accommodation. In the late fifties and early sixties the Afghans had shown keen interest in having their defence personnel trained in the Indian military establishments. But the response from India was faltering and manifestly disappointing. No satisfactory explanation has been forthcoming for this attitude.

Possibly the reason was a firm decision by the Finance Minister to refuse to sanction any funds for this purpose, and the disinclination of the political leadership to override this bureaucratic pusillanimity. Rebuffed by the Indians, the Afghans sought and received open encouragement in all that they asked for from the Soviet Union. On numerous occasions since independence, Pakistan tried to tighten the screw on Afghanistan by curtailing transit facilities for its trade. Every time the Afghans had to turn to the Soviet Union for alternative trade channels when the traditional facilities were denied to them. In 1961, Pak-Afghan relations turned so sour that trade and diplomatic ties totally snapped. This resulted in seriously impinging on the economic rationale for Afghanistan looking southwards.

The Afghans began to look more and more to the Soviet Union. Simultaneously, it provided the Soviet Union with the kind of openings in that country which they would not even have dared seek in the period before independence without risking open confrontation in all its relentless logic with the British authorities. Immediately after partition, India displayed a singular lack of awareness of power realities. With the British taking care of the strategic aspects, the predominant orientation of the freedom movement under the leadership of the Congress was towards issues and objectives which were totally unrelated to exigencies of the exercise of power in the strategic sense.

Possibly, if that bad been one of the inputs, India would have insisted on evolving a reasonable framework to preserve the strategic indivisibility of the sub-continent. It is, however, extremely doubtful if, given the state of mind which the Muslim League leaders had worked themselves into, such an effort would at all have evoked a realistic response. The unhappy context of partition left the leaders of India bitter and indifferent to all that had anything to do with Pakistan. Mahatma Gandhi's proclaimed objectives to dedicate his life to the task of building up bridges of understanding between India and Pakistan fell along with him to the assassin's bullet on January 30, 1948. On its part, Pakistan was even more guilty of total neglect of the strategic imperatives.

Its principal obsession was India. The dividends paid by the policy of confrontation in the period before independence created a fondness to persist with this heady approach. Instead of concentrating its efforts on consolidation of the new State, the leadership of Pakistan launched upon a series of steps calculated to hurt and destabilise India. The net result was that there was a power vacuum in the sub-continent in terms of the strategic indivisibility of the area. Afghanistan had ceased to be a buffer after 1947 not because of anything done by the Soviet Union at that point of time, but because there was no viable power in the sub-continent to sustain that role. Afghanistan was no longer under any obligation to keep equidistance from the superpower to its north. In the early fifties while India and Pakistan were totally unmindful of the strategic indivisibility of the sub-continent, the Americans tried to make inroads into Afghanistan as part of their global strategy to encircle the Soviet Union. The Afghans played it cool and kept open house to both the superpowers--the Soviet Union north of the Hindukush, and USA in the southern flatlands. The American penchant for massive display found full expression in the construction programmes undertaken by them in the south-west of Afghanistan.

In the mid-fifties, they constructed a massive airport at Kandahar, a backward semi-urban town, which would do Delhi, Paris or even London proud in the eighties. Possibly, it had a strategic purpose. But it had no relation to any needs of the people of Afghanistan at that point of time or even now, thirty years later. With the rapid growth of aeronautics, the U.S. lost interest in whatever infrastructural facilities they had created in southern Afghanistan. Thereafter one sees a gradual decline in the U.S. interest in Afghanistan, so that by the early seventies, while the Soviet Union had gradually increased its involvement in that country, the Western powers had continued the process of disengagement. Pakistan was stampeded into its present predicament initially in the summer of 1978 by the misguided enthusiasm of the PNA Ministers belonging to the Jamaat Islami who had emotional and organisational links with the Akhwanul Muslimeen, Hezb-e-Islami, and Jamiat-i-Islami, the three principal platforms of orthodox elements in Afghanistan. The Jamaat not only organised reception and assistance centres for those groups but also mobilised money and resources to help them organise, train and equip groups of volunteers for hostile activities in Afghanistan.

The funds for this programme are believed to have come in abundant measure from the non-official agencies working under the patronage of Saudi Arabia. The flow of refugees had gained considerable momentum by the end of 1978. In early 1979 one came across the possibility of a 'Bangladesh-type operation' being seriously considered in the corridors of power in Islamabad. Around this time the ruling military junta was also getting ready to hang Bhutto. That clearly introduced an element of caution on the part of the Generals. But what really put paid to the proposition was that the Carter administration was tightening the screw on the junta on the twin issues of human rights and the nuclear programme. The U.S. policy around that time was clearly aimed at disciplining Pakistan rather than encouraging it to launch an adventure in Afghanistan. In Afghanistan, the USA was content at that point of time to do its bit only by supplying arms, equipment and funds to the insurgent groups based in Peshawar. But this situation underwent a dramatic change after the election of President Reagan with his proclaimed objective to confront the Soviet Union. The Afghan leaders draw pointed attention to the material culled from the official publications of the Pakistan Government and those articulating the Jamaat point of view to make out a case that hectic activity took place in the tribal areas on the Pakistan side of the Durand Line soon after the emergence of the Khalqi regime and that the earliest clashes took place as far back as September 1978. Although the insurgents are almost everywhere in the country, the Afghan Government policy aims at avoiding any steps which would add to the insecurity of the people. On the other hand, there is a conscious effort to create a vested interest for the people to stay on in the country because this helps to keep the countryside economically productive and politically manageable.

A manifestation of this approach is available from the fact that the Government has instructed its functionaries outside Kabul not to seek to impose their authority on unwilling people and be content in areas where the people, though not willing to support the Government authorities, are inclined to let them be. Overall, the Russian military intervention in Afghanistan is an unmitigated political disaster both within and without the country. Despite that, there is no consideration of a pullout; not without the absolute assurance of their strategic security interests. They are also committed to the viability of the Babrak Karmal Government. There does not also seem to be any inclination to raise the scale of involvement unless they are forced to. A series of well-co-ordinated attacks by insurgents against the Kabul Government, backed by U.S. organised supplies of sophisticated weaponry like surface-to-air missiles and armoured personnel carriers in the hands of the rebels, have not turned out to be adequate provocation for the Soviet Union either to increase the level of their troops or to change their approach in dealing with the insurgents.

The Russians appear to be holding on to their earlier view that they have nothing to gain by escalating or ostentatiously asserting their authority in Kabul. The low profile is a better one to maintain in view of the feelings of the Afghan people. On the rebel side, whatever they think of themselves, they do not add up to a credible power factor capable of forcing the Soviets out. They are disunited and incapable of cohesive action. It may be noted, for instance, that though the Kabul Government in not able to enforce its writ effectively in the countryside, the goods and passenger traffic to and from Kabul keeps flowing smoothly. There is a growing interaction among the authorities and the tribal chiefs with the result that they are getting used to each other. It should be interesting to watch how this process develops. The Reagan administration's policy to confront the Soviet Union has become a major factor in the situation.

As such, unless there is some kind of breakthrough in the overall state of relations between the two superpowers, it is difficult to take an optimistic view of the prospects of a settlement. Pakistan, on its part, led the Islamic Foreign Ministers' Conference at Islamabad in January 1980 to an extreme position on the issue including the suspension of Afghanistan from the membership of the Organisation of Islamic Conference but softened its stand by the time the Islamic Foreign Ministers met again at Islamabad in May 1980 and persuaded the Conference to appoint a Ministerial Committee to explore the prospects of political settlement. But by then the attitude of both Kabul and Moscow had hardened, and a deadlock ensued. The Ministerial

Committee had turned out to be non-starter which further eroded Pakistan's tough posture, and its diplomats began to explore the possibilities of a settlement. Interestingly, the Pakistani Foreign Minister, Agha Shahi, had told newsmen at Islamabad on June 16, 1980, that the positions of Pakistan and the Soviet Union were not "totally different with regard to the solution of the Afghanistan crisis.

In the informal contacts it had been discovered that some elements and proposals for ending the crisis were common between the two sides." Subsequently, in his speech at Loralai in Baluchistan on September 22, 1980, President Zia-ul-Haq reiterated what Pakistan considered as the four principles on which Pakistan would not compromise.

These were: (1) withdrawal of Soviet troops from Afghanistan; (2) creation of conditions favourable for the return of Afghan refugees to their homes in safety and with honour; (3) restoration of the Islamic and non-aligned status of Afghanistan; and (4) the right of the people of Afghanistan to form a Government of their own choice. Before participating in the U.N. talks at Geneva in 1981, Pakistan agreed to a four-point agenda prepared by Diego Cordovez, the special envoy of the U.N. Secretary-General to mediate a settlement on Afghanistan, according to which the discussions would revolve around (a) the withdrawal of foreign troops; (b) non-interference in the internal affairs of the States; (c) international guarantees of non-interference; and (d) the voluntary return of the refugees to their homes. Pakistan officially stated on June 27, 1982, that "in Pakistan's view the return of Afghan refugees was the central issue along with that of the withdrawal of foreign troops from Afghanistan". It would be seen that Pakistan did in fact make a major shift in its position by abandoning its stand on the question of the "restoration of

Islamic and non-aligned status of Afghanistan, and the right of the people of Afghanistan to form a Government of their own choice".

This is so far as the formal position goes but, essentially, both Pakistan and the Soviet Union have, from to time, shown an inclination to be flexible in their approach. During the autumn of 1980, both had carried out extensive diplomatic negotiations in quest of a political settlement. Pakistan's Foreign Secretary visited Moscow on September 16, 1980, when preliminary soundings were taken on a possible Soviet response in case Pakistan opted for a political settlement. Some weeks before Brezhnev's visit to India in December 1980, substantive talks were held in Islamabad between Soviet Ambassador Vitaly Smirnov and Pakistan leaders, including President Zia-ul-Haq. They explored the prospects of a possible breakthrough. Pakistan, it is understood, was willing to offer concrete assurances against interference in the domestic affairs of Afghanistan. Pakistan was also reported to be ready to assure that it would deny the use of its territory to elements engaged in efforts to topple the Babrak Karmal regime. The Soviet Union, on its part, showed readiness to take a sympathetic view of Pakistan's difficulties, especially the large influx of refugees which is proving to be an economic burden, besides being an explosive socio-economic and political factor. These talks provided an acceptable basis for a dialogue.

All that remained was to evolve a suitable framework so that it did not provide a handle to President Zia-ul-Haq's critics to mount an attack against him for surrendering to the Soviets. President Zia-ul-Haq confirmed in a statement in Islamabad on January 30, 1981, that the Soviet Union had recently initiated proposals to resolve the Afghanistan issue which was being carefully considered by Pakistan.

Matters had been going so satisfactorily for both Pakistan and the Soviet Union that when asked by a newsman at Taif as to why the Soviet Union had not been condemned by the Islamic summit in its resolution on Afghanistan, Foreign Minister Agha Shahi remarked: "We have passed the stage of condemnation. It is not appropriate to condemn a person with whom you are going to talk." Press reports throughout October and November 1980, had spoken of the dismay with which USA and the Islamic countries friendly to it viewed Pakistan's lukewarm attitude at the time the U.N. resolution on Afghanistan was being discussed. Later, Pakistan was on an altogether different wavelength from its traditional mentors of the Islamic Conference during the Taif summit (January 24-29, 1981). Around this time the French President mooted his proposal for an international conference to seek political settlement of the problem. An analytical report from Taif published in the *Pakistan Times of* January 29,1981, accused the West of "inspiring" certain countries at the Islamic summit to "take a stiff attitude against negotiations on Afghanistan . . . (they) did not want to have any truck with Kabul in any circumstances".

Even the U.N. Secretary-General was blamed for having played the Western game by having made "his next step in organising talks contingent on the passage of a resolution at the Islamic summit. However, in a total reversal of Pakistan's position at the Taif summit on January 29, 1981, Foreign Minister Agha Shahi called upon the Foreign Ministers of the non-aligned countries at Delhi on February 9, 1981, "to pronounce, formally and unequivocally, on the violation of sovereignty, independence and territorial integrity of Afghanistan". According to the new formulation of Pakistan, the "continuing Soviet military occupation of that country is tantamount not only to a violation of its political independence, sovereignty and territorial integrity but a threat to the stability of the region. It has heightened international tension. It has damaged detente and resulted in the intensification of superpower rivalry and contention in the region of the Indian Ocean and the Gulf."

But that was not the end of the matter. A little while later, Pakistan once again responded favourably to U.N. efforts on the question of a political settlement in Afghanistan. Diego Cordovez had indicated, on the conclusion of the first round of Geneva talks in 1982, that as a result of negotiations he had evolved "a package of understandings". The talks had gone into some very crucial details during which "important political pronouncements and important political decisions were made" he said, and the "level of specificity" of discussions throughout was quite high.

At the second round of Geneva talks in April 1983, it was indicated by a Press release issued by the U.N. representative that "the draft which is near completion sets out the principles and objectives of the comprehensive settlement, defines the interrelationships between the component elements of the settlement and certain provisions including time-frames for implementation". The talks adjourned at this point, presumably to enable participants to formulate their positions on the draft. However, when talks reconvened in June 1983, they concluded without any further progress. The Afghan leaders have publicly stated that the U.S. sabotaged it. Even though Diego Cordovez abandoned his plans for shuttle diplomacy between Kabul, Islamabad and Tehran in 1983, the exercise was revived in early 1984. But the outcome is totally contingent on whether or not the Soviet Union and the USA are able to arrive at an understanding to accommodate each other's interests in South West Asia or at least in the limited context of Pakistan and Afghanistan.

In case the Russians are able to maintain their position in Afghanistan by containment of insurgency to an acceptable level, the USA might well conclude that since they cannot throw the Soviets out, they ought to strike a deal with them whereby the USA stops using Pakistan as a conduit for the supply of cash, equipment and armaments to the insurgent groups operating in Afghanistan, and the Soviet Union could in return hold out an assurance against direct involvement in Iran. The crucial question here would be: Would the Soviet Union acquiesce in an arrangement under which the Americans use Pakistan as a component of its strategic objectives in the Gulf provided the Americans cease their backing for the insurgents in Afghanistan? This point is relevant because in terms of the basic strategic objectives of the USA, Afghanistan is no more than what Henry Kissinger said in respect of Kampuchea--a side-show. The Soviet Union would like to stabilise the regime in Afghanistan. That purpose would be considerably facilitated if the Soviets are able to arrive at an understanding with Pakistan.

However, the Soviet Union cannot afford to yield on any point of substance on its basic position that the political realities arising out of the revolution in Afghanistan are irreversible. Pakistan is not entirely a free agent because of its critical dependence on the U.S. for economic sustenance, which is apart from the supply of military hardware. The equipment used by the Soviet Air Force in Afghanistan is rather primitive and unsophisticated comprising Mi-24 helicopters and MiG-21 aircraft. There are no sophisticated avionics needing extensive ground support. Everything is *manually* operated by the crew members because there is no infrastructure of ground support required for maintenance and operations.

Even so the reaction time has been considerably reduced. They normally hit only known strongholds or attack large insurgent formations on the move, besides undertaking missions to search and destroy insurgent groups. There is no reliable estimate available of the number of aircraft the Soviets have in Afghanistan because this varies according to need with aircraft moving in and out, but at no time has it been noticed that the shortage of aircraft constitutes a constraint on operations. The morale of the insurgents may be affected if they are not able to meet the threat posed by the Soviet aircraft.

If on the contrary they gain access to the equipment they are so desperately demanding, the Soviet involvement will increase. If they do not, the tempo of insurgency would become difficult to sustain. The Afghan Army had about 60,000 troops in 1978. This figure came down to around 20,000 in 1980. Since 1981, the Afghan authorities have been making sustained efforts to reverse the trend and at the moment claim that the Army is almost back to its normal strength. But they do not specify what the number is. This success has been achieved by increasing the period of conscription to three years and the pay from 150 Afghanis (2.60 U.S. dollars) to 3,000 afghanis (54 dollars) per month. Barrack facilities have been substantially improved. Both civil and military personnel are provided free lunch or money in lieu and transport to and fro. The authorities claim that the training of the Afghan troops has been streamlined with adequately equipped modern training schools and regular exercises. A large number of officers and troops requiring specialised training such as paratroopers, signals and armour personnel, are being sent in increasing numbers to the Soviet Union for training. The authorities claim to have brought about a sharp decline in the rate of desertions through political orientation programmes. A separate Political Affairs Department has been set up under the Ministry of Defence and its functionaries are assigned to various units on the Soviet model. The cadres of the People's Democratic Party of Afghanistan in the Army also perform watch-and-ward duty so that the Government is much better informed of what is happening as well as of the mood of the troops. With all these measures, the performance of the Afghan Army vis-a-vis the insurgents is claimed to have registered a distinct improvement. The authorities claim that despite insurgent pressure on Kabul, the situation hardly ever went out of control during the winter of 1982-83. The regime's opponents, however, point to major efforts mounted by them during February 1983, in the course of which they had a clear edge over Government forces. Since the levers of political power vest in the tribal leaders, the regime is going all out to reconcile the tribes and feudal elites.

Television programmes open with recitations from the Holy Quran. All official and party functions also commence similarly. In the last week of November 1983, Babrak Karmal mobilised an impressive array of political elite under the banner of National Fatherland Front. It was an assembly of former ministers under Zahir Shah, retired generals, former members of Assembly, Senate and *Loi Jirgas* besides leaders of "tribes, nationalities and clans". Babrak Karmal addressed the audience as "national patriotic personalities of prideful Afghanistan" and told them that "PDPA members are your younger brothers and sons. . . we have no unbearable and unacceptable demands on you." He asked the invitees to recommend the composition of local committees in whom wide powers would be vested. It remains to be seen if this would work. The tribes never commit to either side.

They act independently in pursuit of their interests, depending on how the situation develops. The participation of the various tribal leaders in the frequent *jirgas* organised by the regime does not necessarily amount to a pledge of loyalty. Traditionally, the custom is never to refuse a *jirga* because that provides one access to the mind of the other side and helps keep one's options open. There has been some talk in recent months about the prospects of Zahir Shah returning to the country. If he returns as the rallying point of Afghan nationalism it may augur well for Afghanistan because, then, even the PDPA might agree to compete as an important component of the national polity. If on the other hand he emerges as the titular head of a grand alliance of the fundamentalist groups operating from Pakistan with U.S. backing and Saudi patronage, the Soviets will frustrate the attempt no matter to what extent they have to go. The PDPA may not amount to much as an effective political factor by itself, but it does draw sustenance from a considerable number of educated and business elite who do not share the religious fanaticism and extremism of the fundamentalist groups.

Education and exposure to modern influences among this class is insubstantial. The process of modernisation during the last twenty years has created a class who would not like the fundamentalists to become the sole arbiters of Afghanistan's destiny. What does the future hold for Afghanistan? Will it become a Finland, an Outer Mongolia or get submerged into the Soviet Union as one of its Central Asian Republics? Unlike Finland, Afghanistan does not have an established power structure enjoying the broad consensus of all segments of the people. Next the neutralisation of Sweden was integral to the Soviet acceptance of Finland as a free country. As against that, Pakistan is the base of an anti-Soviet fight going on in Afghanistan. Afghanistan cannot be an Outer Mongolia because it is not secluded and isolated from the rest of the world. The open borders with Pakistan and Iran rule out any possibility of its withdrawing into a shell like Outer Mongolia. For the same reason, Afghanistan cannot be submerged as the north-western extension of the Central Asian Republics of the Soviet Union. With insurgents able to come in and go out as they please and massive inflow of arms and funds, the very idea of Afghanistan becoming either a Finland or an Outer Mongolia or a Soviet Republic stands ruled out.

The more likely scenario is that Afghanistan will remain Afghanistan. In the nineteenth century the British had come to terms with this fact and chosen to be content with their political pre-eminence, relegating the Czarist Russia to a second place. Now the Soviets will predominate to ensure that Afghanistan does not become a jumping-board for hostile moves against them. For the rest, they will have to learn to live with Afghanistan as a free nation.

India and Afghan Crisis

On 27 December 1979, Kabul Radio announced that Hafizullah Amin had been replaced by Babrak Karmal as President of Afghanistan and a few hours later at 11.15 p.m. the Soviet ambassador in New Delhi informed Foreign Secretary R.D. Sathe that "at the request of Afghan leadership, Soviet troops have been seat to Afghanistan to enable it to resist external aggression and interference." Three days later the United States lifted the ban on the supply of weapons to Pakistan and political observers expected massive US arms aid for Pakistan.

External Interventions in Afghanistan

The trouble in Afghanistan had been brewing up since the beginning of 1979 when the anti-Kabul elements in Afghanistan began receiving assistance directly from Pakistan and indirectly from the United States and China. Available evidence suggests that Pakistan had been feeding the Afghan insurgency from the beginning and that the Chinese and Americans too had been giving training and weapons to Afghan rebels operating from bases across the frontier. The *New York Times* correspondent wrote from Peshawar in June 1979 that "guerilla bands slip into Afghanistan from the camps in Pakistan, which are strung along the Afghan frontier from Chitral...in the north.. .to Baluchistan in the south-west." When the Soviet forces entered Afghanistan, India was in the midst of a fierce election campaign. The Government in New Delhi was headed by a lame-duck Prime Minister with little understanding of, and interest in, international politics. According to a "reasonably reliable account" he could not distinguish South-East Asia's map from Africa's. He had not made any public statement on what had been going on in Afghanistan since the summer of 1979 or on outside interference in the affairs of Afghanistan, though New Delhi claimed consistently good relations with Kabul. Broadly speaking, the Janata and Lok Dal governments did not pay much attention to matters of foreign policy and continued the policies pursued by the previous government.

Their attempts to balance Indo-Soviet friendship with better relations with Washington and Peking had remained counter-productive. Despite Prime Minister Morarji Desai's unilateral declaration that India would not make any nuclear explosion even for peaceful purposes, the United States refused to honour its commitment in respect of the supply of nuclear fuel for the Tarapur plant by continuing to withhold, delay the shipment of nuclear fuel (low enriched Uranium). And then the Vajpayee mission to Peking in February 1979 ended rather abruptly. The Janata leaders wasted much of their energy and time in fighting among themselves, in tarnishing the image of one-another in public and in dislodging one-another from power. They had thus little time left to address themselves to translating into action the promises they had made in their election campaigns, much less any time to plan a coherent foreign policy, to understand the significance and impact of the Sino-Japanese treaty of August 1978, of the Soviet-Vietnam treaty of November 1978 and of the Soviet-Afghan treaty of December 1978, Vice-Premier Deng's visit to the United States in January-February 1979, China's successful attempts to involve the Western powers in the process of modernization of China's industry, agriculture and above all, armed forces. A new structure of power had come into existence and the Janata and Lok Dal Government seemed to believe that this was not likely to endanger India's security. Again, if the trial and judicial murder of Zulfikar Ali Bhutto did not move Prime Minister Morarji Desai, the September 1979 *coup* in Afghanistan and the "death" of President Tarakki soon thereafter did not stir Prime Minister Charan Singh. Perhaps the entry of Soviet troops into Afghanistan would not have stirred him nor perhaps President Carter's warning to President Brezhnev that the latter should withdraw the Soviet forces from Afghanistan or face serious consequences in bilateral relations, but he could not afford to ignore the US decision to resume arms supplies to Pakistan--a country with whom India shares a long border, a country which had attacked India three times since independence. Something had to be done, a decision had to be taken now that the regrouping of American power, the formation of Sino-US-Pak axis, could be seen from our own frontiers.

Thus the Charan Singh Government first expressed its concern on 31 December 1979, to the United States over the reported resumption of arms supply to Pakistan. Eric Gonsalves, Secretary in the Ministry of External Affairs, reminded the American Ambassador in New Delhi that "the supply of arms in the past to Pakistan had invariably led to an increase in the tension in South Asia". Presumably, it struck the South Block that like the Janata Government the Lok Dal Government too was committed to the policy of "genuine" non-alignment; it, therefore, called on the Soviet Union later that day "to pull out from Afghanistan" and warned that the failure to do so would have serious consequences for the region, not realizing that the flow of sophisticated weapons into Pakistan would increase India's dependence on the Soviet Union and, therefore, the call for "pull out" could jeopardise Indo-Soviet links. Meanwhile, President Carter's letter to the Prime Minister concerning the resumption of arms supplies to Pakistan and the events in Afghanistan had been delivered. When the Prime Minister came back to New Delhi in the evening after his hurried election tour, he sent for the Soviet Ambassador and told him that India cherished its traditional and close relationship with Afghanistan and would like Afghan "independence and non-alignment strengthened". According to knowledgable sources, be delivered to long lecture denouncing the Soviet action." Though the Prime Minister did not urge immediate withdrawal of the Soviet forces, he indirectly expressed his disapproval of the Soviet action when he reminded Moscow of the June 1979 joint Indo Soviet resolve to "oppose any interference by outside forces in the internal affairs of Afghanistan." (To be sure, when the joint statement was signed during Prime Minister

Morarji Desai's visit to Moscow, 10-14 June 1979, the parties had in mind intervention by Pakistan, the United States and China.) The Prime Minister further told the Soviet Ambassador that "the presence of Soviet troops will have far-reaching and adverse consequences for this region" and expressed the hope that the Soviet troops would withdraw as soon as possible.

Evidently, the Prime Minister did not think of circumstances which led to the Soviet action; that is, interference in the affairs of Afghanistan by others. He did not realize that Sino-US-Pakistani military linkage demanded strengthening of Indo-Soviet ties. Atal Behari Vajpayee, who was foreign minister in the Janata Government (March 1977 to July. 1979) seemed to have realized the threat to India's security; for he held that the supply of American arms to an "overarmed Pakistan" and Soviet military presence in Afghanistan would imperil peace and stability in South Asia.

He asserted that the Soviet Union "must make a prompt declaration that it will withdraw its forces" and the United States "must not use the developments in Afghanistan to induct arms in Pakistan". But like Prime Minister Charan Singh he failed to take note of interference by powers other than the Soviet Union in the affairs of Afghanistan --interferences to which a reference had been made in the Indo-Soviet joint statement of June 1979 when he headed the Ministry of External Affairs. Though Indira Gandhi had a clear understanding of the issues at stake, what led to the Soviet intervention and the implications of foreign interventions in an area close to our frontier and what response was in India's national and security interests, she too decided to remain somewhat vague when on 31 December 1979, she told press correspondents that "we are against all foreign interventions. But people have been interfering in this area in one way or the other. The whole area is getting so destablized that it is quite a danger to us." Another Congress (I) leader, C.M. Stephen argued that foreign interference in Afghanistan was a continuing process since the Daud regime (1973-1978) and that the United States had no right to complain against the Soviet intervention. Still another Congress (I) leader, A.R. Antulay argued that the turbulence in the neighbouring countries underscored "the need for a stable government that would work"--something which only Mrs. Indira Gandhi could provide. Since the election was close at hand, political parties avoided taking a clear-cut, definite position as they wanted, understandably, votes of all communities and classes.

The CPI and CPI(M), however, made it known that they justified the Soviet military intervention as a step to counter the US-Pakistani interference. Mrs. Indira Gandhi hinted at what would be India's policy if she formed the government when on 3 January 1980, she said that the Soviet action was not a "one-sided affair." Three days later, on the second day of election, 6 January, she was more forthcoming when she said, among other things, "for a long time there has been foreign interference in Afghanistan of one kind and another" and that the Russians had acted in Afghanistan to counter-act what "they regard as western interference." Four days later when she had been asked by the President to form the government, she said in an interview with the French Radio that China had expansionist aims and that Sino-American military cooperation would be "very dangerous for India and the entire region." (This is how she reacted to the US Secretary of Defence Harold Brown's hope, expressed, during his five-day visit to Peking, 6-10 January, that Sino-American "global strategic relations" would broaden and deepen). The drift and ambiguity in India's attitude towards the Afghan crisis and with regard to the new structure of power came to an end soon after the election results revealed the overwhelming victory of Congress (I). The Prime Minister designate had made up her mind indeed. Though she assumed office on 14 January it is she who decided what India's policy should be when the General Assembly debated the Soviet action in Afghanistan on 12 January. Under her instructions, the Indian envoy at the United Nations, Brajesh C. Mishra, in a speech that lasted bare five minutes clearly and categorically stated India's stand on the Afghan issue. It is argued that the Indian government's statement at the UN General Assembly reflected "the switch in the Indian government's stand on Afghanistan with the electoral victory of Indira Gandhi." It would be more appropriate to say that it reflected the determination of the new government to give a definite direction to Indian foreign policy, keeping in mind India's national interests. What other choice was available to India ? It can be said that India could have joined the United States, China and Pakistan and their allies in the General Assembly and voted for the resolution which strongly deplored the Soviet action and called for the withdrawal of Soviet troops But how could New Delhi disregard the fact that the United States had been arming Pakistan since the mid-1950s and that Peking had been supplying arms to Islamabad since the mid-1960s or the fact that in the 1971 India-Pakistan War Pakistan had the support of both china and the United States, but Moscow's full support to India made it difficult for the United States and China' to intervene militarily in the war?

Moreover, since the establishment of Bangladesh, Sino-US links had been further strengthened. Beginning with 1978-79, Washington began taking interest in China's military capability and so did other Western powers and Japan. The new structure of power in Asia made it all the more necessary for India not to rock the boat of Indo-Soviet friendship. This explains why under the Desai regime Indo-Soviet relations improved, though upon assuming office in March 1977 Morarji Desai stated that if the Indo-Soviet treaty meant that India should not have friendship with other countries, then it would have to change. Any censure of the Soviet action in Afghanistan could have undermined friendly relations between India and the USSR at a time when polarization of power in Asia had been taking place and when India was still dependent on the Soviet Union for the supply of sophisticated weapons it needed for its security. It is not that Indira Gandhi acted in a haste as some foreign diplomats and correspondents in New Delhi believed. It is instructive to recall that during the Soviet intervention in Czechoslavakia in 1968, some members of the External Affairs Committee of the Indian Cabinet wanted New Delhi to condemn the Soviet action. But Prime Minister Indira Gandhi pointed out "that this would only alienate Moscow and jeopardise India's supply of arms without any positive benefits to the Czech cause", despite the fact that the Soviet decision to supply lethal weapons to Pakistan in 1968 had caused much resentment in India.

This argument was applicable to the situation in 1980 as well, more so because in 1968 the US was still entangled in the Vietnam war, it had not yet abandoned the policy of containing China and it still considered China its enemy. One thing more needs to be said here. True, India would like Afghanistan to prosper as a completely independent country and it would like the Soviet Union to withdraw its troops from that country. But what is desirable is not always possible. Unfortunately, the revolutionary regime in Kabul did not have a strong and stable organization, nor did it have a large following. When it introduced land and social reforms, the landlords and mullahs joined hands to overthrow the revolutionary regime. In the course of time "Pakistan became a sanctuary for the rebel forces". And Islamabad was not alone in giving support to the rebels. The United States and China were coordinating their strategy along with Pakistan in getting the revolutionary regime overthrown". Pakistan thought that here was an opportunity to instal a government beholden to it in Kabul and thus solve its border problems with Afghanistan. For the United States the objective was to re-establish its presence near Iran in order to influence events in that country. The Chinese too welcomed the possibility of the replacement of a pro-Soviet regime in Kabul with anti-Soviet mullah-dominated regime at the doorsteps of the Soviet Union. As stated by James Reston of the *New York Times,* Moscow, "feared the over-throw of a Marxist government in Kabul and its replacement by a militant Islamic regime" when it decided to send its forces into Afghanistan in December 1979. To be sure, Indian and the Soviet interests converged and could remain secure if the radicals remained in power in Afghanistan rather than be replaced by a pro-Western, pro-Pakistani, mullah-dominated regime. When on 27 December 1979, at 11.15 p.m. the Soviet Ambassador to India informed the Indian foreign Secretary that Soviet troops had been sent to Afghanistan at the request of the Afghan leadership, the Indian political leaders were in the thick of general election, scheduled to begin a week later, the Prime Minister was on an election tour in Uttar Pradesh and other ministers in different parts of the country.

Thus there was nobody in the capital to give direction, with the result that no public statement was issued. Even otherwise, the lame-duck government had been advised by the President to postpone decisions on crucial matters till after the election and in matters of foreign policy the Prime Minister had been following the advice rather strictly. The situation became serious for India when three days later the United States responded by lifting embargo on the supply of weapons to Pakistan; for a while it appeared that the subcontinent was going to become an active theatre of Soviet-American cold war.

The attitude of the political leaders towards the crisis on the whole was cautious and calculated. They certainly had Muslim voters in mind when they desired or demanded the withdrawal of the Soviet troops from Afghanistan. Once the election was over the Prime Minister designate gave a sense of direction to Indian foreign Policy. Vagueness and ambiguity disappeared and from the stand taken by India's permanent representative in the UN General Assembly on 12 January 1980, it was clear that India had at last taken the decision keeping in mind the country's security needs and national interests, though it could be argued that morality required condemnation of the Soviet action. However, Prime Minister Indira Gandhi has often stated that Soviet troops should withdraw from Afghanistan and also that such withdrawal would come about only if the insurgents stopped their activities and outside help and encouragement to them ended. She reiterated this in a press conference in Moscow on 22 September 1982, during her seven-day visit to the Soviet Union, though her hosts did not like the first part of her statement. No wonder the Soviet Embassy in India bulletin *Soviet Review,* did not publish the first portion her statement in its issue entitled Mrs. "Indira Gandhi's Visit to the USSR, September 20 26. 1982".

The re-emergence of superpower politics in South and South West Asia, with the Soviet Union's armed intervention in a traditionally neutral country Afghanistan and the US decision to rearm Pakistan, has created genuine feeling of concern in India regarding the security, stability and peace of the region. The superpower tension has come to India's door-step as South West Asia has become a tension has come to rivalry between the major powers'. Though India's reacation to the present situation is one of subdued caution and calm born out of mature diplomacy and past experience, yet it had conveyed its protests to both the superpowers against their involvement as it would increase tension and instability in the region. But mere condemnation of foreign intervention is not sufficient and India has to take bold initiative to play an active role as a major power in the region to subdue and de-escalate the present crisis and to keep the area from superpower rivalry. However, it is necessary to analysis the circumstances that led the Soviet Union to intervene in Afghanistan and the reasons which prompted the US to seek bases in Pakistan and strengthen it militarily, before making an evaluation of the possible ways and directions in which India could proceed to promote its security and vital national interests. Ever since the 1978 *coup* in Afghanistan, which led to the installation of a leftist government in Afghanistan, Pakistani and the Western scholars had emphasised the fact that the present Russian strategists still uphold the Tsarist ambition to reach warm waters of the Indian Ocean. However, it is necessary here to point out, that the government in Kabul had been pro-Moscow even before the 1978 *coup*. It was so because of the geo-political and economic compulsions which emerged out of Afghanistan being a landlocked country. The conclusion of the friendship treaty between the Soviet Union and Afghanistan in December 1978 and two other *coups* in the following year led by one or another faction of the Communist Party of Afghanistan have been pointed by the West as part of the calculated Soviet moves.

The Russian or the out Communist phobia has been revived by the Western countries to covert their own imperialist and expansionist designs in the strategic South and South West Asia. The American official response to the Afghan developments of December 1979 have been unduly strong and alarmist, in spite of the fact that the Soviet President Leonid Brezhnev, had publicly and vigorously denied expansionist intentions in the area. The Soviet Union justified its action in Afghanistan on the plea that the Afghan government had made a "pressing appeal to the USSR for urgent political, moral and economic assistance including military aid" on the basis of a year old Soviet-Afghan Treaty. It also maintained that its positive response to the Democratic Republic of Afghanistan Government's request was in line with Article 51 of the UN Charter, which provides for the states' inherent right to collective or individual self-defence for repelling aggression and restoring peace. The Afghanistan government too argued in favour of its sovereign right to self-defence by turning for aid to countries with which it had "appropriate international agreement" in accordance with the United Nations Charter. The new Afghan President Babrak Karmal held that the Soviet assistance was sought to defend his country from "external aggression" and he refuted the charges that he had violated the principles of nonalignment by securing military help for his country. A leading Soviet political commentator asserted that the Soviet military presence in Afghanistan was only "a reply action" to "the thrust into Afghanistan undertaken by the USA with the help of Peking and Pakistan's authorities." The Soviet President Leonid Brezhnev accused the US and its allies of launching an "undeclared war" against Afghanistan by sending "thousands of insurgents, armed and trained abroad" into the country. The Soviet Communist Party newspaper, *Pravda* complained that the bulk of weapons and mercenaries used by the imperialists in their struggle against Afghanistan were jumped in Pakistan territory. The Soviet delegate to the UN, Oleg Troyanovsky also stated in the General Assembly that Pakistan was "a major spring-board for the anti-Afghan action." He argued: "If there was no outside intervention in the affairs of Afghanistan, the Soviet Union would not have been called on to provide military assistance there. *Pravda* had warned Pakistan that "it is still not too late for Pakistan to stop meddling in Afghan affairs" and added that the Soviet troops would not pull out of Afghanistan until "foreign interference" had stopped and the Afghan people could "live as they choose."

The Soviet Union made it clear that it would begin withdrawing its troops from Afghanistan when the "country's long wild frontier" with Pakistan was stabilised. The Soviet Union alleged that Pakistan was not alone in providing arms and other aid to the conservative Muslim rebels who were fighting against the leftist government in Afghanistan. It accused the United States and China of coordinating their strategy along with Pakistan in getting the revolutionary regime overthrown in Kabul. The strategy had been worked out with an eye on the entire Gulf region. The entire West, including the US, is dependent for oil on the Gulf area. About 66 per cent of Western Europe's oil imports and 75 per cent of Japan's and 25 per cent of US annual oil imports come from the Gulf. If a conservative mullah-dominated regime could be installed in Kabul with the help of Pakistan and encouragement from both Washington and Peking, then it would not only be a pro-

Pakistan regime, but was expected to be pro-US (despite the fact that the mullah regime in Iran is inimical to the USA) and that it could be instrumental in playing an important role in implementing US objectives and strengthening the American position in the sensitive, strategic Gulf area.

The Soviets believed that then it could be utilised by America to restrain and contain the Soviets and to pressurise the anti-Western forces in this region. The ouster of the Shah and the upsurge against the American-supported rulers of Iran reinforced the need for such a policy. Thus, the Soviet Union, as pointed out earlier, defended its action in Afghanistan on the basis that the activities of Pakistan, China, US and its allies against the revolutionary government in Afghanistan had brought the Soviet Union to Afghanistan. But the US, China, Pakistan and various Western countries rejected the above explanation and justification of the Soviet Union, for they regarded the Soviet action as a clear-cut "aggression" against a nonaligned Muslim country. The Western scholars argued that the callous and brutal actions by the Soviet Union could not be mitigated by argument that the Soviet regime was acting defensively. President Carter said that Soviet attempt to justify its action on the basis of United Nations Charter was a perversion of the world organisation and should be rejected by all its numbers. The US and China maintained firstly that the Soviet action in Afghanistan was "a first step towards the fulfilment of their centuries-old dream of reaching the warm waters of the Indian ocean" The Soviet military action in Afghanistan was regarded as a part of a bigger plan. It has been argued by the *Pakistan Times'* correspondent in London that until there was Soviet involvement in the internal affairs, there was no external threat to Afghanistan. It added. that the threat was internal-

maladministration and conflict. And this threat was used by the Soviet Union to move one step ahead towards the realisation of a 150 year-old ambition.

The third factor, that is alleged to have motivated the Soviet military intervention in Afghanistan, is the Soviet ambition to consolidate its political advance in that country which appeared seriously threatened by the activities of the Muslim guerrilla organisations operating against the Soviet-backed government in Kabul. Fourthly, the rise of Islamic fundamentalism near the borders of the Soviet Union, in Iran, Pakistan and Afghanistan was reportedly perceived by the Soviet leaders as a threat to the Asian republics.

A distinguished writer has argued that the Soviet leaders felt that the religious affinities might be used by anti-communist forces for wooing the Soviet Islamic republics, whose integration into the Soviet Union is certainly less complete than that of the West Russian territories. *The Economist* commented in a similar vein that: "the rise of militant Islamic fundamentalism outside the Soviet Union is beginning to instil fears in Soviet leaders that they may soon have to face militant Muslims within their own borders." Besides the above factors which have been emphasized by the US, China and Pakistan one of the important considerations which might have motivated Soviet moves in Afghanistan, seem to be the Soviet strategy to improve its global position vis-a-vis the US in this region. Moscow, therefore, decided to bolster a friendly Marxist regime in Afghanistan, which is so close to her borders and vital to her security.

The Soviet Prime Minister, Alexei Kosygin warned the US and its allies that "no one should have any doubt that the USSR will not allow any violation of the existing equilibrium of forces in the world to the detriment of its security." With the ambition to preserve the balance of power in this strategic area, Moscow's armed intervention in Afghanistan was a desperate and "emotional" act intended to prevent the overthrow of an Afghan communist regime by Islamic radicals on the Iranian model. To the Soviet occupation in Afghanistan, the West's particularly the USA's reaction was instantaneous, not only because of the Soviet audacity in invading a nonaligned country for the first time since the end of Second World War, but also in view of the formidable US stakes involved. Apart from suspending the *detente* phase of relationship with the Soviet Union, President Carter announced his decision to provide military and economic assistance to Pakistan to meet the situation, which he described as "the greatest threat to world peace since 1945." The White House officials had issued a clear warning to the Soviet Union that "the US is prepared to use force to prevent any further Soviet military moves in South-West Asia". President Carter made it clear that the US would build up Pakistan militarily as a counter- weight to the Soviet Union with arms or arms sale through a consortium in which the West is tipped to take up the role of supplier and Arab states that of financiers.

The US decision to rearm Pakistan had been viewed with much concern, and apprehension by India, Bangladesh, Sri Lanka, Nepal and other countries of the region, as it would convert the South Asian region into a theatre of great power confrontation by reactivating the cold war and increasing the arms-race in the region. India was the most vociferous in its protest to the American efforts to resume its previous policy of rearming Pakistan, a policy which had proved disastrous in the past. The large scale induction of arms in Pakistan by the US and China, India argued, would turn Pakistan virtually into a military cantonment and South Asian region into a threatre of additional rivalry between the Soviet Union and China."

India feared that the arms supplied to the military junta in Pakistan so as to strengthen Pakistan against a Soviet-backed Afghanistan, will be used either against India or against the people of Pakistan, especially against the dissatisfied Baluch and 'Pakhtoon minorities to tighten the unpopular grip over the country. Because it appears from the prevailing mood in Pakistan earlier that it had no intention of getting embroiled in any war against the Soviet Union or to become a pawn in the reviving superpower newly in this region, as it was too anxious, at least exteriorly, to protect and preserve its newly acquired status of nonalignment by remaining aloof from the big power rivalry. Therefore, the government and the Pakistani people, at least this is what the newspaper editorials indicated did not seem to get overexcited by the American offer. This, to some extent, explained the behaviour of President Zia-ul-Haq. He rejected the laid package offered by President Carter and laid down the condition of "no strings," for the acceptance of American military aid.

Generally, it is the donor country that lays down the criteria, but in view of the anxiety of the US to pressurise Pakistan, the international community faces a paradoxical situation of recipient country dictating its own terms for acceptance of aid. These conditions were the following: Firstly, it is pointed out by Pakistan that the aid to it should be on a larger scale and abiding basis "for this emergency will not disappear in a hury." President Zia had described the proposed US aid of $ 400 million as "peanuts", totally inadequate to meet the security needs of Pakistan and demanded $2 billion worth of military and economic aid. Secondly, there should not be any attempt by the US to interfere in Pakistan's nuclear programme, which is well on the way to making a nuclear bomb. Thirdly, Pakistanis argued that the US must understand that the arms would be provided for use against "aggression" whether from the Soviet Union or from India. If Pakistan is involved in a war against India, the US must not place an embargo on spare parts as it did last time. Further, it must train Pakistanis to make their own spare parts so that Pakistan became as self-sufficient eventually as India was. Fourthly, President Zia wanted that the US must not interfere in Pakistan's internal affairs, in other words, no attempt would be made to alter the status of the martial law regime. President Zia did not want the US to put pressure on him for lifting restrictions on Bhutto's widow and daughter or to introduce democratisation and autonomy in Baluchistan and North-West Frontier Province. Lastly, Pakistan made it clear that it would not turn to former aligned status. The two countries would maintain independent approach to each issue in the region, as on a number of issues, the Muslim world does not see eye to eye with Washington. Pakistan wanted that the US should normalize its relations with Iran and the issue of Palestine should be considered *"de novo"*, if it wanted to strengthen its hands against the Soviet threat in South and South West Asia.

In a nutshell, Pakistan rejected the US aid offer because it considered that the time had come to re-examine the terminology of aid or assistance for its practical implications. It was argued that aid is "basically a free and uninterrupted flow of resources", which is what Pakistan needs and what actually is being sought. Brzezinski, the then National Security Adviser to US President, how-eve--, assured Pakistan that the $ 400 million aid offered by Washington was "the beginning of the US response." He stated that"—any attempt by any outside force to gain control of the Persian Gulf region would be regarded as an assault on the vital interest of the US and would be repelled by the use of any means necessary, including military force."

The practical chances of US direct military involvement in the region can be ruled out on the basis of its experience and lesson from Vietnam war. However, the possibility of US motives to increase its influence and hold over the area by strengthening Pakistan via its military aid--direct or through other Muslim countries cannot be overlooked. In this situation, India's primary concern would be to meet its security requirements by defusing the superpower rivalry in this region on the one hand and by neutralising Pakistan's military ambitions, on the other. Actually, it appears that the Afghan crisis had proved a major windfall for President Zia-ul-Haq. Apart from propping up his tottering regime, it has brought him much needed military and economic aid from all directions, particularly from the US which had lately sanctioned $ 32 billion military and economic aid.

India has disapproved of the superpowers' moves to seek military solutions to international problems. Soviet action in Afghanistan was first criticized by the care-taker government headed by Prime Minister Charan Singh and later on by Prime Minister, Mrs. Indira Gandhi. New Delhi had conveyed its deep concern to Moscow because of its apprehension that the Soviet action in Afghanistan may have adverse consequences in the entire region, as Mrs. Gandhi had stated, "one presence attracts another and that is most dangerous." She further added that the Soviet Union by itself would not do anything to them, the situation would depend on what the reactions were to the Soviets and how the situation developed after that. Though, the Soviet move in Afghanistan was to counteract the Western influence or what they described "outside intervention" to topple the' "revolutionary and progressive" regime in Kabul, yet this explanation does not wholly justify the Soviet military occupation of Afghanistan. "That is why, India had expressed her disapproval of the Soviet military action from the very beginning though Mrs. Gandhi viewed that Moscow's action should be viewed in the total context of the situation. The Western response to the presence of Soviet troops in Afghanistan, especially the US decision to arm Pakistan, as alluded to earlier, has caused much alarm and concern in India.

Even an American scholar opined that the US official reaction had revealed a disquieting lack of balance, both in the analysis of the problem and in the response to it. The US decision to rearm Pakistan to meet any threat from the Soviet Union does not seem logical. Actually, India doubts Pakistan's capacity to resist a Soviet incursion, if it occurs, with or without an addition to its muscle power by the U.S. India wanted Washington to seek "diplomatic rather than military solution" to the Afghanistan crisis. It feared that the American efforts to evolve a US-Sino-Pak axis would pose a grave threat to her security. After the opening of Karakoram Highway between China and Pakistan, the transfer of military weapons to Pakistan had already increased, and China had decided to bolster Pakistan's military regime by providing more defence aid in the wake of Afghan crisis. This may lead military junta in Pakistan to adventurism towards India not only to avenge the loss of Bangladesh, but also to distract the attention of its people from internal problems of instability, dissatisfaction, suspicion and distrust regarding its legitimacy to rule over the country. India, therefore criticised the pouring of arms in Pakistan on the following grounds:

Firstly, the supply of arms to Pakistan would heighten tension and instability in the region.

Secondly, it would intensify the arms race in the region and divert the meagre resources from economic development to the military preparedness.

Thirdly, induction of arms in Pakistan would disturb the normalisation of relations between India and Pakistan. The US policy of maintaining an artificial balance of power proved to be one of the important factors disturbing the normalisation of relations between India and Pakistan. Fourthly, induction of arms in Pakistan would undermine its own security and as pointed out earlier would further alienate the people from the Government. This feeling would further alienate the discontented minorities from the Pakistani Government. Fifthly, by the induction of large scale arms, Pakistan would not only earn its neighbours hostility but also that of the Soviet Union's. Lastly, since the proposed US-Chinese arms build up would create an imbalance in the region, it would also under-mine the security of India.

This serious development could drive India into a closer arrangement and relationship with Moscow for seeking security. It would defeat the very purpose of US arms strategy in this region, as American policy makers did not want to push India completely into the lap of Moscow. Thus; India strongly opposed the US and Chinese move to rearm Pakistan.

Of course, it does not want to see disintegration of Pakistan under Soviet impact. On the other hand, it has a vested interest in the viability and stability of Pakistan. But the point is that the rearming of Pakistan would not help in defusing the Afghan crisis or forcing the Soviet

Union to withdraw its forces from Afghanistan. What is required is that conditions should be created in which Afghanistan government can itself ask the Soviet Union to withdraw its troops, which can be possible only when other countries stop meddling with Afghanistan's internal affairs. Therefore, Pakistan should promise, not to render any economic and military assistance to the conservative religious insurgents in Afghanistan. The US and China, too, should refrain from pouring any large scale armament into Pakistan and creating a military imbalance in subcontinent. These conditions would facilitate the Soviet withdrawal and help in reducing the tension and possibly succeed in averting outside intervention on a more permanent basis in this subcontinent. The initial rejection of $ 400 million US aid offer by Pakistan came as a relief to India. But the emphasis on the Islamic links in search of the alternative source of economic and military aid, particularly Saudi Arabia's decision to provide $ 750 million worth of economic and military aid and the US assistances of $ 32 billion later on still pose a grave threat to India's security. Moreover, Pakistanis rejection of US aid was not due to the fact that they were not interested in it but because they did not want to offend the Soviet Union for a 'peanut' donation. However, Pakistan had willingly taken the risk for a larger aid package. The early refusal to accept US aid also indicated that Pakistan was in no mood to go back on its nuclear projects. President Carter's decision to drop the idea introducing legislation authorising the Congress to provide aid to Pakistan, had been interpreted by certain sections that the USA had reconciled itself to a nuclear Pakistan.

But the question arises: is Pakistan going to face the Soviet Union with all the armoury it is receiving from the US? Perhaps, not. President Zia-ul-Haq himself pointed out in this regard that "there is no danger for the Soviet Union, we cannot fight the Soviet Union, we cannot imagine a war against the Soviet Union."

Then against whom the most sophisticated weapons are going to be used, which are not even suited against the Afghan terrain? Probably, it is obvious on the basis of historical facts that these armaments, if they are to be used, would be used against India. It has been mentioned before the US Senate Sub-Committee that of all the deployment of Pakistani forces only two divisions were on the Afghan border, while fourteen were on the Indian border. In this scenerio, India's security is seriously threatened, more so because the military government in Pakistan lacks political legitimacy and military dictators are prone to adopt detrimental and aggressive tactics for their short-term gains.

Therefore, the situation in Afghanistan calls for hectic diplomatic dialogue with the superpowers as well as with the regional countries. Here, the first possible option before New Delhi is that along with other neighbouring countries, it can provide a regional defence system against the intrusion of any superpower. Secondly, since India and the Soviet Union highly value each other's friendship, India can persuade it to withdraw its troops from Afghanistan. This would not only help mitigate the opposition within Afghanistan against the revolutionary government in Kabul, but would also divest USA of an excuse to pour more arms in the subcontinent, Lastly, India itself needs to take a hard look at her nuclear policy. In the context of grave threat to her security and national interest, India might have to seriously weigh the complusion of exercising her options in this field. So research and development programme must immediately provide for that contingency, as India can no longer afford to lag behind. Thus, it can be said that in the wake of Afghanistan crisis, with the US and China's decision to dump armaments in the Indian subcontinent, the South and South West Asian region can become a hot-bed of big power rivalry.

Currently, India is actively participating in reconstruction of New Afghanistan, even at the cost of losing lives of its engineers and other workers. We have to go long. A friendly Afghanistan is in our interest

REFERENCES

A.G. Noorni, "Soviet Ambitions in South Asia," *International Security,* Winter 1979-80, pp. 47-48.

Bhabani Sen Gupta, *The Afghan Syndrom: Haw to Live With Soviet Power,* Delhi, 1982, pp. 15-17.

Dawn Overseas Weekly, Vol. 5, No. 2, 12-18 January 1980, p. 3.

G. Anatolyev, "Afghanistan: Upholding Independence", *New Times,* No. 34, August 1979, pp. 8-9.

Girilal Jain, "Relations With Pakistan: Its Security No Concern of Ours", *Times of India,* 11 Febuary 1982.

Hindustan Times, 2 January 1980. For Afghan representative's arguments see A/ES -6/PV. 1, pp. 19-20.

Indian Express, ed., "Pindi Sets Terms for Accepting US Arms", 17 January 1980.

J.G. Tiwari, "The Story of the Soviet Take Over of Afghanistan", *Organiser,* Vol. 30, No. 39, p. 12.

K. Subrahmanyam, "The Afghan Situation And India's National Interest", *Foreign Affairs Reports,* Vol. 39, No. 8, August 1980, pp. 152-154.

Leslie H. Gelb and Richard H. Ullman, "Keepling Cool At The Khyber Pass", *Foreign Policy,* No. 38, Spring 1980, p 10.

M G. Wainbaum and Gautam Sen, "Pakistan Enters the Middle East", *Orbis,* Vol. 22, No. 3, Fall 1978, p. 609.

Nawa-e-Waqt's views in *The Tribute,* 7 May 1978.

New York Times, 25 June 1979 and *International Herald Tribune,* 16 January 1979.

New York Times, 25 June 1979. Cited in Vidya Prakash Dutt, "Afghan Wat", *Sunday,* 18 February 1980, p. 15.

Radio Kabul as cited in *Hindustan Times,* 4 January 1980.

S.N. Antia, "Afghan Crisis and India's Stakes," *Mainstream,* Vol. 18, No. 24, 9 February 1980, p. *6.*

Selig S Harrison, "After the Afghan Coup: Nightmare in Baluchistan", *Foreign Policy,* No. 32, Fall 1978.

Sunday Tribune, 13 January 1980.

The Tribune, 11 February 1933.

The Tribune, 15 Febuary 1980.

The Tribune, 7 January 180.

Times of India, 8 January 1980.

Vidya Prakash Dutt, "Afghan War", *Sunday,* Vol. 7, No. 32, 10 February 1980, p. 15.

Vijay Sen Badhraj, "India and the Soviet Union", *International Studies,* Vol. 10, Nos. 3-4, July-December 1978, pp. 739-757.

Zareer Masani, *Indira Gandhi: A Biography,* Delhi, 1975, p. 191.

Chapter 5

India and Sri Lanka

Sri Lanka and India are not only two neighbours, they inherit common socio-cultural legacy also. Sri Lanka occupies strategic position in Indian Ocean region. For last many decades Sri Lanka is infested with the problem of Tamil terrorism, i.e. LTTE. India is deeply concerned with this problem as it has many implications in our domestic polity and governance. On the other hand, India is also suffering from Islamic and other terrorist attacks in different parts of the country. Cross-border terrorism and proxy war from Pakistan and recently from Bangladesh have posed a challenge before us. Here, we are highlighting the determinant factors of India-Sri Lanka relations.

The national consensus on the State system as it existed in 1948 when Sri Lanka attained independence has been under severe strain with the assertion of the Sinhalese-Buddhist supremacy in a plural society in 1956. This progressively accentuated and began to acquire the dimensions of a crisis in the seventies-- the constitutional-political framework or the direction of its economic development or in the realm of Sinhalese-Tamil relations. Inherent in such a crisis of consensus has been, on the one hand, an adversarial concept of politics in a highly competitive and volatile political ethos and on the other, a bland and unqualified affirmation of majoritarian principle in a multi-ethnic and scarce-resource society. Consequently, the consensus crisis has manifested at the level of the two major parties, the Sri Lanka Freedom Party (SLFP) and the United National Party (UNP), and at the level of the major minority and the majority communities. The pressures and pulls at the level of the former have been mitigated so far, to some extent, by the phenomenon of their sharing power alternately as a result of fairly regular and periodically held elections. This, however, has not been so in the case of the latter as the very dynamics of the modalities of such power-sharing among the dominantly Sinhalese parties with all its electoral concomitants has tended to push the minority community of the Tamils virtually to a peripheral position in the power structure of the island State. Such a trend has resulted in a diminution of the emotional as well as material stakes of the Tamil community in the system as it operated since 1948. This has run to its logical conclusion of an autonomy demand emerging as a demand for secession.

This Sinhala-Tamil schism ultimately vented itself in the July 1983 violence. By no means the first episode of its kind, the consequence of the events, their causal connection, as well as the pattern of violence and its aftermath, mark it to be qualitatively so different from the past instances that if the quest for a *modus through the All* Parties Conference proves infructuous, a domestic conflict might get internationalised. Underlying such stresses and strains on the political system are the simultaneous and cumulative challenges of participation, distribution, and integration emerging from a complex of factors and forces -- domestic as well as external.

An appraisal of these factors necessitates an overview

of the past and pre-sent contexts of the island States socio-cultural configuration,the nature and character of its power structure the major trends in its economic development and the complex web of external linkages therein.

An appraisal of the various patterns of interactions between the people and the politics of Sri Lanka requires, as a backdrop, (a) a perusal of its socio-cultural pluralism (as reflected in terms of race, religion, language, caste, and family); (b) the nature and tenor of its communicational web; (c) the demographic patterns and trends to the extent they have assumed a criticality in the developmental processes of the country; and (d) the implications and impact of the 'India' factor in its historico-cultural development.

To begin with, the evolution of the island State's multiethnic configuration has been determined to a considerable extent by its geo-political setting of proximity to India and its distance from any other land mass. Thus, intermittent migrational waves from India spanning over several centuries have not only accounted for the bulk of Sri Lanka's population but have also provided the majority-major minority component of its social structure--with the Sinhalese who claim Aryan descent comprising 74 per cent of the total population of 15 million and the Tamils who claim Dravidian descent accounting for 18 per cent of the total population. As for the rest, the Eurasians, Burghers, and Malays--a legacy of the Western colonial era-- constitute about 1 per cent while the Muslims, most of whom claim Moorish identity, account for 7 per cent of the population. Incidentally, a small number of Moors also migrated from India to Sri Lanka.

The pattern of migration from India and the demographic dispersal of the migrants in Sri Lanka has been such that it has resulted in the strengthening of distinct identities of the communities in religio-racial-linguistic terms. Furthermore, the 1981 Census reveals that though island-wise the Tamils are a minority, in eight out of twenty-four districts, the Sinhalese have a minority status in numerical terms. Of these eight districts, the Ceylon Tamils have an absolute majority in five (Jaffna. Mannar, Vavuniya, Batticaloa, and Mullaithivu) and the largest numerical strength in one (Trincomalee) with the Moors and Indian Tamils (settled in Sri Lanka during the British period to work on plantations in the dominantly Sinhalese central and southern parts of the country) having similar position in one each, i.e. Amparai and Nuwara Eliya.

Barring Nuwara Eliya, the heartland of Sri Lanka, the Tamil-dominated districts are contiguous, falling within the boundaries of the northern and eastern provinces. The regional concentration of Ceylon Tamils in the north and east led to the community identifying itself with a "homeland" and thus they had minimal contacts with the rest of the country till the advent of the Western colonial powers. During the colonial era, particularly since the British colonial rule in the eighteenth century, greater interaction took place between the Sinhalese and Ceylon Tamils at various levels, connoting an increasingly competitive but cordial coexistence amongst the Sinhalese-Tamil elites.

Alongside such a pattern of interaction during the colonial era, a fairly compact and developed communication web, of the transport and the mass media--official as well as unofficial--has been buttressed by a high level of literacy (85 per cent), a consequence of the State -initiated policy of compulsory education upto the age of fourteen years and free education upto university level which was introduced as early as 1943. This communication network, however, has tended to be a double-edged sword: of unity as well as division in inter-community as well as inter-community relations.

Closely related to the issue of literacy is the demographic pattern of the island reflecting a bottom-heavy age structure. In 1981, 40 per cent of the population consisted of children below fifteen years of age. The age group of 15-25 years accounted for another one-fifth of the total population. This implies that, first, the heavy child dependency will necessitate adequate resource allocation to meet the basic needs of this segment, particularly in the context of the welfare traditions (of subsidies in food, education, and health), and, secondly, the number of entrants in the active labour force will be considerably large in the years to come, necessitating a large-scale public investment programme that will generate economic activity and thereby mitigate unemployment (a backlog of about 15 per cent).

Looked at in a comparative South Asian context, Sri Lanka was the first Asian country to have universal adult franchise as early as 1931, a right that the electorate has exercised at fairly regular intervals both before independence and after. This has bequeathed Sri Lanka with a tradition of electoral participation as can be seen from the fact that while in the first pre-independent general election in 1947 the aggregate of total votes cast was around 55 per cent, it shot up to 87 per cent in the 1977 election (seventh since independence). Moreover, over the decades, the invalid votes have come down to less than one per cent, thanks to the very high literacy rate.

Another characteristic of the Sri Lanka electoral tradition has been a steady erosion of independents connoting the entrenchment of the party system after a brief spell of a dominant party pattern during the first few years of independence. With the Sinhala Buddhist resurgence which manifested in the general elections of 1956, the dominant party system has yielded place toll two-major party pattern in the Sinhalese areas. Under this system, the UNP and SLFP emerged as two major-parties, having a more or less equally strong support base emerging victorious alternately in ensuing elections and having pre-electoral understanding and post-election coalitional arrangements with the minor parties. The political behaviour of minor parties reflected a consistency in such alignment patterns. Thus, while the predominantly ideologically oriented Left parties--the Trotskyite Lanka Sama Samaj Party (LSSP) and the Moscow-oriented Communist Party of Ceylon (CPC)-- chose the 'centrist' SLFP, the Tamil parties like the Tamil Congress (TC) or the Federal Party (FP) preferred that the UNP perceive it as relatively more secular and less chauvinist than the SLFP.

During 1956-1970, the coalition governments, though reflecting the diverse pressures and pulls within the Cabinet and leading at times to the edging out of one of the minor partners, marked continuous efforts to evolve a consensus on major issues of public policies. This was due to: (a) the marginal majority of the ruling party and its need to keep the support of at least some of the minor parties; and (b) the imperative to maintain a certain degree of continuity in governance in view of one of the two major parties being alternately in power.

In the process, two major trends emerged. First, both the parties, having their major support base in the predominantly Sinhalese areas, competed one with the other in being more Sinhalese-Buddhist; and, consequently, both alienated the Tamil minority in varying degrees which however stopped short of breaking point. Second, though differing from each other in their respective economic strategies to cope with the developmental challenges, they accommodated each other's legacies to advantage when in power. Such an accommodation went along with a shift in emphasis in their respective economic strategies reflecting to a considerable extent such divergence in their foreign policy orientations and avocations. Thus, the national consensus on economic political, and ethnic issues, though increasingly tenuous. was apparently maintained till the 1970 elections.

If 1956 was a watershed in Sri Lankan politics in evoking a Sinhalese-Buddhist ascendancy, so too was the 1970 election--but in a different context. To begin with, unlike the 1956 elections in which Bandaranaike's Mahajana Eksath Peramuna (People's United Front} had a precarious majority of 51 in an elected house of 95, the United Left front headed by his widow, had won 115 out of a total of 151 elective seats in 1970.

Secondly, in 1956 barring the breakaway group of the LSSP, which was one of the constituents of the MEP, the major left parties, the LSSP and the Communists, had pre-electoral arrangements on some seats but had remained in opposition, promising the ruling front only 'critical support'. In the 1970 elections both of them were the electoral partners of the SLFP in the United Front (UF), winning nineteen and six seats, respectively.

However, even without its Left allies, the SLFP had acquired a cohesive majority of ninety scats, with the UNP limping behind with seventeen. Even so, the UNP's debacle in terms of seats (from sixty-six seats in 1965 to seventeen in 1970) did not reflect its electoral strength. In fact, in terms of the total votes polled it had bagged the maximum number of votes: 38 percent, with the SLFP polling 37 per cent. The system of first-past-the-pole coupled with the formation of the United Front; the phenomenon of polarised contests, with a substantive number of them being between the SLFP/LSSP/CP and the UNP; and, last but not the least, the hazards of ruling--all led to the UNP's loss of seats in many constituencies.

Also, unlike the 1956 elections in which socio-cultural issues had an edge over the economic questions, the economic issues provided the major thrust to the 1970 elections. The "open door" policies of the UNP could not cope with the widespread and increasing unemployment of vernacular-educated rural youth. Finally, the electoral verdict reflected a gradually entrenched psyche of the Sinhalese electorate; the choice of its electoral option underlined not so much is *preference* for an alternate party as the *rejection* of the ruling regime.

In the electoral arena, however, the UNP-UF confrontation was mainly in the dominant Sinhalese-Buddhist areas. Such polarisation was weakest in the Tamil-dominated northern and eastern provinces. There the issues were somewhat different, revolving around the effectiveness or otherwise of the regional parties, like the Federal Party and the Tamil Congress, for having a co-operative or coalitional arrangement with one of the two major parties and in remaining within the framework of an integrated unitary structure, even though they complained that such a structure did not adequately reckon with their community/regional identity and aspirations in socio-economic terms. However, for the first time, the magnitude of the UF electoral strength had totally neutralised the role of the regional parties as a "balancing" force between the two major parties consequently, their bargaining strength and manoeuvrability vis-a-vis the Centre was considerably reduced.

It is noteworthy that, as in the past, a considerably large number of members of Parliament and the "core" of Government--the Cabinet--continued to be drawn from the upper strata of Sri Lankan society. The only major difference in the 1970 elections from the earlier ones was a decrease in the number of English-educated wealthy MPs and an increase in the Sinhala-educated MPs few of whom had a relatively humbler rural background. Even so, the number of land-owners, businessmen, and lawyers and other professionals continued to be dominant--a phenomenon that hardly changed in the 1977 legislature.

Despite such a convergence amongst the parliamentary elite in socio-economic terms, the pressures and pulls from their respective support bases, coupled with the divergence in their ethnic as well as socio-economic perspectives, pulled them in different directions even though a broad countrywide consensus had emerged a new constitutional framework replacing the Soulbury Constitution of 1945 which, with certain modifications, had been operative since independence. Even so, before the new Constitution could be finalised, the climate of consensus had been vitiated and its erosion had set in, as was evident from the insurgency of April 1971, followed by the promulgation of a long-drawn-out national emergency; the walk-out of the Federal party in June 1971 from the Constituent Assembly and, finally, the rejection of the Constitution in the final voting by the UNP in May 1972.

Notwithstanding the walk-out or the vehement dissent of virtually the entire opposition, in view of its massive majority, the United Front pushed through the new Constitution for which it had no doubt, in principle, a national mandate, but had failed to ensure a nation-wide, all-party consensus. Such a consensus-erosion leading to a consensus breakdown on the constitutional framework, occurred in the main in two critical areas: the degree of economic radicalisation and secularisation, and at two levels: the UF-UNP level and the UF regional or Tamil parties level.

The major points of contention between the United Front and the Tamil parties, particularly the Federal Party (which had won thirteen out of nineteen seats in the northern and eastern provinces) revolved around the sections pertaining to unitary structure, religion, language, and citizenship. The Federal party, while questioning the primacy accorded to Buddhism as the "foremost religion" in the Constitution as well as the non-justiciable nature of fundamental rights, was particularly agitated over the unitary structure incorporated in the draft Constitution and the position of the Tamil language therein. It demanded a federal constitutional framework which provided for a greater devolution of powers. It also reiterated its demand for making both Tamil and Sinhala the official languages.

Since 1956 when Sinhala was made the official language, as against the earlier understanding of both the UNP and the SLFP for providing parity of status between Sinhala and Tamil, the language issue had emerged as the focal point of the increasing chasm between the two communities. And though the Tamil Language Special Provisions Act of 1958 did provide certain safeguards in this respect, the implementation regulation for the "reasonable use of Tamil" Act was not provided for as late as 1966. What is more, during the debate in the Constituent Assembly the legal validity of the 1966 regulations was questioned by Felix R. Dias Bandaranaike, a leading member of the United Front, adding thereby to the Federal party's suspicions regarding the intentions and bonafides of the Sinhalese majority in the implementation of the 1958 Act. As such, after failing to ensure the safeguards for the use of Tamil in Tamil-dominated areas as well as its official status in the rest of the country, coupled with the other issues already mentioned, virtually all the Tamil members of Parliament walked out of the Constituent Assembly and formed a Tamil United Front in 1972. The non-compliance of the requisite safeguards for the Tamils in the constitutional document reflected that certain issues affecting ethnic relations were virtually non-negotiable with the Centre. In the process It had also underlined an increasing hardening of inter-community racial prejudices, reinforcing racial stereotypes as perceived by one vis-a-vis the other.

Significantly, in view of both the UNP and the SLFP sharing their support base amongst the Sinhalese Buddhists and attempting to edge out each other in a highly competitive system, there was a near-unanimity between the two on provisions relating to religion and, to a considerable extent language. And though the UNP criticised the United Front for its "parochial" attitude vis-a-vis the Tamils, its major disagreement with the United Front lay on the broad parameters of the Constitution as such, in which the classical balance of powers, between the various organs of the Government was not as maintained: judiciary was given a back seat and bureaucracy was politicised. The "socialist mobilist" orientations of the Constitution (alongside the exclusion of the right of private property in fundamental rights), it was feared by the UNP, would usher in a system of "State capitalism" and "prime-ministerial" Government without recourse to participative channels.

That the apprehensions of the UNP were to a considerable extent well founded was evident from the modalities and implementation of various law pertaining to land reforms, nationalisation, and the Business Acquisition Act which, though radical in content, were tardily implemented, and often became avenues of patronage distribution by those in power. As for its efforts to create mechanisms for devolution of power through the creation of the District Political Authority (with the MPs of the area being at the power apex), it did not go a long way either, for often the devolution of funds was partisan and its implementation tardy. Further, the economic policies of the United Front led to the widening of a State sector with poor performance and its efforts towards economic self-sufficiency in various economic commodities, through rigid quotas and State control, led to scarcities and long queues. Nor could it accelerate the economic activities on a large scale so as to generate greater employment opportunities. Finally, the contradictions and "power tussle within the United Front increasingly surfaced leading to the ouster of the LSSP in 1975 and the breakaway of the Communist party on the eve of the 1977 election."

The fragmentation of the United Front was disastrous for the SLFP, but more so for the LSSP and the Communist party in the 1977 election. For the first time in the electoral history of Sri Lanka, the LSSP and Communists drew a blank. The total rout of the Left parties in the electoral verdict could be ascribed to the absence of the traditional no contest pact with the SLFP the fragmentation of the Left forces which were contending with each other in many constituencies; their credibility crisis as the junior partners of the centrist United Front regime; and their limited capability to turn populist measures into performance in the wake of the SLFP dominance in decision-making. In the process, their image as "progressive" parties had been tarnished and their support base constricted as was evident from the low percentage of votes polled by both of them.

As for the SLFP, its numerical strength went down from ninety to eight. The UNP won 140 out of 168 seats and, ironical as it may seem, the Tamil United Front, christened in 1976 as Tamil United Liberation Front (TULF) and having a separate State as its electoral mandate, emerged as the largest opposition party, with its leader A. Amirthalingam becoming the leader of the opposition.

The 1977 election has been a critical landmark not only because of the UNP's unprecedented victory but more so because of the manner in which it interpreted the mandate as a sanction to cast the entire system in virtually a new mould, with a view to gain political stability and rapid economic modernisation.

To a considerable extent, this is what the United Front also had in view earlier. And though the strategies of both, due to their divergent orientations and perspectives, varied, particularly in the economic realm and to a certain extent in the politico-constitutional realm, the compulsions of mass politics as well as the imperatives of governance and power sustenance have led both to adopt populism; increasing centralisation of power; intensive induction of emergency provisions; and frequent use of the coercive apparatus of the State. While denouncing such measures when in opposition, both resorted to them when in power, eroding, in the process, the democratic norms without attempting to evolve a nation-wide consensus on an economic or a constitutional framework viable enough to accommodate the socio-cultural diversities.

To begin with, in the promulgation of the 1978

Constitution, the tyranny of the majority prevailed as much as it did in 1972, depriving the new Constitution national sanction if not legitimacy. The major point of criticism of the opposition as a whole has been the change-over from the Westminster model of parliamentary system to a de Gaullist type presidential system. The major explanation behind the promulgation of the presidential system has been that a judicious balance between democratic participation and stability for the implementation of the developmental processes would be best realised in such a system for, the President, unlike the legislators, would be free from the "constituency" considerations which conditioned the attitudes of the MPs. As such, despite the parliamentary politics and a plethora of shifting alliance systems between and amongst the legislators, the President would ensure speed and continuity in policy implementation. However, what has emerged in the process is a top-heavy system which has become highly personalised rather than institutionally channelled. Consequently, it signals the portents for the eighties and thereafter.

For one, it brings in its wake the issue of the stature and capability of the President's successor to manage such over-arching powers judiciously. For another, it has affected the equilibrium between the various governmental organs. While the judiciary has been sidetracked in the name of the sovereignty of the people's elected assembly, in the legislature, the tyrannical majority of the ruling regime has neutralised the requirements of accountability (as is evident from the speed with which some of the critical legislation has been rushed through). Furthermore, in view of the President being also the chief of the UNP, the ruling party MPs have had little leeway, in effect, for autonomy and independence within the legislature.

The very fact that soon after the advanced presidential election in October 1982, and the declaration of referendum a month later to elicit popular mandate for the extension of Parliament by another term (i.e. upto 1989), the President had already had undated letters of resignation of all his party MPs, reflected the untrammelled powers at his disposal for a made-to-order Parliament. This has been particularly so due to the system of proportional representation and the "list" principle in the new Constitution under which, in the event of the resignation of an MP, his party has the right to nominate his successor. What is more, about one-half of the governmental MPs have been ministers of one sort or an other, i.e., Cabinet ministers, deputy ministers, ministers without portfolio, district ministers, etc. Nearly half of them thus wear two hats, combining the legislative as well as the executive role.

Under such a situation (with the over-arching powers of the President to hire and fire any MP) Parliament, despite its so-called sovereign powers, has become an appendage of the executive. Yet, the legislature has been endowed with sufficient powers to subordinate: the judiciary. Thus, Bills which in the view of the Cabinet of Ministers are "urgent in the national interest" must be scrutinised by the judiciary within twenty-four hours. Existing laws which are inconsistent with the Constitution are allowed to stand. And finally, there is no judicial review of *enacted legislation,* and the Constitution envisages only "prospective annulment" In sum, thus, the balance between executive and democratic participation has been on several occasions tilted in the-direction of a strong, stable executive.

Further, ironically as it: may seem, the holding of too many elections--the presidential election; the urban-rural council elections; the referendum followed by a mini-election--has made the people election-weary. The referendum has also heralded certain regressive tendencies in the electoral dynamics, followed by an increasing erosion of a competitive party system and ensuring continuance of the present regime till 1989. Consequently, the modes of protest and dissent which might have found expression in the electoral arena in 1983 (had the election been held) have increasingly resorted to extra-constitutional means, the worst manifestation of this being in the ethnic realm.

It seems that the President, acutely aware of the intensity of the grievances of the Tamils, had hoped in vain (as it now seems) that he would be able to evolve a political solution of the 'Tamil' issue through negotiations. Apparently he had expected that schemes of decentralisation in the form of District Councils and rapid economic development would have their spill-over effects in the Tamil as much as the Sinhalese areas.

It is in such a context that the economic package of the UNP needs to be appraised. Unlike the SLFP, the developmental perspectives of which hinged around State control and monopoly, import substitution, and greater foreign exchange restrictions, the focal point of the UNP's economic policies has been an export-oriented economy with a fairly heavy induction of foreign aid and investments. As such, its policies have envisioned: (i) an open-door economy, with the accent on free enterprise based on free market forces; (ii) liberalising the foreign exchange and import regulations; (iii) divesting the import monopolies of the State, except in the case of a few basic food items; (iv) generally providing an attractive incentive package to foreign investors; (v) telescoping the span of the Mahaweli project from thirty to six years to accelerate irrigation facilities, land settlements, and self-sufficiency in food, particularly rice; and (vi) abolishing food subsidies for everyone and instead, introducing the 'food stamp' scheme for those earning less than 500 rupees per month with a view to cushioning the relatively poor strata.

As for the social subsidies, the UNP has succeeded in cutting down the budgetary expenditure on social services from 43 per cent in 1970-71 to an estimated 17 per cent in 1982. In the context of the overall economic framework of the UNP, the social implications in renouncing the subsidy component have the tremendous potential of enhancing inequalities in income distribution and affecting the process of distributive justice-- unless and until it succeeds in increasing the productivity and income opportunities of the poor through its growth strategies, bridging thereby the gap between investment and output, between capital outlay and productive employment. And though in the initial years, due to the massive foreign loans and aid, mostly from the West, the UNP did succeed in generating an impressive record of employment opportunities, this has gradually petered down.

With regard to the overall economic performance of the UNP the comments of the World Bank in 1982 are revealing. After appraising the various sectors of its economy it concluded that the process was "accompanied by growing deficits in the budget and in the current balance of payments which reached unsustainable levels in 1980. Good progress toward the restoration of economic stability was made during 1981, yet it would now appear that this progress will not be maintained in 1982 and 1983. Accordingly, it recommended pruning in the budget expenditure, circumspection in introducing new projects, further reduction of the "burden" of consumer subsidies, and devaluation of the rupee.

The recommendations, telling as they are, indicate that the major problem of Sri Lanka is that of the adverse balance of payments due to a combination of slow export volume growth and a large deterioration in the terms of trade. During 1979-81 for instance, the current account balance had a deficit of about 2,000 million Sri Lankan rupees. Added to this has been an unprecedented foreign debt accumulation which has been more than doubled during 1977-1981. As for the debt servicing payments, they had a threefold increase during this period. Also, the widening budget deficit and the continuing high growth in money supply led to increasing inflationary trends. In the context of such inflationary trends, the unemployment problem, because of a backlog coupled with the magnitude of the new entrants in the active labour force, has its criticality too.

Meanwhile, it is noteworthy that since 1977, the multilateral agencies like the World Bank, the International Monetary Fund (IMF), the International Development Association (IDA) and Ceylon Aid Consortium have pumped massive aid, mostly in soft loans, into Sri Lanka. However, whether such a massive dose of aid from these agencies would be forthcoming after a couple of years is uncertain. And in view of its financial commitments, Sri Lanka may need, in dire situations, to resort to loans from commercial banks as it did in 1981 when the World Bank delayed its payment. Such a situation may severely strain its economic capabilities and add to its economic fragility. The other major avenue on which in any case its economic perspectives hinge to a considerable extent is that of a massive flow of foreign investment, which has yet to reach the quantum to substitute for the multilateral aid.

Earlier it was believed that, given a lease of life for

another six years, the UNP would complete the Mahaweli project which will give an impetus to economic growth in many ways. Besides, being now assured of the continuity of the regime, greater foreign investment may come from countries like the USA, West Germany, and Japan; and with the induction of such foreign investment the export-oriented economy may have its take-off stage by the end of the eighties. Such a perspective however has been considerably vitiated by the July 1983 violence which has not only given a severe setback to the economic development in terms of economic losses incurred during the violence but, what is more, has entailed an environment which may not be considered "congenial" by the foreign investors.

Even so, there may not be an economic "crash", but rather a situation of a "limping" economy in the sustenance of which the strategic and economic considerations of the West assume equal significance. To begin with, continued economic support to a less developed country having a "participatory" framework of politics, experimenting with the open-market economy could make it a "model" for the Third World. And in any event, the smallness of Sri Lanka makes the task of managing its economy not far too burdensome. More so, in view of the aid and investment flow, even in economic terms, the West may develop a stake in the health of its economy. What it may require in this context is a continuity in the "right" environment for investment, and action; and, if need be, strengthen the centre, through aid and other wherewithal, to help facilitate political order and the integrity of the country. As for the *quid pro quo,* Sri Lanka need not be a "surrogate" but simply be "amenable to the strategic requirements of the West.

For an indication of the extent to which Sri Lanka can

go along in "accommodating" the requirements of the West, a quick perusal of its foreign policy is necessary. Traditionally, within the non-aligned framework, while the relations of the UNP have been cordial with China and Russia, they have been close with the Western powers. As for Mrs. Sirimavo Bandaranaike, her cordiality has been critical of the "rapacious West".

The differences in foreign policy between the UNP and the SLFP, while reflecting their respective ideological proclivities, appear to have emanated from their divergent approaches towards the development of the domestic economy. Following from this, there has been a difference in style and a shift in emphasis too. While the SLFP has had an outward-looking foreign policy, that of the UNP has been relatively inward looking. Finally, the new orientation" of the UNP foreign policy has been in its emphasis on "economics" and not on "politics". "I seek to make foreign policy an effective instrument of economic advancement", stated Foreign Minister A.C.S. Hameed, as early as 1977. "I do not want to cut a figure in the international scene. I do not want to play diplomacy. This is a luxury. We are departing from the path of over-emphasising politics."

Such a shift in emphasis coupled with the economic orientations of the UNP has been reflected in its foreign policy behaviour, as well as the gamut of foreign economic transactions. Thus in the input of the massive foreign aid, the share of the Soviet Union and China has been rather negligible. Besides, as regards China, the two decades old rubber-rice agreement has undergone a significant change in 1983. The latest agreement has replaced the traditional barter arrangements with a cash agreement thereby opening options for Sri Lanka to have trade exchange with free market economics. Besides there has been a continuous decline in Sri Lanka's imports from China which in the sixties had ranked amongst the first five in trade imports. Instead, Saudi Arabia held the first position in imports to be followed by Japan and the USA in 1981. As regards exports, the USA and the UK shared one-fifth of its total exports in the same year.

The sheer magnitude of aid, investment loans, and trade with countries like the UK and the USA is massive, and the political spill-over effects of such closeness have already been felt in some cases. Thus Sri Lanka's soft-pedalling on the issue of Diego Garcia at the non-aligned summit; its response on the Falkland islands supporting the British case; its rather subdued response on the controversial map published in a U.S. Joint Chiefs of Staff pamphlet showing Trincomalee as one of the ports available to the U.S. Navy personnel for rest-and-recreational facilities; its grant of certain significant facilities to the Voice of America under the renewed agreement of 1983, making Sri Lanka in the process an important "listening post" of the U.S.--all these do seem to be the political pay-offs for economic support.

Added to these has been the issue of leasing of ninety-nine unused oil tanks in the China Bay near Trincomalee, the tender for which has been finally given to a Singapore-West German-Swiss consortium of firms allegedly having links with the U.S. and Pakistan. Besides, during the UNP regime the ban on all foreign naval vessels visiting the Trincomalee harbour--imposed during the United Front regime--has been lifted. While the considerations for lifting such a ban, according to the President, were purely economic--the earning of much-needed foreign exchange--it is not without significance that some of the controversial issues related to foreign policy have revolved around Trincomalee--one of the finest harbours in the world (and a former British naval base) having a strategic importance in the Indian Ocean. As a naval base or "facility" it has the tremendous potential of filling in a gap between West Asia and Thailand--to the north of the Indian Ocean, in the ring of U.S. bases and facilities.

So far, the President has shown, to the extent possible, a remarkable degree of circumspection and finesse in his diplomatic overtures. His handling of the "Scott" episode leading to recall of Scott, the First Secretary in the U.S. Embassy, was a signal as well as a warning to those at home as well as outside. According to observers, Scott's "undiplomatic" comments were as much responsible for his recall as his "hobnobbing" with the Eelamists. The message was clear: President Jayewardene's pro-Western tilt had to be on his terms and in his style.

Such an independent gesture, however, may not be easy in the event of the increasing economic dependence of Sri Lanka on the Western powers in addition to this is the acceleration of military linkages in view of the separatist movement in Sri Lanka.

In the event of the movement gathering momentum, economic exigencies and political expediency may lead to a greater acquiescence of the Centre to the West, with compromising postures in the realm of foreign and strategic affairs.

Ironical though it may seem, during the Jayewardene regime a number of measures were adopted to assuage the Tamil sense of grievance for example, the status of Tamil as an associate national language greater autonomy in district administration and the deletion of certain provisions in the university administration which were perceived by Ceylon Tamils as discriminatory.

However, the President has had a formidable legacy to cope with. Such conciliatory gestures, if they had been made in the fifties and even in the sixties might not have led to the present impasse. Coming as they did in the late seventies, they were perceived as "too little and too late" and, in any case, were not adequately implemented.

As such, they did not go very far in assuaging the sense of relative deprivation of the Tamil youth. If at all, in the power structure of the seventies with the tyrannical majorities of the ruling regime, coupled with the vagaries of patronage politics, he perceived himself increasingly marginalised and peripheral in the process of governance.

Revolving around the issues of language, employment, regional autonomy, land settlements or colonisation, the Ceylon Tamil sense of grievance has not been in terms of self-prestige alone as a community. It has sharp economic edges too. In fact, even during the UNP regime overall bonanza in the employment market, out of 140,000 jobs only 1,000 had gone to the Tamils. In the governmental services too their share had shown a consistent decline. In addition there has been the issue of land settlement in the context of which the Tamil leaders charged the present Government as well as its predecessors that the Sinhalese-dominated Centre had been turning the majority Tamil areas into minority Tamil ones.

Consequently, economic opportunities for the "sons of the soil" had been shrinking even in their traditional "home land", not to talk of other areas. As for the issue of regional autonomy, even when the institutional structure was evolved to impart a certain degree of autonomy at the district level, the long-drawn-out tradition of a unitary political framework adduced several constraints in its functioning.

Finally, the imparting of education through one's mother tongue and the impasse on the language issue resulted in widening the segregation of the two communities, particularly its younger component who could not communicate with one another. Also, in their respective text-books they received different sets of historical interpretation which at times conflicted and perpetually reinforced cultural prejudice and racial distrust. The insularity of the Tamil youth from the Centre consequently grew. His diminishing stakes--emotional as well as material--in the Centre coupled with his perception, whether real or exaggerated, of relative deprivation as a Tamil, found the sheet-anchor of the demand for Eelam to be pursued through peaceful or violent means.

The "Indian" Tamils, in view of their ambivalent political status but more so due to their demographic setting, did not envision an Eelam as a panacea for their sense of grievance. Nonetheless, in the wake of the recurrent, communal violence in which they have also been affected and the role of the law-and-order machinery, they have expressed sympathy with the grievances of the Tamils without either supporting Eelam or its violent means. The Muslim community, in view of its spatial dispersal coupled with the nature and scope of its economic activities all over the country, has maintained that Eelam is neither "desirable nor feasible. It is dangerous to our self-preservation as a community" Even so, occasional Sinhalese-Muslim violence and terrorist-military confrontations have created anxiety and uncertainties over the political future and security of the large number of Muslims residing in the eastern province which encompasses the territorial confines of the Tamil Eelam. Among the Sinhalese, while the moderates have been in favour of an accommodative stance vis-a-vis some of the Tamil demands, virtually all of them view the secessionist demand as a non-negotiable one. Apart from the fact that such a demand means an onslaught on the territorial unity and integrity of the island State--the Sinhala Dwipa--historical memories condition the attitude of the majority community too. These memories, by no means pleasant ones, are fostered by a selective use of myths and symbols to portray the Sinhalese as the vanquished and besieged in the past through sporadic Tamil invasions followed by the conquest of the island by the Chola and Pandya kings in the medieval period and the induction of the Indian Tamils during the British colonial period. There is then, the geophysical reality which adds to this "burden of history". The prospects of the Tamils of Tamil Nadu and the Sri Lanka Tamils "swamping" the Sinhalese is ever present in the Sinhalese psyche. This leads to a complex situation of the majority community having a minority complex, in the shadow of India. Such a complex of subjective factors has manifested itself in a particularly exaggerated fashion because of the competitive politics as it has evolved in Sri Lanka over the last three decades.

The inability of the Tamil and the Sinhalese leaders to work out a *modus vivendi,* despite years of tortuous dialogue between the two, has resulted in the growth of an impatient extremist element in both the communities, with its all-or-nothing demand leading at times to an enmeshing of three types of violence: (a) that of the Tamil terrorist; (b) the counter-violence wrought by the policc and military; and (c) communal violence, which reached a new height in the ethnic conflagration of July 1983. This has had a critical spill-over effect on the domestic politics of India and has adversely impinged on the relationship between Delhi and Colombo.

In comparison with some of the other neighbouring States, India's relationship with Sri Lanka was characterised by cordiality marked by negotiated settlements on bilateral irritants, e.g. the question of Kachchativu as well as the political status of the "Indian" Tamils in Sri Lanka. To some extent, the systemic congruence provided a positive thrust to bilateral relations. Moreover, inhibitions and complexes emanating from too much dependence on the big neighbour, as in the case of Nepal, or psychological hangovers inherent and embedded in the very inception of countries such as Pakistan and Bangladesh, did not seem to cloud India-Sri Lanka relations.

Yet, there is a marked congruence in the perception of all the neighbours of India characterised by a certain degree of adulation for its achievements and a sense of insecurity vis-avis its pressure-exerting capabilities. The extent of such a perception of the colossus of the north may have, at times, been exaggerated; but there in no doubt that it is deeply ingrained in the psyche of the Sri Lankans, particularly the Sinhalese. Such a perception has surfaced time and again in the context of the ethnic crisis in Sri Lanka during which, while on the one hand Delhi has tended to adopt a restraining approach and made efforts to mediate to diffuse the crisis, on the other hand a segment of the Tamil Nadu leadership has openly called for an interventionist approach.

The fact of the refuge of the Eelamists in Tamil Nadu has also to be taken into account. While military training to them has been officially denied, it is nonetheless admitted that such support might have been provided by individuals and groups sympathetic to the Tamil "cause". The open and competitive electoral politics in both the countries has also been characterised by the dichotomies and contradictions emanating from the imperatives of the wresting or sustaining of political power. The proceedings of the All Parties' Conference (APC) in Sri Lanka to find a negotiated settlement on the "Tamil" issue, the initial reluctance of the SLFP to join it and its subsequent withdrawal reflect to some extent the electoral consideration of the opposition party in the island State. Similarly, the shrill voice of the opposition, particularly the leadership of the Dravida Munnetra Kazhagam (DMK), indicates the imperatives of electoral winds in Tamil Nadu too.

Understandably, the Sinhalese and Tamil perceptions vis-avis India's role (on the Tamil issue) show a wide divergence. And even within these communities a range of perceptions can be discerned. To begin with, the TULF, the middle class, the petty and big Tamil industrialists, many of whom in effect are for a negotiated settlement, believe that India's persuasion and mediation can facilitate greater concessions from Colombo on issues of autonomy and security.

On the other hand, the Tamil terrorists feel that positive help from India, either towards an organised military solution acceptable to them or sufficient support for their activities towards achieving Eelam, can also serve India's interest in containing "excessive" Western presence. Often, the word "support" from

India implies support from South India. Further, while some groups envisage a separate and independent Eelam, there are others who do not rule out a political nexus of Tamil Nadu and Eelam. Still others believe that the continuous support of India to the APC and thereby a prop to the TULF will harm the human rights of Tamils, including the right of self-determination. India should therefore take a "bold stand" to help a progressive People's Party to work actively in Eelam areas. In this respect, the prerequisites of India's role should be to urge the Government of Sri Lanka to: (a) withdraw the armed forces in the cordned area of Jaffna; (b) repeal the Prevention of Detention Act; and (c) provide a package proposal acceptable to the Tamils. Tamils who are in exile or in asylum in South India should be ensured the right to move freely in Tamil areas in Sri Lanka. Only then can such a group conducively help to preserve law and order and thereby contain the different Tamil groups in Sri Lanka under the banner of the party.

The Tamil points of view thus reflect options (as envisaged for India) ranging from military intervention to that of political pressure (national as well as international) to mediation.

Virtually all Sinhalese view the first two options with irritation and trepidation and would like the third option to be effective when sought for. Thus, looking back, it would seem that, as in 1971 when Mrs. Bandaranaike sought assistance in order to quell the group insurrection, President Jayewardene also welcomed Indian intervention for mediation. In both the cases, it seems that India's assistance had been sought when the political system of the country had been threatened.

In the context of the proceedings of the APC--which the Minister of National Security, Lalit Athulathmudali, frankly acknowledged in a recent interview had been on the Indian initiative--President Jayewardene's assertion in an interview in April 1984 to the news magazine *India Today* that Mrs. Gandhi should stop talking to Amirthalingam stands in sharp contrast. Apparently, what has brought about this shift in President Jayewardene's approach is a degree of self-confidence that he is in a position to contain both the terrorist activities in Jaffna and its repercussions on the Sinhalese option in the rest of the country. Coupled with this is his vastly improved and considerably expanded naval capabilities to cut the terrorist traffic across the Palk Straits. He appears to have succeeded in doing so with the assistance--the military wherewithal and the training--from the Western countries. While at this juncture it may seem that there is a shift in the President's approach inasmuch as his actions are directed at treating the Tamil question as a law-and-order problem, he has eventually to find a solution to the causes for this "law and order" situation. It is in this context that the outcome of the APC needs to be foreseen. The proceedings so far reveal that while the President has not had any great problem in securing a consensus on the issue of giving citizenship to the "stateless" or the necessity of devolution of power levels, he has come up with almost elemental opposition from the Sinhalese to any restructuring that remotely concedes the conversion of territorial integrity into unification of the Tamil areas in the north and the east. A reconciliation of widely differing perceptions and aspirations is not likely to be easy in this context. As such the outcome of the APC which would predictably be long-drawn-out would depend largely on the ability of the President to evolve a national consensus on an equitable sharing of power.

In sum, the present political situation in Sri Lanka indicates (a) the continuance of a protracted state of internal war; (b) an increasing "corporatism" with the UNP staying in power till the end of the decade and the virtual absence of a political alternative at this juncture; and (c) the economic orientation of the UNP, resulting in an enmeshing of its economy with the West Which will have its inevitable politico-strategic consequences.

As for India-Sri Lanka relations, given its disparate power equation with Sri Lanka, coupled with the propensity of the Sinhalese to suffer from the small-power complex and the "Tamil" factor in bilateral relations particularly during 1983-84, it seems that, first, Sri Lanka will continue with greater alacrity the maximisation of its external options to diversify its linkages with extra-regional powers and also with other regional powers placed in a similar situation. Secondly, there would not be a congruity of foreign policy approaches and response except in general terms. Finally, Sri Lanka will continue to harp on the issue of its autonomy, sovereignty and integrity vis-a-vis India as and when so impelled. "The Indian Government" retorted the President, "keeps saying: 'Don't enter into this pact or that.' But why should they tell me what I shoulder shouldn't do? That goes against my grain." As for Sri Lanka leasing out the tank farm at Trincomalee to a consortium of firms; the President declared that the Indians, if they so wish, may also join the consortium. "If they have fears about the U.S. Navy coming to Trinco, I can't help it. We're not interested in their shouting, their sabre-rattling. I am not going to be frightened by India."

India thus has entered a new phase in its relationship with Sri Lanka which is marked by overt suspicion as well as apprehension and a distant cordiality. And this phase is likely to continue in the eighties.

We will discuss India's role in the Sri Lankan conflict from the standpoint of two inter-related levels: one, the organization of hegemony with respect to the Tamil liberation struggle; and two, the consolidation of a regional hegemony in South Asia. Insofar as all issues are relative, conditional, temporary, representing contradictions in reality, they must be understood and analysed within the range of their particular historical moments. In this respect, it is important to highlight three key developments in the situation within which India undertook its role in the Sri Lankan Tamils' War of Liberation in the period between 1982-1987.

First is the. breakup of Pakistan and the emergence of Bangladesh, including India's direct military intervention. We have already indicated in Chapter 9 that India emerged as a regional power in South Asia, following its military victory over Pakistan in the wake of the nationalist struggle in Bangladesh in 1971. In the backdrop of the government-sponsored agricultural and industrial policies favourable to 10 per cent of the population, surging military expenditures, massive poverty, not to mention the consolidation of the hegemonic politics of centralization, the Indian ruling class succeeded in winning the support of the majority of the population in the campaign to make India the pre-eminent power in South Asia. Not surprisingly, therefore, in the 1980s, a certain section of the Indian intellectuals had sought to glorify the 1971 event less in connection to the emergence of Bangladesh as an independent state and more in relation to the emergence of India as a regional power in South Asia.

Vyas statement indicates two important points: first, the maturing of the Indian foreign policy in the hegemonic construction of a great and strong India; and second, the establishment of a more cohesive strategic-defence foreign policy, or rather a broad consensus among the policy-makers with regard to the means, for building a great and strong India. Given the fact that Vyas' article was published in 1986, both the above-stated points remain important in the context of the Sri Lankan issue, which had then gained momentum. While the former seeks to consolidate or rather demonstrate India's pre-eminent position in South Asia attained in 1971, the latter prepares the stage for a more direct role of India in the Sri Lankan civil war.

Also important here is the fact that, while the Soviet Union, as we have indicated, had already recognized India as the *de facto* regional power in South Asia in 1971, the United States only changed its policy towards the sub-continent in the mid-1970s. Instead of supporting Pakistan and attempting to balance its power with India, the United States recognized the latter as the dominant power in South Asia [Nayar, 1979: 138]. India, therefore, had secured vital international consent with regard to its position as a 'regional power' in South Asia, several years prior to the qualitative transformation of the Tamil liberation struggle. Such consent, in fact, allowed India to undertake its role in the Sri Lankan conflict quite freely, independent of the wishes of the extra-regional powers or, for that matter, the superpowers.

A second important development is the emergence of India as a nuclear power. We have already indicated that India, following its first nuclear explosion in 1974, went ahead with the policy to further militarize its nuclear programme. In this connection, the Indian Government invested heavily in the development of military-related space technologies. Indeed, several critics have pointed out that its nuclear policy bears testimony to an attempt on the part of India to emerge as a great power or even a superpower in the image of a modern 'Western' state.

Sharma, however, remains unaware of the intrinsic relationship between the hegemonic aspirations of the Indian ruling class and the nuclearization of India. Only with respect to the current leadership (i.e. of the 1980s) does Sharma sees a quantum leap in India's nuclear programme. While it is true that there was a development of India's nuclear programme in the mid-1970s and 1980s, and is, therefore, far more observable, it nevertheless remains a development within the realm of the hegemonic constitution of the post-independence state of India.

What is, however, unique in Sharma's representation is the nature of the consent organized by the Indian ruling class, with respect to the country's defence strategy, i.e. the policy of nuclear deterrence. Not only do we see here a statist interpretation of Asoka's policy but also the projection of nuclear defence strategy as something historically justifiable and *natural* to the country's security. Indeed, the successful organization of the national consent in favour of nuclear development allows the Indian Government to periodically raise the military or military-related expenditures and to divert substantial resources, which could otherwise be used to alleviate the social condition of the ruled class.

Put differently, the nuclearization of India, far from creating conditions for the national development, reflects a consolidation towards the task of building a great and strong India, which at this historical conjuncture, remains identified with the task of reproducing India's pre-eminent position in South Asia.

A final development is the consolidation of domination of the Indian ruling class following shifts in governmental power, limited, however, to the representatives of the different factions of the ruling class. We have Already indicated that the fragmentation of the Congress Party led to a qualitative shift in the reproduction of hegemony of the ruling class. In the context of changes in the governmental power, it reached a critical stage in 1975 when Indira Gandhi proclaimed a nation-wide state of emergency to pat down a massive anti-Government movement. In 1977, however, the Indira Government had to step down following its defeat at the hands of a combined opposition group, led by the Organisational Congress, renamed the Janata Party. The latter, however, fell apart in less than two years, which saw the return of Indira Gandhi's Congress to power in 1980. Following Indira Gandhi's assassination in 1984, the Indira-Congress nominated her son, Rajiv Gandhi, to the prime ministership. In the 1984 elections, Rajiv Gandhi defeated his rivals easily, but failing to meet the growing aspirations of the masses and facing a renewed anti-Indira Congress alliance, he lost the 1989 -elections. The Janata Dal-led alliance, which formed the Government, not only remained closely linked to the Hindu communal organizations but also to the interests of the caste conscious rural *kulaks* [i.e. landed interests].

What is, indeed, interesting in all these changes is that governmental power shifted among the representatives of the different factions of the ruling class. We have already indicated this development in detail. In this respect, not only was there no qualitative or even significant change with respect to the hegemonic politics of development and centralization but also no such changes took place with respect to the international dimension of the state. Put differently, there was a broad consensus among the representatives of the different factions of the ruling class with regard to the kind of politics to be undertaken in building a great and strong India.

In the beginning of the 1980s and well into the period between 1982-1987, the above-stated developments constituted the historical moment within which India undertook its role in the Sri Lankan Tamils' War of Liberation. The significance of the time period (i.e. 1982-1987), however, has less to do with the dynamics of India's politics and more to do with those of the Tamil liberation struggle.

Hegemony and the Tamil Liberation Struggle

In the context of the Tamil liberation struggle, the Indian ruling class organized hegemony on two critical fronts: one, among the Sri Lankan Tamil population; and two, among the Indian population. Insofar as this includes the national-international dimensions (i.e. the 'horizontal-vertical' as well as the Vertical-horizontal' reciprocities) of both India and Sri Lanka, any exposition of India's role in the Sri Lankan Tamils' War of Liberation must also include the dynamics of the national-international dimension of the state of Sri Lanka. We shall, however, limit our exposition of the latter to those features which have a direct bearing on India's role in the Tamil liberation struggle.

Hegemony Organisation Among the Tamils

The Tamil liberation struggle had its roots in the constitution of the post-independence state of Ceylon (renamed Sri Lanka since 1972), which by way of undermining the interests of the predominantly Hindu Tamil minority', came to be identified with the 'Buddhist-Sinhala majority' of the island. In the absence of a well-developed counter-hegemony favourable to all religio-ethnic groups as well as to the members of the ruled class, the Sri Lankan ruling class successfully organized hegemony over the majority of the people of Sri Lanka by appealing to their Buddhist-Sinhala identity. The latter's success, however, alienated the Hindu Tamils for it undermined their interests--from language to landholdings, from commercial enterprises to military services [Schwarz, (1975) 1988: 10]. While there was already a close social relationship between the Hindu Tamils of India and Sri Lanka, the Sri Lankan Tamils looked across the Palk Strait and sought the help of India to offset the consolidation of domination of the forces related to the 'Buddhist-Sinhala majority'. This could not but facilitate the Indian ruling class efforts to organize hegemony over the Sri Lankan Tamils, one which allowed the former to take control and direct the Tamil liberation struggle to its advantage.

Apart from the issue of the Sri Lankan Tamils, India had more specific reasons to be attentive to the Tamil question in Sri Lanka. The Tamil population in Sri Lanka remains divided into two: one, Sri Lankan Tamils; and two, Tamils of the Indian origin. While the former have been living on the island, particularly in the northern and eastern regions, for a couple of thousand years and also ruled large parts of it before the arrival of the Europeans in the sixteenth century, the latter were mainly brought to Sri Lanka from southern India during the nineteenth and early part of the twentieth centuries to work as labourers in rubber, tea and coffee plantations situated in the central highlands of the island. In this respect, Tamils of Indian origin differed from the Sri Lankan Tamils not only in their place of residence but also in their occupation. The former, in fact, were more impoverished and less educated than the Sri Lankan Tamils, a factor which alienated them even from the Sri Lankan Tamils.

Following Sri Lanka's independence, however, Tamils of Indian origin became the first victims of the organisation of the post-independence state of Sri Lanka. In 1948 and

1949, the Sri Lankan Government enacted the Ceylon Citizenship Act and the Indian and Pakistan Residents (Citizenship) Act respectively, both of which formally denied citizenship and voting rights to the Tamils of Indian origin. This made them practically stateless. Nearly all the Sinhalese Members of Parliament together with a majority of the Sri Lankan Tamil MPs voted in 1948 and 1949 for the political deprivation of the Tamils of Indian origin [Laiq, 1985: 766]. In fact, there existed a broad consensus at the time of independence to deport these Tamils back to India.

If there was a broad consensus within Sri Lanka to deport the Tamils of Indian origin, India in the beginning was outrightly reluctant to take them back. The failure to resolve this issue poisoned not only the relationship between the Sinhalese and Tamils in Sri Lanka but also between India and Sri Lanka. But despite its reluctance to take the Tamils back, the Indian Government did not hide the fact that it was sensitive to the issue. The matter was finally resolved after 38 years of negotiations, which included three major agreements (1964, 1974 and 1986). Both India and Sri Lanka, amidst accusation by critics, mainly Sri Lankan, of a governmental sell-out in the face of India's pressures, shared the last of the 975,000 Tamils of Indian origin between them in an agreement signed in January 1986.

While it is true that India became a party in Sri Lanka's internal affairs, largely as a result of the latter's policy of disenfranchising Tamils of the Indian origin, its success remained more directly related to the consolidation of domination of the hegemonic forces related to the 'Buddhist-Sinhala majority'. There is no question, however, that the Sinhalese, and occasionally even the Sri Lankan Tamils as well as Tamils of south India, attempted to fuse the liberation struggle of the Sri Lankan Tamils with that of the problems faced by Tamils of Indian origin [Udayashankar, 1986]. But the latter factor was only a peripheral issue in the Tamil liberation struggle. In fact, the intensification of the Sinhala domination pushed the indigenous Hindu Tamils towards India. In this respect, frequent anti-Tamil riots contributed to a situation where India found it easy to lend support to the cause of the Sri Lankan Tamils and bring them to its side.

While anti-Tamil riots occurred periodically and more frequently since independence, it reached a situation of utmost gravity, primarily due to the direct participation of the Sri Lankan police and military, in July-August 1981. Following this riot, many Tamil 'militants' left Sri Lanka for Tamilnadu (India), where within a year of their arrival they began recruiting Tamil refugees (numbering 100,000 in the aftermath of the July 1983 riot) for military operations to free the northern and eastern regions of Sri Lanka and establish an independent state of *Eelam* [Jayawardena, 1988: 144]. This marked the beginning of a new phase in the Tamil liberation struggle, not only from the standpoint of the Sri Lankan Tamils but also from the standpoint of India. The Indian Government, for its part, provided food and shelter to the Tamil refugees and offered training facilities and military equipment to the Tamil guerrillas, under the direct supervision of its intelligence agency, the Research and Analysis Wing [Kodikara, 1989: 718]. It is not difficult to see here that by providing food and shelter to the Tamil refugees and training facilities and military equipments to the Tamil guerrillas, India not only became a party to the Tamil cause in Sri Lanka but also won over a large section of the Sri Lankan Tamils.

However, what seems to have deepened India's influence over the Tamil liberation struggle had to do not only with the kind of support it provided to the Tamil refugees and guerrillas but also the presence of an intense rivalry among the different Tamil militant groups. By 1982, a large section of the Tamil population, abandoned the path of non-violence and constitutional means in favour of the armed insurrection. They began supporting several militant groups which included, among others, the Liberation Tigers of Tamil Eelam (LTTE), the Peoples' Liberation Organization of Eelam [PLOTE], the Eelam Peoples' Revolutionary Liberation Front [EPRLF], the Tamil Eelam Liberation Organization [TELO], and the Eelam Revolutionory Organization of Students [EROS]. Despite the formation of a loose alliance (with the exception of PLOTE) under the banner of Eelam National Liberation Front [ENLF] in April 1985, these groups did not cooperate to any extent. There were, in fact, incidents of inter-group fighting while these groups were stationed in Tamilnadu as early as 1982 [Ponnambalam, 1983: 218]. But more serious ones were witnessed in 1985-1986, about which we shall return later. Both the State and the Union Governments of India intervened to settle the inter-group fighting, which only deepened India's influence over these militant groups.

In this respect, two developments could be highlighted. First, with Tamil guerrilla bases in Tamilnadu, it became easy for India to influence the militant groups, even to the point of using one group against the other to ensure its preponderant role in the struggle; and second, in order to enhance their power and position, some of the militant groups become quite willing to please India by linking their own strategy with that of India's. Both these developments, insofar as they created conflicts between the different militant groups, considerably weakened the struggle of the Tamils against the Sri Lankan military. In fact, division among the Tamil militant groups increased their dependence on India, a factor which was very much resented by one particular group, the LTTE.

In this light, equally devastating for the Tamil cause was the conflict between the Tamil United Liberation Front [TULF], the established political party of the Tamils, and the militant groups. The former, in marked contrast to the latter, used parliamentary democratic processes to obtain *Eelam.* While there was growing public (predominantly Tamil) resentment against the policies of the TULF, particularly after the 1981 anti-Tamil riot, for failing to protect Tamil lives and interests, the political struggle of the TULF became practically ineffective after the enactment of the Sixth Amendment in August 1983, which made all activities related to separation or secession unconstitutional [Hennayake, 1989: 402]. The TULF members, in fact, fled to India immediately after the approval of the Amendment in the Sri Lankan Parliament. But by then the TULF had already lost its position to the various militant groups, already engaged in the armed struggle against the Sri Lankan Government. It practically became just another group vying for India's support to boost its position.

It is not very difficult to see here that no single Tamil political party or group attained leadership of the liberation struggle. None could draw the line as to what strategy the Tamils should undertake to attain *Eelam.* In fact, conflict between the various militant groups, as well as between the TULF and the militant groups, aided in no small measure by the decision of the militant groups to establish bases in Tamilnadu, brought India to the scene, making it a key party in the Tamil liberation struggle. Put differently, the Tamil liberation struggle itself became dependent on

India's role in the issue. With this pronouncement, India could not but be emboldened to carry out measures to consolidate its preeminent position in South Asia.

The Organization of Hegemony Among the Indian Population

While for reasons of culture, ethnicity and religion, support for the Sri Lankan Tamils was always strong in the Indian State of Tamilnadu, it depended further following anti-Tamil riots of 1981 and 1983. Immediately following the July 1983 riot, the people of Tamilnadu wholeheartedly supported an all-party call for a State-wide *bandh* (work stoppage) to condemn the indiscriminate killings of the Tamils and show solidarity with the Tamil liberation struggle. Both the ruling and the main opposition parties of Tamilnadu (the All-India Anna Dravida Munnetra Kazhagam [AIADMK] and the Dravida Munnetra Kazhagam [DMK] respectively) strongly protested the suppression of the Tamils in Sri Lanka. They had, however, marked differences on the plan of action. While the AIADMK took a moderate approach, sending only a high-level delegation to New Delhi to request Prime Minister Indira Gandhi to put pressure on the Sri Lankan Government to stop the anti-Tamil violence there, the DMK, in line with its traditional support for Tamil sub-state nationalism, described the action of Sri Lanka as genocide against the Tamils and called on the Indian Government to send its armed forces to Sri Lanka in order to save the Tamils [Jayawardena, 1988: 145], But despite such differences, both of them urged the central government to take more active measures against Sri Lanka and rescue the Sri Lankan Tamils from their current plight.

The central government, under Prime Minister Indira Gandhi, welcomed the show of support for the Sri Lankan Tamils in Tamilnadu. In this connection, Indira Gandhi requested all political parties in India, including those of Tamilnadu, to support her government's efforts to tackle the problem in Sri Lanka [IRS, 1984:19]. In fact, the central government was not only ready to sympathize and show solidarity with the people and politicians of Tamilnadu on Sri Lanka but was also ready to undertake an active role against Sri Lanka on a more broad 'national' (i.e. Indian) terms in a bid to resolve the anti-Tamil violence in the island. Such a 'national' approach, however, was difficult to undertake if the problem in Sri Lanka was not addressed beyond Tamilnadu's provincial concern. The rest of India was not Tamilian and do not share the unique cultural and ethnic bond that existed between the people of Tamilnadu and the Sri Lankan Tamils. The only exception, however, was religious affiliation. Like Sri Lankan and South Indian Tamils, the majority of the Indian people are Hindus. Indeed, once the government had dubbed the conflict in Sri Lanka a grave problem for India as well, the hegemonic forces began highlighting certain key elements central to the conflict, largely to attract the majority of the Indian people to the side of the government so that it could initiate a strong and unified role against Sri Lanka.

This resolution could be looked at in one of two ways: first, it could be referring specifically to the 'Tamils of Indian origin'. In that case, it is worth pointing out here that the main victims of the July 1983 anti-Tamil riot were not the Tamils of the Indian origin but rather the Sri Lankan Tamils; secondly, if the resolution intended to include the Sri Lankan Tamils as 'people of the Indian origin" as well then it would be subscribing to a pan-Indian vision based primarily on the factor of religious affiliation (i.e. Hinduism), for the Buddhist-Sinhalese, who are also, in one way or another, people of the Indian origin, are, in this case, implicitly left out and rebuked.

Whichever way one looks at this resolution, both remain related, with some differences in degree, to the Hindu majority of India.

The significance of this projection can hardly be minimised. Once the conflict in Sri Lanka is identified in religious terms, it becomes easy for the Hindu majority of India to identify themselves with the cause of the Sri Lankan Tamils. Indeed, the Indian ruling class understood very well that it could easily mobilize the majority of the Indian people on the side of the government on the Sri Lankan issue by appealing to their religious affiliation or more tactfully, as in the case of the Ruling Congress, by highlighting the pitiful condition of the people of Indian origin in Sri Lanka.

This point is a critical one for it highlights the fact that insofar as the question of religious affiliation or the factor of the people of the Indian origin organized support for the government on the Sri Lankan issue, it readily reproduced the politics of centralization catering to the hegemonic construction of a great and strong India. Such an outcome, however, sacrificed the more important dimension of the conflict, and that is, the question of the nationalist aspirations of the Tamils. This is because once the government had the mandate to enforce its policy on Sri Lanka on a more broad 'national' (i.e. Indian) terms, it readily utilised the Tamil liberation struggle to meet its own hegemonic objectives, i.e. to consolidate India's pre-eminent position in South Asia. Put differently, the Indian government put a lid on the form and content of the Tamil liberation struggle to suit its own interests in the region. Such a situation became evident by 1985, with implications within the political forces of both Tamilnadu and, more importantly, the Tamil liberation struggle. In the case of the latter, for example, it radically transformed the strategy of the Tamil militants, namely, that of the Tamil Tigers, thus far favourable to the role of the Indian government in the conflict.

But a 'national' approach to the Sri Lankan conflict could not be sustained simply by appealing to the Hindu majority. Such an appeal had to be more extensive so that it could provide a sense of urgency to the whole country, irrespective of religious or communal affiliations, of the need to confront the problem in Sri Lanka. In this respect, the question of 'national security' acquired greater significance. Indeed, in the aftermath of the July 1983 anti-Tamil riot, when India began contemplating its role in the Sri Lankan conflict, Indira Gandhi raised fears about a possible foreign intervention in the region [Manchanda, 1986: 574].

In this campaign, however, Indira Gandhi was not alone; other high-ranking government officials, including the media, spoke of foreign powers intervention in the region in the name of defending Sri Lanka from India. For example, on August 1, 1983, major Indian newspapers published a UPI (news agency) dispatch indicating that the 'riot-battered Sri Lanka, appealed for pledges of military assistance from the USA, Britain, Pakistan and Bangladesh, in the event of a foreign invasion (suggestively India)' [IRS, 1984: 24]. But despite official denial from the Sri Lankan Government that such a request had been made, as well as from the US State Department and the British Foreign Office that such a request had been received by them, the Indian Foreign Minister Narasimha Rao told the Indian Parliament on the following day that "there is substance in the report" [Manchanda, 1986: 575]. Such a campaign, no doubt, created conditions for patriotic fervour, likely to unite the people on the side of the government against foreign powers, including Sri Lanka.

But apart from organizing popular support against Sri Lanka, the question of national security rationalized larger allocations of the government military spending, which by 1984 reached nearly 20 per cent of all government spending [Robinson, 1989: 181]. We have already indicated in Chapter 9 how this condition is looked upon favourably by the commercial and industrial section of the Indian ruling class. Indeed, the prospect of military conflict, to the point of waging a limited war, as we have pointed out in the previous chapter, is sometimes welcomed by the capitalists for it tends to improve their relative position in the economy. In this sense, the question of national security, insofar as it allows the Government to rationalize high levels of defence expenditure, remains related to the politics of development.

The successful reproduction of the politics of development, however, like the reproduction of the politics of centralization, limits India's support for the Tamil nationalist aspirations. This is because the question of national security, followed as it is by higher defence expenditure, creates momentum within the Government circle, commercial and industrial interests and, no doubt, military establishment to participate directly in the conflict and not be satisfied, as in this case, simply by performing the task of arming the militants from Sri Lanka. In fact, the government and military officials, as well as the capitalists were all eager to demonstrate India's military capability, which had become an important yardstick of modern development. This would ensure and reproduce public support for the military, particularly its ever-increasing budget, But the more such demonstrations of military capability are made, the more the Tamil liberation struggle, insofar as it is dependent on India's support, was sacrificed for reasons peculiar to India's military and development.

The governmental support for the Tamil cause became even more acute and restricted in the face of a national consensus devoid of any inputs from the counter-hegemonic forces. Indeed, the bulk of the members of the ruled class, without having a counter-hegemony to rally behind, accepted religious and national appeals and supported the Government on Sri Lanka. The role of the political parties linked to counter-hegemonic practices, namely the Communist parties, was no better [Nauriya, 1987: 982]. None of the Communist parties, in fact, provided any significant policy options on Sri Lanka contrary to the role of the Indian government. Instead, some (like the CPI [Marxist-Leninist]) supported certain militant Tamil factions stationed in Tamilnadu, while others (like the CPI) refrained from supporting the militants but upheld the cause of the Sri Lankan Tamils in the same way as did the government [O'Ballance, 1989: 75; Jayewardene and Jayewardene, 1987: 235].

Put differently, the counter-hegemonic forces, either directly or indirectly, supported the government on Sri Lanka. This provided the government with a free hand to shape and control the Sri Lankan conflict in ways suited to its interests and objectives. This brings us to the second level of our discussion of India's role in the Sri Lankan Tamils' War of Liberation, where we shall see how the successful organization of hegemony among the struggling Tamils and the Indian population allowed the Indian government freely to transform the Tamil nationalist struggle into an Indo-Lanka affair, consolidating thereby India's pre-eminent position in South Asia.

THE CONSOLIDATION OF REGIONAL HEGEMONY IN SOUTH ASIA

The Indian Doctrine

Immediately following the July 1983 anti-Tamil riot, when India was already partially involved in the Sri Lankan conflict (remindful here of the fact that it was already a year since India began sheltering and arming the Tamil militants), high-ranking Government officials, including the Prime Minister, Indira Gandhi, spoke about, although not in any clear textual form, India's special position in the region [IRS, 1984: 25].

The image of the infamous Monroe Doctrine is clear here, only reconstructed this time in a qualitatively different historical setting, not to mention different geographical location. The Indian Doctrine, however, although referring to all South Asian neighbours of India, focused primarily on Sri Lanka. This is clear not only from Gupta's assertion that the doctrine had been spawned by the conflict in Sri Lanka but also, and more importantly, from the timing of its announcement by the Indian ruling class. But insofar as the doctrine focused on Sri Lanka, it had two key forces, both central to the conflict, to deal with.

1. The Sri Lankan government, or more specifically, the Government under Junius R. Jayawardene. The Indian government resented the latter's hobnobbing with the Western powers, particularly the United States and Pakistan [Manchanda, 1986; Akram, 1987]. After capturing governmental power in July 1977, Jayawardene opted for a free-market economy, making Sri Lanka increasingly receptive to Western capital and technology. At the same time Sri Lanka's relationship with Pakistan improved dramatically, although much of it, apart from Pakistan's closer relationship with the West, came from the desire of

the Sri Lankan government to distance itself from India. Both of these developments were in marked contrast to the previous regime under Sirimavo Bandaranaike [1970-1977], which favoured, at least in public, socialist and non-aligned principles, and remained somewhat more friendly to India. Jayawardene's overtures to the West and India's tradition 'enemy', Pakistan, therefore, came as a rude shock to the Indian ruling class, which singled them out as a challenge to India's pre-eminent position in the region.

The suppression of the Sri Lankan Tamils, then, provided the Indian government with a golden opportunity to put pressure on Sri Lanka. Apart from sheltering and arming the Tamil militants, the Indian ruling class blew out of proportion some of the features of Sri Lanka's relationship with the United States and Pakistan. Apart from the question of military supplies from these two countries, which was anything but spectacular (Manchanda, 1986), the Indian government highlighted two issues, both related to the United States, as evidence of foreign intervention in the region.

The first one referred to the oil facilities in the port city of Trincomalee in eastern Sri Lanka. Trincomalee remained a focal point of contention between Indian and Sri Lanka for reasons of oil exploration in the vicinity. The Sri Lanka government had favoured a U.S.-related multinational for the job, sidestepping the offer made by the Indian Oil Corporation [Rao, 1984]. To make this issue a security concern for India, Government officials and the media dubbed the 'oil contract' testimony to Sri Lanka's willingness to make naval facilities at Trincomalee available to the United States in exchange for a defence pact [Manchanda, 1986: 576-578]. The U.S. government immediately denied this report. More fundamentally, however, India's accusation made little sense for it does not explain why the United States would be interested by a defence pact with Sri Lanka, not to mention by Trincomalee when the United States already had Diego Garcia in the Indian Ocean at its disposal. It was otherwise becoming increasingly evident that the Indian government disapproved of the Trincomalee oil deal and was only looking for an excuse to put pressure on the Sri Lankan government.

The second issue related to the question of providing greater operational facilities to the *Voice of America* [VOA]. The latter received permission to operate in Sri Lanka soon after Jayawardene's coming to power. But no sooner did the VOA have the rights to operate from Sri Lanka, then it requested greater control over the programmes broadcast so that it could avoid Sri Lankan restrictions [Manchanda, 1986: 576]. The Indian government viewed this development with concern, describing the U.S. radio station in Sri Lanka as a foreign listening post and, therefore, a security risk to India.

The U.S. government, however, not only denied India's allegations but also reiterated U.S. acknowledgement of India's regional hegemony in South Asia. In this connection, it is important to understand here that what mattered was not so much the fear of the United States or for that matter Pakistan, but rather the audacity of the Sri Lankan government in approaching the United States and Pakistan over the shoulder of India and challenging India's pre-eminent position in South Asia. The Indian Doctrine, taking note of these developments, cautioned the Sri Lankan government to refrain from adopting policies contrary to the hegemonic goals of India.

2. The struggling Tamils, particularly the Tamil militants. With the unfolding of the civil strife in Sri Lanka, the Sri Lankan ruling class, in so far as it has remained glued to the 'Buddhist-Sinhala majority', lost its influence over the Sri Lankan Tamils. This is more true in the case of the Sri Lankan government under Jayawardene, which openly opted for a military solution to curb the nationalist aspirations of the Tamils. In this light, Indian pressure (whether political or military) on the Sri Lankan government does not automatically translate into Indian pressure on the Sri Lankan Tamils. In fact, the reverse is often true, i.e. the Indian pressure on the Sri Lankan government could mean a measure of Indian support for the struggling Tamils. In a situation like this, the Sri Lankan Tamils remained immune from the pressure that was brought upon the Sri Lankan government by the proclamation of the Indian Doctrine.

At the same time, however, this does not mean that the Sri Lankan Tamils are totally immune from the restrictions imposed by the Indian Doctrine. Indeed, to the extent that they were waging their struggle under the leadership of various militant groups and to the extent that their goal was the creation of an independent state of *Eelam,* the Sri Lankan Tamils also fell within the purview of the Indian Doctrine. Like the Sri Lankan government, although not in the same category, the Sri Lankan Tamils or more precisely, the Tamil militants were inhibited from undertaking activities contrary to the hegemonic interests of India. In this connection, three issues could be highlighted.

First, the Indian government never shared the Tamil militants goal of *Eelam.* In fact, immediately after the July 1983 anti-Tamil riot, Indira Gandhi told the *Lok*

Sabha that her government was ready to assist the Sri Lankan government in finding a federal solution to the Sri Lankan conflict [O'Ballance, 1989: 27]. This otherwise indicated that, although the Indian government was ready to provide shelter and arms to the Tamil militants, it was unwilling to support the cause of *Eelam,* i.e. the Indian government was eager to put pressure on the Sri Lankan government on the question of foreign intervention or issues challenging India's hegemony, but not on the question of meeting the nationalist aspirations of the Tamils. The Tamil militants, in light of the hegemonic projection of the Indian Doctrine, understood this very well. But the dependence on India was so deep that, save the Tamil Tigers, none of the Tamil militant groups could adopt a strategy independent of India. Not surprisingly, the wrath of the Indian government fell very shortly on the Tamil Tigers.

The second issue was the question of oil facilities in Trincomalee. We have already indicated how the Indian government viewed the oil facilities in Trincomalee as a matter of India's concern. What is, however, equally important in this context is the fact that the port city of Trincomalee, as part of the eastern province of Sri Lanka, was at the centre of the Sri Lankan conflict. The Sri Lankan Tamils viewed the eastern province as part of the Tamil homeland. In this respect, whatever the outcome of the Tamil liberation struggle--whether increased autonomy or a separate state--the Sri Lankan Tamils would have to come to terms with the Indian government on the question of oil facilities in Trincomalee. Like the Sri Lankan government, they too were limited in their ability to initiate a role independent of India on the matter.

And lastly, although the Indian government was

providing the maximum political support, and most of the arms and ammunitions, to the Tamil militants, it became increasingly worried about their international connections, particularly with sympathizers based in Europe and the United States. In this respect, the first World Eelam Tamil Conference, held in New York in July 1982 was significant for it was attended by various Tamil militant groups, including the Tamil Tigers [Ponnambalam, 1983: 219]. The latter had the organized capability to attract other internationally known militant groups, and consequently international arms trading and unknown international forces [Jayawardena & Jayawardena, 1987: 195-196; Fernando, 1986: 248]. This was unacceptable to India, which wanted to keep the military side of the Tamil liberation struggle, including the flow of arms to the militants, under its control. The Indian government understood very well that any organized shipment of arms from international sources to the Tamil militants could free the latter from its hold and in the long-run invite forces contrary to India's interests into the region. In this connection, the Indian Doctrine made clear to the Tamil militants what was expected from them. Only the Tamil Tigers dared to flout it openly, which soon led to a qualitative transformation of India's role in the Sri Lankan conflict, to the detriment of the Tamil nationalist struggle.

Indo-Lanka Agreement (1987) and Rise of the Tamil Tigers

The presence of intense rivalry among the different Tamil militant groups, all of which were engaged in armed resistance against the Sri Lankan government. Although all of them at the start of the armed struggle agreed on the creation of *Eelam* through violent force, they differed on the question of leadership and the extent to which India ought to help them. Among the various militant groups, the Tamil Tigers took the most extreme and uncompromising position on these two issues. Not only were they seeking absolute control of the liberation struggle, they also wanted to keep India's support limited to the task of providing training facilities and arms without itself getting involved in the conflict. In the light of the lack of overwhelming support among the Tamils and India's deepening influence over some of the Tamil militant groups, it became impossible for the Tigers to make their position acceptable to all the militant groups. To achieve their objective, however, the Tigers resorted to a campaign of alliance and annihilation against rival militant groups.

Although instances of open clashes between rival groups, particularly those involving the Tamil Tigers, could be found as early as 1982, it reached a new height in 1985-1986, beginning with clashes between Tamil Tigers and PLOTE in March 1985. Most of the members of the PLOTE, including its leader, Uma Mahaswaram, formerly belonged to the Tamil Tigers [O'Ballance, 1989: 49]. It is probably for this reason that the Tamil Tigers made PLOTE their first target. The attack on the PLOTE, however, was only one aspect of the Tamil Tiger strategy to become a paramount military force in the Tamil liberation struggle. In April 1985, for example, barely a month after attacking the PLOTE, the Tamil Tigers welcomed the formation of a loose alliance between the various militant groups (with the exception, however, of PLOTE) under the banner of Eelam National Liberation Front [ENLF]. In addition to the Tamil Tigers, the Front include TELO, EPRLF and EROS [Jayewardene-find Jayewardene, 1987: 138].

From the standpoint of the Tamil Tigers, however, the formation of the ENLF was only a stopgap. Apart from enabling them to attract the rank and file of rival militant groups, it allowed them to neutralise these groups from coming to the aid of PLOTE. The strategy worked well, for within a year the military wing of the PLOTE was virtually wiped out, its members either killed, underground, or in the Tamil Tigers. But no sooner had the Tamil Tigers succeeded in routing out the PLOTE, then they shifted their attention to another militant group. This time it was TELO. In May 1986, the Tamil Tigers attacked the military strongholds of TELO in the Jaffna area of northern Sri Lanka and quickly brought the group's demise. Those who survived the attack either went underground or later joined the Tamil Tigers. Next in line was the EPRLF, against whom the Tamil Tigers launched an all-out offensive in December 1986.

In this case, however, the Tamil Tigers failed to inactivate the military wing of the EPRLF completely [O'Ballance, 1989: 67]. But whatever may have been the outcome of this particular offensive, the fact remains that by the beginning of 1987, the Tamil Tigers, with the aid of their campaign of alliance and annihilation, had emerged as the paramount military force in the Tamil liberation struggle. This was a kind of development that disturbed the Indian government greatly. There were two reasons for this: first, the Indian government from the beginning of the armed struggle provided training facilities and arms to all the Tamil militant groups, itself remaining agnostic about their rivalry, out of sheer prudence. Apart from keeping a face of neutrality, it enabled the Indian government, as indicated earlier, to deepen its influence over the militant groups. In this respect, the military action of the Tamil Tigers against rival militant groups represented a serious challenge to the Indian government for it indirectly undermined the latter's support for them. And as for the second reason, the Indian government feared that the predominant military position of the Tamil Tigers, insofar as it had the potential of attracting the Tamil population (the majority of whom, although supportive of *Eelam,* were yet to rally behind one single militant group), could embolden the Tamil Tigers to carry out the armed struggle on their own, independent of India. This fear was not unfounded.

In April 1985, Indian customs seized a huge container, almost the size of a railway wagon, full of arms and ammunition destined for the Tamil militants and allegedly sent by Tamil expatriates in Europe [Jayewardene and Jayewardene, 1987: 137]. This incidentally was one of the many arms shipments that Indian customs successfully detected and seized, although it is possible that many more may have slipped through. If anything it indicated the extent to which the Tamil militants were unwilling to rely totally on the Indian Government for arms and ammunition. The Indian government, however, as indicated earlier, could not tolerate this free flow of arms to the Tamil militants, lest its control over them weaken. In this context, the secret arms shipments, many of which were later linked to the Tamil Tigers [Jayewardene and Jayewardene 1987: 196], and the rise of the latter as a paramount military force, set the stage for the Indian government to abandon the Tamil Tigers and concurrently, the Tamil liberation struggle itself.

The rise of the Tamil Tigers also had a corresponding impact on the Sri Lankan government. In the earlier stage of the armed struggle with so many Tamil militant groups around, the Sri Lankan government had a hard time identifying the principle antagonist with which it could come to terms politically and failing that, militarily, or vice versa. In fact, it was hoping that inter-group rivalry would weaken the Tamil liberation struggle. Not surprisingly, in May 1986, when Tamil Tigers and TELO fought each other, the Sri Lankan government simply kept quiet and monitored the internecine battle [O'Ballance, 1989: 62]. The rise of the Tamil Tigers in 1987, however, changed all this. Not only did the Sri Lankan government now fear the prospect of a more consolidated armed struggle in the island, it also had a clear opponent to deal with. Hoping to campaign on the dissatisfaction of the rival militant groups with the Tamil Tigers and to resolve the Tamil question militarily, the Sri Lankan government launched an all-out offensive against the Tamil Tigers in May 1987.

The May offensive of the Sri Lankan government, however, did not go very far. The Indian government, realizing it was losing control of the Sri Lankan conflict, openly condemned the military action and threatened to come to the Sri Lankan Tamils' rescue. To make its threat credible, it used some interventionist postures. In the guise of a humanitarian mission and without prior permission of the Sri Lankan government, five Indian transport planes, with the aid of four combat planes, dropped 22 tons of relief supplies on the Jaffna Peninsula on June 4, 1987 [Nauriya, 1987; O'Ballance, 1989: 86]. The relief supplies were specifically meant for the Sri Lankan Tamils. The following week the Sri Lankan government called off the military offensive and began earnestly to consider the peace plan put forward by the Indian government. At this stage, the role of the Indian government in the Sri Lankan Tamils' War of Liberation became crystal clear. While, on the one hand, it had no intention of providing a free hand to the Sri Lankan government to resolve the civil strife on its own terms, lest it would put into question India's pre-eminent position in the region, on the other hand, it saw the rise of the Tamil Tigers as a threat to its own role in the Tamil liberation struggle and therefore, equally damaging to India's pre-eminent position in the region. The peace plan offered to the Sri Lankan government in July 1987 had been designed to meet, as we shall shortly see, the Indian government's concern on both these fronts. The Sri Lankan government, without being able to attract any regional or extra-regional powers in the campaign to deter India and, at the same time, being content with the Indian government's opposition to the independent role of the Tamil Tigers, succumbed to the former's pressure and signed the Indo-Lanka Agreement (i.e. Agreement, Annexure and Letters) on July 29, 1987 [MEA, 1987]. By coming to terms with the Sri Lankan government, the Indian government, however, successfully transformed the Tamil nationalist struggle into an Indo-Lanka affair and consolidated India's pre-eminent position in South Asia. A closer exposition of the Agreement will make this clear.

The July 1987 Indo-Lanka Agreement featured three key relationships; one conflicting, the other two co-operative. These include: one, the relationship of co-operation between the governments of Sri Lanka and India; two, a relationship of conflict between the India government and the Tamil Tigers; and three, the relationship of co-operation between the Indian government and the pro-Indian representatives of the Sri Lankan Tamils. Although neither the Tamil Tigers nor the pro-Indian representatives of the Sri-Lankan Tamils were signatories of or even mentioned in the Agreement, both had their representations implicitly referred to in the Agreement. We shall begin with the last relationship.

In the wake of the armed struggle, particularly in a situation of intense rivalry among the various Tamil militant groups, the Indian government had deepened its influence over most, if not all, of these groups. The names of EPRLF, TELO and PLOTE can easily be mentioned in this regard. The rise of the Tamil Tigers further saw these militant groups lean heavily towards the Indian government, which soon earned the reputation of being the pro-Indian representatives of the Sri Lankan Tamils. By July 1987, it became possible for the Indian government to obtain their consent with respect to its peace plan. The provisions which directly concerned them and required their tacit support include:

1. The merger of the Northern and Eastern Provinces into one administrative unit (Agreement, Art. 2.2).
2. The people of the Eastern Province must confirm the merger of the Provinces through a referendum (Agreement, Art. 2.3).
3. Beside Sinhala, Tamil and English, will also be the official languages of Sri Lanka (Agreement, Art. 2.18).

What this amounted to is the acceptance of greater *Tamil autonomy,* albeit within the framework of the Sri Lankan unity, on the part of the pro-Indian representatives of the Sri Lankan Tamils. But since it fell far short of an independent state of *Eelam,* the Tamil Tigers refused to support the Agreement. This brings us to the second relationship--between the Indian government and the Tamil Tigers.

The Indian government was bent upon limiting the powers of the Tamil Tigers. The following provision, make this clear:

1. India will take all necessary steps to ensure that

Indian territory is not used for activities prejudicial to the unity, integrity and security of Sri Lanka (Agreement, Art. 2.16 A).

2. The Indian Navy will co-operation with the Sri Lankan Navy in preventing Tamil militant activities from affecting Sri Lanka (Agreement, Art. 2.16 B).
3. The Indian government will give military assistance to the Sri Lankan government as and when required to implement the provisions of the Agreement (Agreement, Art. 2.16 C and Letters).
4. Tamil militants must surrender their arms. The surrender shall take place in the presence of representatives from the Indian and Sri Lankan Red Cross (Annexure, Art. 4).
5. India will deport all the Sri Lankan citizens, who are found to be engaging in terrorist activities or advocating separatism or secessionism (Letters).

This, no doubt, represented a complete U-turn on the part of the Indian government with respect to its policy of providing political and moral support, including training facilities and arms, to the Tamil militants. The Tamil Tigers, therefore, saw this as a clear sign of betrayal of the Indian government of the Tamil nationalist cause. The stage was now set for the Indian government, in collusion with the Sri Lankan government, to put down the Tamil Tigers and make its policy in the Sri Lankan conflict prevail. This brings us to the first relationship--between the governments of India and Sri Lanka.

Understandably, insofar as the crushing of the Tamil militants, particularly the Tamil Tigers, was concerned, nothing could have been more ideal from the standpoint of the Sri Lankan government. But for nothing did the Indian government agree to co-operate on this matter with the Sri Lankan government. The latter agreed to:

1. Accept an Indian role in the internal affairs of Sri Lanka. This included, among others, co-operating in implementing the merger of the Eastern and Northern Provinces (Agreement, Art. 2.14), rehabilitating militant youth (Agreement, Art. 2.11), ensuring the physical safety of Sri Lankan Tamils (Agreement, Art. 2.16 E), supervising elections (Agreement, Art. 2.17), and monitoring the cessation of hostilities (Annexure, Art. 5).
2. Reach an early understanding about the relevance and employment of the foreign military and intelligence personnel in Sri Lanka (Letters).
3. Not to make Trincomalee or any other ports in Sri Lanka available for military use by any country in a manner prejudicial to India's interests (Letters).
4. Work with India in restoring and operating the Trincomalee Oil Tank (Letters).
5. Review Sri Lanka's agreements with foreign broadcasting organizations to ensure that any facilities set up by them in Sri Lanka are used solely as public broadcasting facilities and not for any military or intelligence purposes (Letters).

It is not difficult to see here that the Sri Lankan government had to agree to the Indian government's expression of interest in the region in some concrete terms in order to get its co-operation in limiting the powers of the Tamil militants. And once the Sri Lankan government agreed to the terms laid down by the Indian government, the latter had little problem in disowning the Tamil liberation struggle. The July 1987 Indo-Lanka Agreement, while symbolizing the transformation of the Tamil liberation struggle into an Indo-Lanka affair, marked the consolidation of India's regional hegemony in South Asia. In this context, the imagination of the 'knowing subject', with respect to both general and particular categories, proved central to the task of organizing hegemony among the Tamil and Indian population and transforming the Tamil liberation struggle into an Indo-Lanka affair.

In the context of the consolidation of the hegemonic construction of a great and strong India in the image of the modern 'Western' state, India's role in the Sri Lanka Tamils' War of Liberation remains critical in several respects. First, within a week of signing the July 1987 Agreement, Indian troops, under the designation of the Indian Peace-Keeping Force, landed in northern Sri Lanka and six weeks later began to round up and attack the Tamil Tigers. This set an example for India's military role in the internal affairs of a neighbouring country with the consent of its government. The ruling class of a neighbouring country can thus, in return for some favourable gestures, 'invite' the Indian Army to resolve its conflicts at home. And India, in the guise of peace-keeping, could attract some concessions and deepen its power over that country. Second, there was hardly any activities on the part of the Indian ruling class to seek international consent with respect to India's role in the Sri Lankan conflict.

This was in marked contrast to India's role in Bangladesh's War of Liberation in 1971. Indeed, the superpowers' acceptance of India's pre-eminent position in South Asia has provided the Indian government a free hand to pressurize (in this case) Sri Lanka into accepting conditions favourable to India's interests in the region. The July 1987 Indo-Lankan Agreement is a clear case in this context. And finally, with the landing of the Indian troops in northern Sri Lanka, the Indian ruling class had accomplished a vital task not only had it warned the hegemonic forces of Sri Lanka but also the Sri Lankan Tamils not to challenge India's regional status. Both of them, in fact, were told that India could go either way if it was threatened or challenged in anyway. In this sense, the Indian ruling class had qualitatively transformed the nature of inter-state relationship in the region, with itself having the power to determine what the relationship ought to be. The complete withdrawal of the Indian troops in March 1990, after a stay of more than two and half years, did not change the situation in any fundamental way. The Indian government otherwise, while organizing hegemony among both the Indian and the Sri Lankan Tamil population, succeeded in transforming the Tamil liberation struggle into an Indo-Sri Lanka affair and in the process consolidated India's pre-eminent position in South Asia.

Rajiv Gandhi, the former Prime Minister of India was assassinated at the hands of LTTE. India paid heavy price for its efforts to solve the Tamil problem in Sri Lanka. However, both India and Sri Lanka have to share many things and have to march unitedly in many respects for maintaining peace in the region.

CHAPTER 6

India and Bangladesh

> Mistakes are costly and somebody must pay. The time to correct a mistake is before it is made. The causes of mistakes are, first. "I didn't know"; second, "I didn't think"; third, "I didn't care."
>
> —*Henry H. Buckley*

There is no exaggeration in saying that Bangladesh emerged on the World map with active support of India. India sacrificed thousands of its defence personnel and civilians in the liberation war of Bangladesh. For some years, Indo-Bangladesh relations remained amicable and cordial. But after Mujib era, Muslim fundamentalist groups made headway in Bangla polity and governance. Now Balgladesh has forgotten India's contribution to its liberation. Bangladesh-ISI nexus is strengthening day by day. Bangladesh has harboured militants and terrorists from our North-eastern states. Terrorist training camps of so-called Islamic Jehadis are being run in Bangladesh. Illegal infiltration of Bangladeshi migrants have posed serious challenge before India. The demographic profile of Assam and other north-eastern states, West Bengal etc. have changed. Criminal and terrorist activities have increased.

The present chapter highlights some salient features of Indo-Bangladesh relations. This chapter also addressed to India's role in Bangladesh's War of Liberation in 1971—from the time of Pakistan's military crackdown on the unarmed Bangalees in March 1971 to the liberation of Bangladesh in the wake of direct military intervention by India in December 1971.

India's role in Bangladesh's War of Liberation can be understood from the standpoint of two inter-related levels: one, the organization of hegemony with respect to the nationalist struggle in Bangladesh; and two, the constitution of regional hegemony in South Asia. It is important to keep in mind here that insofar as all issues, are relative, conditional, temporary, and representing contradictions in reality, they must be understood and analysed within the range of their particular historical moments. Towards the end of the 1960s, three important developments constituted the historical moment in the backdrop of which India undertook its role in Bangladesh's Liberation war.

First is the consolidation of domination of the ruling class in the light of the fragmentation of the Congress. We have already indicated that in the post-1969 period we find a qualitative development with respect to the reproduction of hegemony. This is referred to the formal split of the Congress, making the latter both the party of the Government (i.e. the 'Ruling Congress') and of the opposition (i.e. the 'Organizational Congress'). Such a situation not only consolidated the hegemonic politics of development but also the hegemonic politics of centralization, making the Hindu majority a decisive factor in the reproduction of hegemony favourable to the ruling class.

While one could see this situation already well developed by the end of the 1960s, the victory of Indira Gandhi in the elections of March 1971 helped further to fuse the Ruling Congress and the Government into a single entity. But apart from the fact that both the Ruling and Organizational Congress shared identical national and international goals and in this sense remained equally committed to the reproduction of hegemony, the major Communist parties also lent critical support to the Ruling Congress in the domestic and international affairs, which only proved conducive to the latter's reproduction. Following the split of the Congress in 1969, Indira Gandhi relied on the support of the Communist members of the Parliament (43 votes of the CPI and CPI [Marxist]) to run her minority government [Hiro, 1976: 80]. This ushered in a situation favourable to the consolidation of Indo-Soviet relationship, one which, at that particular historical conjuncture, was also desired and actively sought by the Government of India.

Second is the deterioration in the relationship between India and its neighbours, leading to wars with China and Pakistan in 1962 and 1965 respectively. While war with China centered on the conflicting territorial demands in the border areas (in Aksai Chin and Arunachal Pradesh regions), India's war with Pakistan in 1965 was directly related to India's policy in Kashmir. We have already indicated the sub-state nationalist aspirations of the Kashmiris in the face of the 'illegal' merger of Kashmir into the Union of India. In the midst of growing alienation of the Kashmiris, Pakistan attacked India, hoping it would bring the (Indian) Kashmiris into the fold. This did not materialise. Rather, the Pakistani attack proved fatal to the Kashmiris (at least for some time) for it allowed the Indian Government to present the Kashmiri struggle as foreign sponsored.

Both these wars, however, concretized what Ashok Kapur has called Nehru's creation of "a [foreign policy] strategy similar to Kautilya's 'circle of state'" [1976: 47], i.e. in order to offset the hostile position of China and Pakistan, India quickly sought the friendship of China's and Pakistan's 'enemy'--the Soviet Union. During the 1965 Indo-Pakistan war, the Soviet Union played the role of an honest broker, which culminated in the 1966 Tashkent Summit. But by the end of 1969, with Sino-Soviet border conflict and consolidation of Sino-Pakistan relationship, the Soviet Union tilted more openly towards India. Moscow terminated its aid relationship with Pakistan and extended an additional $150 million military aid contract to India [Ahmed, 1984: 113].

For India, this also meant a significant shift from its well-proclaimed policy of peaceful co-existence and non-alignment (the latter understood more in the sense of preserving a noticeable distance from both the superpowers) to a close and more promising relationship with the Soviet Union. We have already indicated how the policy of peaceful co-existence came to hold a central place in India's relationship with China, particularly in the face of India's relative weakness vis-a-vis China. The policy, however, suffered a major setback in 1962, following the outbreak of war between the two countries.

The humiliation that India suffered in the war helped the Government to win public support for a more selective approach towards the superpowers. Indeed, in the wake of increasing hostility between China and the Soviet Union and the presence of an historical relationship between Pakistan and the United States (the former had joined the U.S.-led CENTO and SEATO military pacts in mid-1950s), India found the task of befriending the Soviet Union not only prudent but also politically more attractive. Lastly is the development of the military. We have already indicated the correlation between defence and industrial development.

India had little difficulty in accelerating the pace of its military industrial development following the outbreak of the 1962 and 1965 wars.

By the end of the 1960s India not only began to produce sophisticated conventional weaponries (which included since 1964 the production of MiG-21s under the joint Indo-Soviet collaboration) but also stepped up its effort to become a nuclear power [Deshingkar, 1983]. At the same time, India acquired sophisticated weapons from abroad to modernize its military. To overcome the Western powers' refusal to provide sophisticated weapons, India sought the help from the Soviet Union. By the end of 1969 India was already a formidable military power armed with locally produced as well as imported weapons, not to mention possessing an army of 980,000 troops (identically thrice the size of Pakistan's armed forces at the time) [Robinson, 1989: 181-205]. Indeed, with respect to the development of the military, India had come a long way from its declaration of Asokan ideals of non-violence and peaceful co-existence to possessing violent means, ready to project and materialise its power and prestige in the region. Towards the end of the 1960s and prior to the beginning of India's role in Bangladesh's War of Liberation, the above-stated developments constituted the historical moment in the backdrop of which India undertook its role in 1971.

Hegemony and Bangladesh's War of Liberation

With respect to the nationalist struggle in Bangladesh, the Indian ruling class organized hegemony on two critical fronts: one, among the struggling Bangladeshis; and two, among the Indian population. It is not difficult to see here that from a practical standpoint this includes the national-international dimensions (i.e. the 'horizontal-vertical' as well as 'vertical-horizontal' reciprocities) of both India and

Bangladesh. In this light, any exposition of India's role in Bangladesh's War of Liberation must also include the dynamics of the national-international dimension of the state of Bangladesh. It may be noted here that the Indian ruling class organized hegemony on both fronts simultaneously, allowing India to take control of the event and direct it to its advantage.

The Organization of Hegemony among the Struggling Bangladeshis

At the outset, one thing must be made clear--the emergence of Bangladesh is *not* an outcome of a conspiracy by India. The movement towards an independent Bangladesh was a product of the cumulation of the contradictions inherent in the formation of the state of Pakistan. As we are primarily concerned here with India's role in Bangladesh's War of Liberation, we shall refrain from discussing it in detail. Suffice it to point out here that the *genocide* in Bangladesh in 1971 was but the climax of the overtly national oppression of the Bangalees at the hands of the (West) Pakistani ruling class. Indeed, given the post-1947 history of domination of the eastern wing of Pakistan (i.e. Bangladesh) and the struggle of the Bangalees, particularly after 1966 under the leadership of Sheikh Mujibur Rahman and his party-the Awami League, it was not very difficult to predict the break up of the state of Pakistan. Time was the only factor. And it is on this time issue that India came to play a decisive role in the liberation struggle of Bangladesh. The barbaric action of the Pakistani military on the people of Bangladesh on the night of March 25, 1971 produced an atmosphere of death and terror.

The natural instinct of the people was to escape from it. The choice was India not because of any romantic enthusiasm for India's democracy or secularism but simply because of the geographical proximity and the common reflection of the Kautilyan dictum that 'the enemy of my enemy is my friend'. The mass killing which by April rose to more than 300,000 people, in effect saw a flow of refugees of 60,000 a day [Mullick, 1972: 22]. The resultant situation was, of course, a qualitatively different one from that which prevailed before. A projection of the crisis was needed and India lost no time on that. Indeed, to give effect to this cautious approach, India at first described through its media, representatives, and other means, the condition in Bangladesh and its consequence to India, particularly with respect to the flow of refugees. India, however, lost no time in taking certain diplomatic measures, not only to awaken the conscience of the world but also to build a national consensus and, at the same time, attract the Bangladeshis to its fold. At mid-day of March 27 Calcutta Radio, interrupting its normal programs, began to play Bangla patriotic songs and music, with continuous broadcast of the news of the military crackdown in Bangladesh.

One particular song of Rabindranath Tagore--*Amar shonar Bangla* [My golden Bengal], which had already been declared the national anthem of Bangladesh by the students of Dhaka some time in mid-March--was played time and again. Unaware of India's position at the time, the music was undoubtedly welcomed by the Bangladeshis. In fact, the music immediately created an atmosphere of friendliness and projected the support of India to the national liberation movement of Bangladesh. Soon the Bangladeshi political and military officials, not to mention the general population, began to reach India to seek refuge, help and advice. The music played its part. Also important was India's careful choice (particularly by the members of the Indian Government) of key words having political connotations. This case is unique from four varied viewpoints: first, the terminology satisfied the people of Bangladesh, particularly in a situation where the word 'East Pakistan' was abhorred by them; second, despite Swaran Singh's assertion to the contrary [MEA, 1972: 690], it was to impress upon the Bangalees of West Bengal (a State of the Indian Union) that the national liberation struggle in Bangladesh was essentially a struggle of the people of 'East Bengal' and not of 'West Bengal'; third, using only 'Bangladesh' would have meant giving public recognition to Bangladesh's claim to statehood, a fact which would have strengthened Pakistan's argument that India was sponsoring the nationalist struggle in Bangladesh; and lastly, it was a tactical projection--India was waiting for world public opinion to get familiarised with the term 'Bangladesh'.

Indira Gandhi kept referring to the eastern wing of Pakistan as both 'East Bengal' and 'Bangladesh' until September 1971. After September, she dropped 'East Bengal' and used only 'Bangladesh'. By that time, however, India was already considering the military option. One must, indeed, appreciate India's *kutaniti* (diplomacy), in winning the support of the Bangladeshis, without making its effort seem as a gross interference in Pakistan's internal affairs. India further impressed the Bangladeshis with its efficient management of the refugees. The Bangladeshis were provided with food, shelter and security on their arrival to India.

By June 1971 Bangladeshis were crossing the Indian border at the rate of 100,000 a day, putting tremendous pressure on India's economy [Quaderi, 1972: 150-153]. Indeed, given India's poor economic condition, the friendly response of the Indians to the flow of refugees was welcomed by the Bangladeshis. Moreover, from the standpoint of the

Bangladesh Government-in-exile, the refugees provided a practical solution to the task of guerrilla recruitment and training. The daily arrival of the refugees offered a huge supply of freedom fighters who could be trained in safe locations in India and then sent home to fight the Pakistan army. However, within the Indian population, the flow of refugees, particularly their religious composition, contributed to a qualitatively different set of calculations more favourable to India's undertaking of the military option. Nothing, however, acted so strongly in bringing about a favourable attitude by the Bangladeshis towards India than the support provided by the latter to the establishment of the Bangladesh Government-in-exile and its various functionaries (*Swadhin Bangla Betar Kendra* [Free Radio Bangladesh], the *Mukti Bahini* [Liberation Force], etc.).

A Provisional Government, manned entirely by the members of the Awami League, was inaugurated at Baddayanattala (renamed 'Mujib Nagar') near the Bangladesh-India border in April. Under pressure from the Pakistan army, it quickly shifted to India, making Calcutta its headquarters. It may be pointed out here that a large part of the Provisional Government's administrative expenditures was borne by India [Umar, 1974: 88; Siddiqui, 1975: 9]. This allowed the Provisional Government to champion the cause of Bangladesh quite freely and extensively in the major centers of the world. India also helped to establish and run Free Radio Bangladesh. Officed in one of the floors of the Calcutta Radio Station, Free Radio Bangladesh began regular service in Bangla and English in June 1971 [Kabir, 1984].

With the help of India's transmission networks, Free Radio Bangladesh was able to relay its programmes throughout Bangladesh. The service provided by the Free Radio Bangladesh, apart from boosting the morale of the Bangladeshis and providing them with news of the activities of the Bangladesh Government-in-exile, highlighted the new-found friendship between India and Bangladesh. Indeed, so effective was the role played by Free Radio Bangladesh that Bangladeshis not only accepted news from the Indian sources but also rejected the broadcasts of Radio Pakistan as sheer propaganda. Also important was India's support in building the *Mukti Bahini* [Liberation Force]. While recruitment to the *Mukti Bahini* required prior approval of the Awami League and the Bangladesh Government-in-exile, it generally included the Bangalee members of the regular Pakistan Army and the police force which revolted after the March 25 crackdown, as well as students and workers. Even before the establishment of the *Mukti Bahini* the Bangladeshi guerrillas received training and weapons from India, mainly from the Indian Border Security Force. With the formation of the *Mukti Bahini* in April, however, the task of training and arming the new recruits fell primarily to the Indian Army [Sisson and Rose, 1990: 182].

The strategy of the liberation war, however, was undertaken by the senior officials of the *Mukti Bahini,* under the leadership of M.A.G. Osmani, the Commander-in-Chief of the force. This strategy, which later became known as the Teliapara Document, basically involved the use of both guerrilla and regular units of the *Mukti Bahini* in the liberation of Bangladesh [Maniruzzaman, 1980 (1988): 112-113]. Indeed, it is on this basis that the Indian Army began training the Bangladeshis in both guerrilla and conventional warfare in different military centres across the country. The Teliapara Document excluded the use of the Indian Army in any form in the task of liberating

Bangladesh. In this respect, the *Mukti Bahini,* although trained and armed by the Indian Army, remained relatively free in areas of recruitment and planning, a factor which later contributed to the growing disappointment of the Indian Government with the *Mukti Bahini.* In fact, it led India to build a parallel (pro-Indian) force under the name of *Mujib Bahini* [Mujib Force].

There is no question that India, with the kind of help it provided following the March 25 military crackdown, succeeded in making a strong impression on the people of Bangladesh. Many in the Awami League and the Bangladesh Government-in-exile, for example, began openly to espouse the view that India's military support was vital to ensure a quick victory over the Pakistan occupation army [Siddiqui, 1975]. This only emboldened the Indian Government to carry out measures more restricted to fulfilling the hegemonic interests of the ruling class in the region.

Organization of Hegemony among the Indian Population

Apart from humanitarian concern, the immediate bond that the majority of the people of India had with the Bangladeshi refugees was with respect to the latter's religious identity. According to one estimates, 80 to 90 per cent of the refugees, which reached nearly 10 million by November 1971, were from the Hindu community [Maniruzzaman, 1980 (1988): 125]. While this high percentage of the Hindu refugees could be debated, it is certain that the number of Hindu refugees as compared to the Muslims was very large. This is because the Pakistan Army made the Hindus the major target of its wrath on the Bangalees. Following the March 25 military crackdown and after weeks of indiscriminate killings, the Pakistan Army targeted the people of Bangladesh more selectively in the campaign to suppress the nationalist movement.

In this latter phase of the military campaign, which ran almost until the final days of the Pakistan Army's stay in Bangladesh, the Hindus--aside from (mainly Muslim) nationalist politicians, intellectuals and students -- became the major target of arrests, torture and death. The Pakistan Army undertook this policy of selective targeting with the intention of making the civil war into a Hindu-Muslim conflict and thereby attempting to win back the support of the predominantly Muslim population of Bangladesh. Little did the Pakistan Government of the time realize that 1971 was not 1947! Given the post-1969 reproduction of the politics of centralization in India, particularly with respect to the consolidation of the majority of the Indian population under the hegemonic representation of monolithic Hinduism, it was not very difficult to predict that the majority people of India (i.e. the Hindus) would be particularly disturbed with regard to the high percentage of the Hindu refugees in the wake of military action in Bangladesh.

Indeed, some political parties, like the Jan Sangh, did not fail to grant importance to the crisis in Bangladesh on the basis of Hindu atrocities there. The Government, however, attempted to down-play this position, lest it transform the historic upsurge of the 75 million people of Bangladesh (in the manner of the Pakistan Government) into another Hindu-Muslim conflict.

The Indian Government at the time was particularly wary of the fact that a communal interpretation of the civil war in Bangladesh, while lending weight to the Pakistan Government's position, would surely alienate the majority of the people of Bangladesh. But if this showed signs of political prudence on the part of the Indian Government, the uneasiness of the Hindu majority about the situation in Bangladesh still remained. There was widespread feeling that the independence of Bangladesh in view of its predominant Muslim population would usher in a second Islamic state in South Asia [Aziz, 1976; Chowdhury, 1980; Hassan, 1988]. This led to the fear that it would complicate the return of the Hindu refugees to Bangladesh after independence. Therefore, in order to secure the support of the Hindu majority, it became important for the Indian Government to act in a manner that would ensure the safe return of the Hindu refugees once Bangladesh became independent.

The Indian Government attempted to downplay the communal coloration of the civil war in Bangladesh by referring to Awami League's record on secularism [MEA, 1972: 670]. The Indians, however, knew the implications of the practice of secularism all too well. In the case of Bangladesh, where the majority of the people belonged to one particular religion (more than 86 per cent Muslims), the practice of secularism not only remained uncertain but predictably one-sided. Indeed, the Hindu majority of India, although felt some comfort from Awami League's support for secular policy, preferred a more direct role for their country in the liberation of Bangladesh, to mitigate their concern. The commercial and industrial section of the Indian ruling class came out openly and quite early in favour of a free Bangladesh. Apart from reasons of profit-making, which could, however, only be relatively small in scale if not insignificant (more on this shortly), it had strong historical appeal. The latter related to the fact that until 1965 India and the eastern wing of Pakistan had a viable trade relationship. The Pakistan Government put an end to this following the outbreak of the Indo-Pakistan war in 1965.

There was a strong feeling in India that with the independence of Bangladesh the old trade relationship would resume and that the latter would provide a 'natural market' for Indian goods [Guha, 1971: 983; Bhattacharjee, 1971: 1323]. This position is interesting, although it remains somewhat mystified. Given India's industrial structure, directed as it is towards a limited yet deepened home market, as indicated, it is certain that the Bangladesh market does not fall into the priority list of the Indian capitalists in the latter's business of profit-making. Why was the 'market question' then so eagerly championed in the wake of the crisis in Bangladesh? Two factors, both related to the immediate situation, seem to be responsible for this. First is the state of the economy of the eastern region of India, particularly West Bengal. We have already indicated the failure of the Central Government and the Ruling Congress to deliver to West Bengal the benefits of the Green Revolution. In this connection, we also indicated the development of a massive peasant movement [i.e. the Naxalite movement] in West Bengal in 1967-1972. To recover the lost support of the people of West Bengal, a measure which almost became essential in the wake of the crisis in Bangladesh, a persisting campaign was undertaken projecting the future prosperity of West Bengal, or that of the eastern region as a whole, with the emergence of a free and independent Bangladesh. This not only downplayed the failure of the hegemonic forces to arrest the post-independence discontent of the people of West Bengal and of the eastern region but also provided fresh (much of it, false) hope to these people that an independent Bangladesh would change their current pitiful condition. And all this for the purpose of enlisting their support in the hegemonic construction of a great and strong India, an outcome now easily made possible with the civil war in Pakistan and the possibility of an India-backed birth of Bangladesh. Second is the prospect of lucrative profits from war. Not only arms manufacturers and contractors but also producers of non-military goods (transport, textiles, leather, etc.) profit from wars or conditions of war.

Much of their profits come from government spending, a factor which only increases their support of the government's belligerent position against the enemy state. Moreover, war or its possibility, particularly on a limited scale, creates conditions within the economy favourable to the ruling class [Nauriya, 1987: 982]. In this respect, it may be pointed out here that if the prosperity of Bengal and of the eastern region was an over-extended ploy, albeit as a part of the hegemonic campaign to attract the support of the population to the event in Bangladesh, the commercial and industrial section of the Indian ruling class found the prospect of lucrative profits from another Indo-Pakistan war highly attractive. What is, however, more significant is the pressure that is built upon the industrial and agricultural, section of the ruled class to postpone their demands for higher wages, better working conditions, protection from inflation or lay offs, etc., during any national crisis or war. It may be noted here that in the course of India's role in the liberation of Bangladesh not only did the Indian Government succeed in putting down the Naxalite movement decisively but also the Ruling Congress came out victorious, defeating the powerful Communists, in the West Bengal State elections in 1972. It is, however, important to keep in mind here that the counter-hegemonic forces, in view of their practical absence in the organization of hegemony in the international dimension of the state of India contributed very little to India's role in the Bangladesh crisis.

Indeed, following the military crackdown in Bangladesh, both the CPI and the CPI [Marxist] not only supported the

Indian Government's stand on the issue but also were one step ahead of the Government in placing their demand for official recognition of the state of Bangladesh [CPI, 1972: 393; Sisson and Rose, 1990: 180]. There was hardly anything real to distinguish their role from that of the Ruling Congress and the Government. The only possible exception, however, could be the direct links that the CPI and the CPI [Marxist], and even the CPI [Marxist-Leninist], had established with their counterparts in Bangladesh in 1971 [Maniruzzaman, 1980 (1988): 141-149; Sisson and Rose, 1990: 180]. But even in this case, the role of the Indian Communist parties was limited because the Communists in Bangladesh were struggling to free their country under the hegemony of the Awami League and the Bangladesh Government-in-exile. The counter-hegemonic forces all accepted either directly or indirectly the Government's position on the Bangladesh issue, leaving the latter a free hand on the subject.

This brings us to the second level of our discussion of India's role in Bangladesh's war of liberation where we shall see how the successful organization of hegemony among the struggling Bangladeshis and the Indian population allowed the Indian Government to transform freely the nationalist struggle in Bangladesh into an Indo-Pakistan affair in the direction of constructing a great and strong India.

The Constitution of Regional Hegemony in South Asia

We shall divide this section into three sub-sections. In sub-section one, we shall focus on the consolidation of domination of India over the nationalist struggle of Bangladesh prior to the former's undertaking of the military operation in favour of the latter. Sub-section two will focus on the organization of international consent, one which provided India a relatively free hand in bringing the

Bangladesh crisis to an end. And sub-section three will focus on India's military operation and the surrender of the Pakistan Army to the Indian Armed Forces. A closer exposition of each of these sub-sections will allow us to understand how the Indian Government succeeded in making the nationalist struggle of Bangladesh into an Indo-Pakistan affair, ensuring thereby India's predominant position in South Asia.

The Consolidation of Domination

It is no secret that the Indian Government's support of the nationalist struggle of Bangladesh was made conditional on its being led by the Awami League [Maniruzzaman, 1980 (1988): 113]. The official position was that such a leadership would create a favourable public opinion both at home and abroad since the Awami League had just won the general election in Pakistan. Although this was true, it also opened up other more significant possibilities for India. In fact, the Indian Government felt that it could best influence the outcome of the Bangladesh crisis by establishing a special relationship with the Awami League since the latter had already organized hegemony over the nationalist struggle in Bangladesh. As for the Awami League, almost panicked by the military crackdown and the absence of their leader, Sheikh Mujibur Rahman (the latter was arrested on the night of March 25 and flown to West Pakistan), the Indian Government's move was a favourable one destined to keep it in power. In essence, however, the power was very much illusive. It only signalled the beginning of the end of the, Awami League's role and the beginning of India's role in the liberation of Bangladesh. The Indian Government, however, was not wholly content with its new found relationship with the Awami League. It felt somewhat disturbed with respect to the military side of the nationalist struggle, particularly the role of the *Mukti Bahini,* which, as indicated earlier, despite being armed and trained by the Indian Army, remained relatively free in areas of recruitment and planning. This prompted the Indian Government to support and build a parallel (pro-Indian) force, called the *Mujib Bahini.*

From the Awami League's side, the formation of such a force was understandable, although it is widely held that Prime Minister Tajuddin Ahmed and some other prominent Awami Leaguers in the Provisional Government opposed it. The support for its formation, however, came from the 'youth wing' of the Awami League, with Mujib's nephew, Sheikh Fazlul Huq Moni, as one of its key leaders, who feared the increasing popularity of the *Mukti Bahini.* The members of the *Mujib Bahini* not only received training and better weapons under the direct supervision of the Indian Government's foreign intelligence organization, the Research and Analysis Wing [RAW], but also were allowed to operate outside the authority of the Bangladesh Government-in-exile [Hasan, 1986: 7]. Indeed, from India's side, the policy served well not militarily (probably it was never intended to) but politically. The formation of the *Mujib Bahini* brought home suspicions and frictions amongst the Bangladeshis fighting the liberation war, making it easy for the Indian Government to act decisively when the time was ripe.

The military operation of the *Mukti Bahini,* however, came under the sole command of the Indian Armed Forces with the formation of the *Mitra Bahini* (Joint Command] on December 10, 1971--four days after India's official recognition of Bangladesh and seven days after the outbreak of the Indo-Pakistan war [Chakrabarti, 1978: 214]. The *Mitra Bahini* Agreement was signed by the Acting President,

Nazrul Islam and Prime Minister Tajuddin Ahmed on behalf of the Bangladesh Government, while General Sam Manekshaw, the chairman of the Chiefs of Staff Committee of the Indian Armed Forces and D.P. Dhar, the chairman of the Policy Planning Committee, signed it on behalf of the Indian Government: [Maniruzzaman, 1988: 140]. It is interesting to note here that neither the Prime Minister of India, Indira Gandhi, nor the chief of the *Mukti Bahini,* M.A.G. Osmani, signed the document. In fact, the inclusion of D.P. Dhar severely undermined the importance of this Agreement, particularly when the counterpart was being represented by the Acting President and the Prime Minister. Furthermore, in that document, the Indian Armed Forces were described as 'supporting forces' [Maniruzzaman, 1980 (1988): 140], although in practice India had already assumed the sole military authority in the liberation war of Bangladesh. Indeed, the formation of the *Mitra Bahini* provided India the necessary legal coverage for the final military onslaught, demonstrating thereby the extent to which India had consolidated its domination over the nationalist struggle of Bangladesh.

Organization of International Consent

In July 1971, K. Subrahmanyam, the Director of India's Institute for Defence Studies and Analysis deliberately leaked to the world press a confidential document, advocating direct military intervention [Shelly, 1979: 64]. In the paper, titled 'Bangladesh and India's National Security--the Options for India,' Subrahmanyam argued that 'by such pre-emptory military moves India could ensure her security by preventing a radically left-oriented leadership from being installed in power in a free Bangladesh' [Shelly, 1979: 64]. Both the timing and the content of this document are interesting. While it is true that Subrahmanyam had consistently been calling for a more active Indian policy against Pakistan ever since the crisis began in March (he, in fact, is recorded to have said on March 31, just six days after the military crackdown, 'What India must realise is the fact that the break up of Pakistan is in our interest, an opportunity the like of which will never come again' [Siddiqui, 1975: 8]), the timing and content of this document are more significant from the standpoint of India's organization of international consent.

We have already indicated earlier the development of a well-anchored relationship between Pakistan and the United States and also between Pakistan and China. In July 1971 these relationships took special meaning in view of the United States' attempt to open up a relationship with China [Ahmed, 1984; 1985]. It was from Pakistan that Henry Kissinger secretly visited Peking in the second week of July 1971 [Jackson, 1975: 65]. In the backdrop of this event, the Indian ruling class undertook two seemingly contradictory policies, set to fulfill, however, a common goal of organizing international consent. The first policy specifically relates to the content found in Subrahmanyam's document--the fear of the left power in Bangladesh. It is not surprising that a section of the organic intellectuals, linked to the hegemonic project, would attempt to win the support of the United States or at least its neutrality in the Bangladesh crisis by putting forth such fears. Indeed, the left-phobia was so well orchestrated in India that even the U.S. Defence Intelligence Agency, among others, did not fail to report it [Sisson and Rose [1990: 303].

The left-phobia, however, was a classic red herring. Apart from the fact that the Awami League had already established its hegemony over the nationalist struggle, none of the leftist political parties at the time, whether pro-Peking or pro-Moscow, despite their direct participation in the armed resistance against the Pakistan Army, had the strength or the organizational capability to capture and hold power in Bangladesh. If anything, the left-phobia suited India to convince the United States to back its role in Bangladesh, while at the same time, it suited the United States to convince the domestic public opinion that a neutral position or accepting India's role in Bangladesh was a far better option than facing a Communist Bangladesh. In this respect, Subrahmanyam's July document was timely and useful to India in the task of acquiring an international consent to its military role in Bangladesh. But the Indian Government could hardly remain content with the outcome of the hegemonic dissemination of left-phobia, particularly with regard to its impact on the United States at a time when the latter was busy opening up to China. Moreover, the Indian Government had to deal more directly with China, whose impending rapprochement with the United States posed the possibility of threatening India's hegemonic aspirations in the region.

This led the Indian Government to concentrate on the second policy, that of establishing a special relationship with the Soviet Union. In July 1971 the Indian Government quickly accepted a two-year-old Soviet offer for a security-based friendship treaty [Sisson and Rose, 1990: 198], This was officially concluded on August 9, 1971 when the Soviet Foreign Minister A.A. Gromyko came to New Delhi to sign the treaty. Article IX of the treaty provided India with the necessary assurance that its impending goal had the backing of a superpower [Mullick, 1972: 24-28]. The Soviet Union also made arrangements for the immediate supply of advanced military weapons. These weapons, valued over $500 million, were to reach India by December 1971 [Maniruzzaman, 1980 (1988): 127].

In the process of organizing international consent, India came to be recognized as a *de facto* regional power of South Asia, not by both the superpowers at this stage, but by the Soviet Union. The special relationship that India established with the Soviet Union provided the former a relatively free hand in initiating a direct military role in the Bangladesh nationalist struggle. It took the United States, however, another six years, i.e., until the Carter Administration in 1977, to recognize officially India as the leader of South Asia [Nayar, 1979: 171]. But even in 1971 the United States, despite its tilt towards Pakistan, did practically nothing to stop the hegemonic aspirations of India in the region. Indeed, in the course of its organization of international consent, the Indian Government became confident that the U.S. support of Pakistan would fall far short of any direct military involvement on its part. With the signing of the Indo-Soviet treaty, such a possibility, even if it was contemplated by certain sections within India, further diminished.

It is not difficult to see here that by mid-1971 the Indian ruling class organized multifold, seemingly contradictory, policies to ensure international consent with respect to India's military role in the Bangladesh crisis. But the monsoon season had to pass before an all-out field operation could be launched in Bangladesh, not to mention the completion of the military supply from the Soviet Union. Indeed, from a military standpoint and from India's position, the Bangladesh theatre was ready for war by the end of November. But for the Indian Government there were also other pressing reasons to undertake the military operation in the month of November.

The Military OperaTION and the Surrender of the Pakistan Army

The *Mukti Bahini* adopted on their own the strategy of

the liberation war. This strategy, also referred to as the Telia-para Document, recommended a three-phase military struggle to defeat the Pakistan Army in Bangladesh: first, guerrilla operation by the guerrilla forces of the *Mukti Bahini;* second, guerrilla operation by the guerrilla and regular forces of the *Mukti Bahini;* and third, a full-scale conventional attack by the regular forces of the *Mukti Bahini* [Maniruzzaman, 1980 (1988): 113]. By November 1971, the *Mukti Bahinis* were already in phase two of their strategy, i.e. both the guerrilla and regular forces of the *Mukti Bahini* were making significant progress in insurgent operations against the Pakistan Army [Hasan, 1986: 130]. But before the *Mukti Bahini* could embark upon the third phase of the Teliapara strategy, the Indian Armed Forces entered Bangladesh.

In fact, on November 21 a notable skirmish between the Indian and the Pakistani troops occurred around a in the Jessore district of Bangladesh [Ayoob and Subrahmanyam, 1972: 208]. On November 30, Indira Gandhi announced in the Indian Parliament that India would not withdraw its troops from the border areas unless Pakistan troops vacated Bangladesh' [Mullick, 1972: 63]. A panicky Pakistan then attempted to play its last card daring to declare war on India on December 3, 1971. The aim, of course, was to internationalize the issue and force a cease-fire on India. But given India's successful organization of international consent, particularly the support of the Soviet Union at the United Nations (the latter vetoed three ceasefire-related resolutions), not to mention the swiftness with which the Indian Armed Forces, albeit with the aid of the *Mukti Bahini,* moved inside Bangladesh, the war strategy of Pakistan failed completely.

Significant here is the fact that with India's direct

military intervention, the Indian Armed Forces robbed the third phase of the Teliapara strategy (i.e., full-scale conventional attack) from the *Mukti Bahini*. Moreover, with India's intervention, the regular forces of the *Mukti Bahini* became, ironically, the supporting forces in their own land. Indeed, in the light of this development, the *Mitra Bahini* Agreement of December 10, 1971, which provided the Indian Armed Forces, as we have indicated earlier, the role and status of supporting forces simply became devoid of any practical significance, if not farcical.

From the standpoint of the *Mukti Bahini,* however, there was hardly any reason to become pessimistic about the outcome of the third phase of the Teliapara strategy under its own command. In this context, two important factors could be highlighted. The first is the huge cost of Pakistan's military machinery in Bangladesh. According to the figures released by the Institute of Strategic Studies (London), Islamabad was spending at least one crore [ten million] of rupees a day on its war in Bangladesh [Srivastava, 1972: 143]. Indeed, this colossal expenditure was beyond Pakistan's economic capability, particularly in the face of the complete stoppage of export (jute, tea, and other capital-earning commodities) from Bangladesh. In a situation like this, the collapse of Pakistan's military machinery in Bangladesh only became a question of time. Second is the increasing strength of the *Mukti Bahini.*

By October 1971, the *Mukti Bahinis* were 100,000 strong and another 100,000 were being trained [Ayoob and Subrahmanyam, 1972: 207; Maniruzzaman, 1980 (1988): 114]. A sheer trained and militarized human weight, coupled with the complete support of the population and the difficulties faced by the Pakistan Army in terms of geography, resources and morale, ensured the eventual victory of the *Mukti Bahini*. And this was without any direct military intervention of the Indian Armed Forces. It may be pointed Out here that even if the Indian Army had restricted its attacks to the Pakistani posts in the border areas, as with the case of the Boyra incident of November 21, the Pakistan Army would have collapsed very soon. In fact, by late November with the Indian Army posted in the border areas, the *Mukti Bahini* practically cornered the Pakistan Army by simultaneously launching attacks on the border posts and in the cities [Khan, 1973: 128; Ayoob and Subrahmanyam, 1972: 208-209].

The Indian Army, however, did not wait for the *Mukti Bahini* to defeat the Pakistan Army alone. It swiftly moved towards Dhaka, albeit aided by the opportunity provided by Pakistan's declaration of war against India, and quickly brought about the surrender of the Pakistan Army. Does this then show that the Indian Government was merely *using* the *Mukti Bahini* to finish the spadework so that its forces could have a smooth ride towards Dhaka? The question is a viable one in a situation where the task outlined by the Teliapara strategy remained unaccomplished at a critical stage. Indeed, with India's direct military intervention in the nationalist struggle of Bangladesh, the *Mukti Bahini* after doing all the spadework since its formation in May 1971 was rendered a secondary force at a crucial period. Both the ultimatum call and the surrender document bear testimony to our contention.

Indeed not only did the surrender document refrain from giving any role to the *Mukti Bahini* (nor did the latter have any representation in counter-signing the document), it also provided the Indian Armed Forces with the sole authority to determine the fate of the Pakistan Army in Bangladesh. In this respect, three critical points may be highlighted. First, the document assured the Pakistan forces in Bangladesh that they were all surrendering to the Indian Armed Forces. It also made clear that the decision of Lieutenant-General Aurora was final with regard to the surrender process. This meant that Bangladesh essentially did not have any *right* to influence the fete of the Pakistani prisoners-of-war, a fact which later proved disadvantageous to Bangladesh in opening up negotiations with Pakistan regarding the transfer of assets, mutual exchange of the Bangladeshi and Pakistani citizens who were stranded during the war, division of foreign aid-related liabilities, etc. Second, with the signing of the surrender document all arms and ammunitions of the Pakistan Eastern Command came under the control of the Indian Armed Forces. The latter, therefore, had legal grounds to transfer all the weapons surrendered by the Pakistan Army in Bangladesh to India. It may be pointed out here that this issue was very much resented by the *Mukti Bahini;* in fact, one of its sector commanders, Major M.A. Jalil found himself sacked and jailed for protesting the transfer of Pakistani weapons to India. And third, the surrender document failed to mention *genocide* or mass killings committed by the Pakistan military and para-military forces.

It is estimated that the number of victims of the Pakistani atrocities ranged from the official Indian, as well as the most acceptable, figure of three million to the most conservative figure of 300,000 [Sisson and Rose, 1990: 306]. Contrary to these horrifying death figures and well-documented evidence of war-crimes [Quaderi, 1972; Chaudhuri, 1972; Payne, 1973], the surrender document guaranteed 'safety and well-being' to all Pakistan military and para-military forces. If anything, this effectively cancelled the possibility of bringing the members of the

Pakistan military and para-military forces to trial for committing atrocities against the civilian population of Bangladesh.

For all practical purpose, the surrender document sacrificed certain basic interests of Bangladesh at the expense of making room for India so that it could redefine its relationship with Pakistan. It otherwise symbolized the transformation of the nationalist struggle of Bangladesh into an Indo-Pakistan affair. The Indian Government, however, was careful as not to raise the resentment of the Bangladeshis to the point of inviting hostility. Indeed, after ensuring the necessary security measures, it quickly flew home the all-Awami League Bangladesh Government-in-exile from Calcutta.

In the context of the hegemonic construction of a great and strong India in the image of the modern 'Western' state, India's role in Bangladesh's War of Liberation remains critical in several respects. First, following the military crackdown of the Pakistan Army on unarmed Bangalees, the Indian ruling class successfully organized hegemony over the nationalist struggle of Bangladesh. As such, it remained directed primarily towards fulfilling the latter's hegemonic aspirations in South Asia.

In this respect, while the Indian Government openly contributed to the success of the liberation war in Bangladesh, it used the occasion to consolidate India's position in the region. Second, the Indian ruling class successfully organized hegemony among the Indian population with respect to the nationalist struggle in Bangladesh. This task proved relativcly easy not only because the Indian ruling class already had established hegemony in India's foreign policy but also because the counter-hegemonic forces all accepted either directly or indirectly the Indian Government's position on the Bangladesh issue. In this respect, it is important to keep in mind here that the post-1969 reproduction of the hegemonic politics of development and centralization ensured the consent of the majority of the population to the Government's policy of direct military intervention in the nationalist struggle of Bangladesh. Third, the Indian ruling class successfully organized international consent to back India's role in the Bangladesh crisis. In the process, particularly following the signing of the Indo-Soviet friendship treaty, India came to be recognised as a *de facto* regional power of South Asia by the Soviet Union.

The Indian ruling class also managed to limit the role of the United States and China in the conflict, particularly their support of Pakistan, which further allowed India to consolidate its position in the region. In this context, the imagination of the 'knowing subject', with respect to both general and particular categories, proved central to the task of organizing consent both at the national and international dimensions of the state. And finally, with the direct military intervention and, following that, with the signing of the surrender document, the Indian ruling class dominated the outcome of the liberation war of Bangladesh.

In fact, in the wake of transforming the nationalist struggle of Bangladesh into an Indo-Pakistan affair, India not only redefined its relationship with Pakistan (the latter brought down in size, both in terms of area and population) but also emerged as a regional power in South Asia.

Glossary

Accords: International agreements originally thought to be for lesser subjects than covered by treaties , but now really treaties by a different name.

Ad Referendum: An agreement reached ad referendum means an agreement reached by negotiators at the table, subject to the subsequent concurrence of their governments.

Agrément: Diplomatic courtesy requires that before a state appoints a new chief of diplomatic mission to represent it in another state, it must be first ascertained whether the proposed appointee is acceptable to the receiving state.The acquiescence of the receiving state is signified by its granting its agrément to the appointment.It is unusual for an agrément to be refused, but it occasionally happens.

Aide Mémoire: A written summary of the key points made by a diplomat in an official conversation.Literally, a document left with the other party to the conversation, either at the time of the conversation or subsequently, as an aid to memory.

Alternat: When an agreement is signed between two states, or among several states, each signatory keeps an official copy for itself.Alternat refers to the principle which provides that a state's own name will be listed ahead of the other signatory, or signatories, in its own official copy.It is a practice devised centuries ago to handle sensitivities over precedence.

Ambassador Extraordinary and Plenipotentiary: The chief of a diplomatic mission; the ranking official diplomatic representative of his country to the country to which he is accredited, and the personal representative of his own head of state to the head of state of the host country.The term “extraordinary” has no real meaning.Years ago it was given only to nonresident ambassadors on temporary missions and was used to distinguish them from regular resident ambassadors.The latter resented others having this appellation, as it seemed to imply a lesser position for themselves.Eventually therefore, it was accorded to them as well.“Plenipotentiary” also comes down through the years.Today it simply means possessed of full power to do an ambassador’s normal job.Ambassador is capitalized when referring to a specific person (i.e.Ambassador Smith).

Ambassador-Designate: An official who has been named to be an ambassador, but who has not yet taken his oath of office.

Ambassadress: A term often used to denote the wife of an ambassador, and misused to denote a woman chief of mission.The latter is an ambassador, not an ambassadress.

Asylum: Used in diplomacy to mean the giving of refuge in two senses: first, within the extraterritorial grounds of an embassy (not generally done in American embassies); and second, when one states allows someone to live within its borders, out of reach of the authority of a second state from which the person seeks protection.

Attaché: Civilian attachés are either junior officers in an embassy or, if more senior, officers who have a professional specialization such as "labor attaché", "commercial attaché", "cultural attaché", etc.On the military side, an embassy will generally have either an army attaché, naval attaché, or air attaché - and often all three.In American embassies, the senior of the three is called the defense attaché and is in charge of all military attaché activities.These consist largely of liaison work with local military authorities and of keeping informed on host country order of battle.

Bag, The: See "Pouch".Bag is the British term."Bag Day" is the day the pouch is sealed and sent to the home office.Hence, bag day is the day when all non-telegraphic reporting must be finalized and dispatched.

Belligerency: A state of belligerency is a state of armed conflict.Belligerents are direct participants in the conflict.

Bilateral: Bilateral discussions or negotiations are between a state and one other.A bilateral treaty is between one state and one other."Multilateral" is used when more than two states are involved.

Bout de Papier: A very informal means of conveying written information; more informal than an aide mémoire or a memorandum.

Breaking Relations: The formal act of severing diplomatic relations with another state to underscore disapproval of its actions or policies.It is generally an unwise step, because when relations between states are most strained is when the maintaining of diplomatic relations is most important.It makes little sense to keep diplomats on the scene when things are going relatively well and then take them away when they are most needed.An intermediate step which indicates serious displeasure but stops short of an actual diplomatic break is for a government to recall its ambassador indefinitely.This is preferable to a break in relations as his embassy will continue to function; but again this comes under the heading of cutting one's nose to spite one's face.If a dramatic gesture of this kind is needed, it is far better promptly and publicly to recall an ambassador for consultations, and then just as promptly return him to his post.

Calls and Calling Cards: "Calling" has largely disappeared from private life, but it is a practice which is still useful in a diplomatic community where the early establishment of extensive contacts is a must.Soon after a diplomat's arrival at a new post, therefore, he will embark on a program of call on those with whom he will be dealing - and whom he must lose no time in getting to know.In modern, less formal times, calling cards do not have nearly the same role in diplomatic life they once did.But with the traditional initials, p.p.(pour présenter); p.f.(pour féliciter); p.c.(pour condoléance); p.r.(pour remercier); or p.p.c.(pour prendre congé) inscribed at their bottom left-hand corner, they remain a still useful and accepted way to convey simple messages of presentation, congratulation, condolence, thanks, and farewell.

Casus Belli: An action by one state regarded as so contrary to the interests of another state as to be considered by that second state as a cause for war.

Chancelleries: As in "chancelleries of Europe," i.e.foreign offices.

Chancery: The office where the chief of mission and his

staff work.This office is often called the embassy but this is a misnomer.Technically, the embassy is where the ambassador lives, not where he works, although in earlier times when diplomatic missions were smaller, this was usually the same building.Today, for clarity's sake, many diplomats now distinguish between the two by using the terms "embassy residence" and "embassy office".

Chancery, Head of: An important position in British embassies not found in American diplomatic establishments.An officer, usually head of the political section, charged with coordinating the substantive and administrative performance of the embassy.In an American embassy, the ambassador looks to the deputy chief of mission to do this.

Chief of Mission: The ranking officer in an embassy, permanent mission, legation, consulate general or consulate (i.e.an ambassador always, and a minister, consul general, or consul when no more senior officer is assigned to the post).A "chief of mission" can also be the head of a special and temporary diplomatic mission, but the term is usually reserved for the earlier listed examples.

Clearances: A message or other document conveying a policy or an instruction is "cleared" in a foreign office, or large embassy, when all officials who have responsibility for any of its specific aspects have signified their approval by initialing it.Some officers gain a reputation for insisting on changing, even if only in minor ways, everything that is places before them - and it is occasionally alleged they would do so even if it were in the Ten Commandments being presented to them. Conversely, others are occasionally so casual that their clearance seems to mean only that the document in question does not appear to take away any of their jurisdiction.A clearance procedure in some form is essential for adequate coordination, but when overdone (as it often is), it can be a stifling, time-consuming process, and a bane of diplomatic life.

Communiqué: A brief public summary statement issued following important bilateral or multilateral meetings.These tend to be bland and full of stock phrases such as "full and frank discussions", and the like.Occasionally, getting an agreement on the communiqué turns out to be the most difficult part of the meeting.

Conciliation: An effort to achieve agreement and, hopefully, increased goodwill between two opposed parties.

Concordat: A treaty to which the Pope is a party.

Conference or Congress: International meetings.In the diplomatic sense, a congress has the same meaning as a conference.

Consular Agent: An official doing consular work for a nation in a locality where it does not maintain a regular consulate.This official is usually a national of his host state, and his work is usually part-time.

Consulate: An office established by one state in an important city of another state for the purpose of supporting and protecting its citizens traveling or residing there.In addition, these offices are charges with performing other important administrative duties such as issuing visas (where this is required) to host country nationals wishing to travel to the country the consulate represents.All consulates, whether located in the capital city or in other communities, are administratively under the ambassador and the embassy.In addition to carrying out their consular duties, they often serve as branch offices for the embassy, supporting, for example, the latter's political and economic responsibilities.Consulates are expected to play a particularly significant role in connection with the promotion of their own country's exports and other commercial activities.Officers performing consular duties are known as consuls or, if more junior, vice consuls.The chief of the consulate is known as the consul.

Consulate General: A bigger and more important consulate, presided over by a consul-general.

Consul, Honorary: A host-country national appointed by a foreign state to perform limited consular functions in a locality here the appointing state has no other consular representation.

Convention: An agreement between two or more states, often more, concerning matters of common interest.While supposedly used for lesser matters than embraced in a treaty, it often deals with important subjects indeed - international postal and copyright laws, for example, of the law of the sea.

Counselor of Embassy: A senior diplomatic title ranking just behind an ambassador and a minister.In many embassies there is no minister, and the counselor is the number two man, i.e., the deputy chief of mission.(In a very small embassy, the second may not have this rank).In a large embassy, the second ranking officer may be a minister, or minister-counselor, in which case the heads of the more important sections have counselor rank.Thus, for example, the embassy's political counselor, economic counselor, an administrative counselor are well-known and much-respected positions in diplomatic life.

Country Desk: State departments and foreign offices generally have an office for each country with which the have active dealings.These offices are often called country desks, and if a large country is involves and there is a large embassy to support there, the desk is likely to be staffed by a large number of officers.A smaller country may require a one-officer desk only.

Country Team: An American diplomatic term meaning the ambassador's cabinet.It consists of his deputy chief of mission, heads of all important embassy sections, and the chiefs of all other elements (military, agricultural, aid, information, and cultural, etc.) working under him in the "embassy community".

Credentials: The name for letters given to an ambassador by his chief of state, and addressed to the chief of state of his host country.They are delivered to the latter by ambassadors in a formal credentials ceremony, which generally takes place shortly after his arrival at a new post.Until this ceremony has taken place he is not formally recognized by the host country, and he cannot officially act as an ambassador.The letters are termed "letters of credence" because they request the receiving chief of state to give "full credence" to what the ambassador will say of behalf of his government.

Declaration: This can have two quite distinct meanings in diplomacy.It can first, of course, mean a unilateral statement by one state, ranging from an expression of opinion or policy to a declaration of war.It can also mean a joint statement by two or more states having the same binding effect as a treaty.In this latter connection declarations can be put forward either in their own right or appended to a treaty as an added understanding or interpretation.

Delegation: Again used in two senses in diplomacy."Delegation" can be the term used to refer to the specific powers delegates by his government to a diplomat acting in certain specific circumstances.It also refers to an official party sent to an international conference or on some other special diplomatic mission.

Demarché: An approach, a making of representations.Still very common term used by diplomats to indicate the official raising of a matter with host country officials, often accompanied by a specific request for some type of action or decision in connection with it.

Détente: An easing of tension between states.

Diplomatic Agent: A generic term denoting a person who carries out regular diplomatic relations of the nation he/she represents in the nation to which he/she has been accredited.

Diplomatic Corps: The body of foreign diplomats assembled at a nation's capital.In cities where consuls and consul general are resident, the are collectively known as the consular corps.The dean of both corps is usually that official who had been at his post the longest.There are exceptions to this later rule, however.For example, in some Catholic countries, the papal nuncio is always the dean.The dean represents the corps in collective dealings with host country officials on matters of a ceremonial or administrative character affecting the corps as a whole.

Diplomatic Illness: The practice of feigning illness to

avoid participation in a diplomatic event of one kind or another and at the same time to avoid giving formal offense."Diplomatic deafness" is a somewhat related concept whereby older diplomats allegedly turn this infirmity to advantage by not hearing what they prefer not to hear.

Diplomatic Immunity: Exemption of foreign diplomatic agents or representatives from local jurisdiction.Also see Diplomatic Immunity.

Diplomatic Note: A formal written means of communication among embassies.

Diplomatic Privileges and Immunities: Historically accorded in recognition that the diplomat represents (and is responsible to) a different sovereignty; also in order that the legitimate pursuit of his official duties will not be impeded in any unnecessary way.They include inviolability of person and premises and exemption from taxation and the civil and criminal jurisdiction of local courts.Also see Diplomatic Immunity.

Diplomatist: It has the same meaning as "diplomat".An outdated word rarely used now in spoken diplomacy but occasionally still appearing in the literature of diplomacy.

Dual Accreditation: Having two or more responsibilities, such as an ambassador who is simultaneously accredited to two nations.

Economic Officer: A career diplomat who specialized in economics rather than political, administrative, or other matters.

Embassy: The residence of an ambassador.In recent years, also inaccurately used to denote the building which contains the offices of the ambassador and other key members of his staff.The proper term for the latter, as noted above, is the "chancery".As also noted above, confusion is nowadays avoided through the practice of using the two terms "embassy residence" and "embassy office".

Entente: Denotes a close understanding between certain nations.It suggests mutual and complementary efforts, and a sense of compatible objectives.It can be agreed on orally or in writing, but as a concept is generally less binding than a treaty relationship.

Envoy: Nowadays used to refer to any senior diplomat.Earlier it had a specific hierarchical connotation, being used to designate diplomatic agents of less than the highest rank.

Excellency: An archaic but still much-used title for addressing an ambassador.Theoretically, an American ambassador is not supposed to be addressed this way, but he generally is - along with all his other ambassadorial colleagues."Mr.Ambassador" is more accurate and less silly.That he is; he may or may not be "excellent."

Exchange of Notes: A common way of recording an agreement.The contents of the notes are, of course, agreed upon in advance by the two nations participating in the exchange.

Exequatur: A document issued to a consul by the host country government authorizing him to carry out his consular duties.

Ex Gracia: Something which is done as a gesture of good will and not on the basis of an accepted legal obligation.

Extradition: The term for the process, governed by formally concluded agreements, by which fugitives fleeing justice from one country are returned from the country where they have sought refuge.It does not apply to political offenses.

Extraterritoriality: The exercise by one nation, as a result of formally concluded agreements, of certain sovereign functions within the territory of another state.A curtailment of the jurisdiction of the latter state in certain specified areas and/or in certain specified respects.

Final Act (Acte Final): A formal summary statement, drawn up at the conclusion of a conference.

Foggy Bottom: The name given to a once marsh like area near Washington's Potomac River, and now somewhat irreverently bequeathed to the U.S.Department of State, one of that area's best-known modern occupants.

Foreign Affairs Community: An American government term used to denote the State Department and other government departments and agencies (Defense, Commerce, Agriculture, Treasury, U.S.Information Agency, the Central Intelligence Agency, the Agency for International Development, etc.) which have special interests and responsibilities in the foreign affairs field.

Full Powers: A document which authorizes a diplomat to conduct and consummate special business on behalf of his government, such as the settlement of a dispute or the negotiation and signing of a treaty.Before signing a treaty, a diplomat is obligated to show his full-powers document to the other parties involved.

Good Offices: An effort by a third state, or by an individual or an international body, designed to stimulate the processes of settlement in a dispute between two other states.

Guarantee, Treaty of: A treaty which requires signatories to guarantee that situations agreed upon will be maintained.The honoring of such commitments can precipitate armed conflicts.

High Commission: A diplomatic mission of one Commonwealth country in another.For example, Canada has a High Commission in Canberra, Australia.

High Commissioner: The chief of a high commission.Similar to what an ambassador is to an embassy.

Legation: These are rare now, but they were once very common.A legation is a diplomatic mission similar for most practical purposes to an embassy, but lower in rank, and presided over by a minister rather than an ambassador.For most of the last century, American diplomatic representation abroad was limited to legations, and for much of this century, the U.S.was represented in more countries by legations than it was by embassies.

Letters of Recall: Also presented by a new ambassador, along with his letter of credence, to the chief of state of his host country during his credentials-presentation ceremony.It is the official document which formally recalls his predecessor.

Minister, Minister-Counselor: Apart from its cabinet-officer connotation (i.e."foreign minister"), a minister has traditionally been a chief of diplomatic mission who headed a legation rather than an embassy.As so few legations are left, the title is now borrowed more and more to designate the second-ranking officer of a large embassy.It has, therefore, come increasingly to mean the senior counselor under the ambassador.To avoid confusion with the old connotation, the United States and a number of governments designate these senior deputy chiefs of mission by the hyphenated title "minister-counselor".

Mission: A generic term for embassy.Mission also describes the entirety of official representation in a given foreign country which functions under the supervision of the Ambassador, including civilian and military personnel.

Passport: The official document issued to a person by his/her government certifying citizenship and requesting foreign governments to grant the individual safe passage, lawful aid and protection while under that government's jurisdiction.

Precedence: Priority; the right to superior honor on a ceremonial or formal occasion; for ambassadors in a country, precedence is determined by the order in which they presented their credentials to the host government.

Protocol: Another name for an agreement.Originally a protocol was considered a somewhat less formal document than a treaty, but that is a distinction no longer valid.A protocol may be an agreement in its own right.It also may constitute added sections which clarify or alter an agreement, or it may be used to add new subjects of agreement to the original document.

Rapporteur: The official of a committee or subcommittee whose job is to prepare a summary report of its discussions and conclusions.

Rapprochment: The establishment of improved relations.

Ratification: The act, subsequent to a treaty's having been negotiated, by which a government commits itself to adhere to that treaty.In the United States, it is inaccurate to speak of the Senate's ratifying a treaty.The executive does this, but only after the Senate has given its consent.

Recognition: Commonly used in connection with the recognition by one state of 1) the existence of another state (for example when a new one is formed), or 2) the existence of a government which is in effective control of a state.The term "de facto recognition" means recognition that a state, or a government of a state, in fact exists - but it also means the withholding of full official recognition of this.When the latter is extended, it is termed "de jure recognition".It is a distinction based more on diplomatic convenience than on logic.

Seventh Floor: Shorthand for the most senior leadership of the U.S.State Department.It is where the offices of the Secretary of State and his most senior aides are located.

Short-Timer: A diplomat whose assignment at a foreign post is nearing its close.A phrase borrowed from the military.

Sixth Floor: Where many of the U.S.State Department's regional and other assistant secretaries have their offices.Shorthand for the assistant secretary level of the department's leadership.

Treaty: A formal mutually binding agreement between countries.The term comes from traiter, to negotiate.

Ultimatum: A last statement indicating a final position.On occasion a prelude to the initiation of military action.

Unfriendly Act: A term used when one government wishes to tell another that an action the latter has taken is regarded as so serious that it might lead to a military action against it.An action which risks war.

Vice Consul: A junior ranking consular officer.

Visa: Written authority to enter a country for either temporary or permanent residence, depending on its wording.

Bibliography

Ashok K. Mehta, "Maoist Insurgency in Nepal", *The Hindustan Times* (Delhi) February 6, 1998.

Asoka Mehta, *Changing Alignments in Asia,* New Delhi, 1984.

Atulanada Chakrabarti, "Peking for Race?", *Organiser,* September 11, 1971, pp. 7-8.

B. Vivekanandan, 'Afghanistan Invasion Viewed from India,' *Asia Pacific Community,* Tokyo, Fall 1980, no. 9, pp. 66-69.

Bhabani Sen Gupta, "India's Role in Sri Lanka Pluses and Minuses", *Lanka Guardian,* Vol. 10, No. 14, November 5, 1987.

Brij Mohan Toofan, "India and International Scene," *Janata,* March 14, 1971, pp. 3-4.

C. Rajagopalachari and J.C. Kumarappa (eds.), *The Nation's Voice.* Ahmedabad, 1932.

Charles H. Kennedy, "Politics of Ethnicity in Sindh," *Asian Survey,* No 10, October 1991.

Chintamani Mahapatra, "The US Pressure on Pakistan: Wasim's Mission to Washington", *Strategic Analysis,* October 1991.

Clement R. Attle, *Empire into Commonwealth,* London: OUP, 1961.

Dev Dutt, "The Bharatiya Jan Sangh," in Chatterji, *Political Prospects,* p. 106.

Dinesh Singh, "The Indian Parliament and Foreign Policy," *Parliamentarian,* 51 (July 1970), p. 160.

Edith T. Penrose, *The Large International Firm in Developing Countries: The International Petroleum Industry,* Cambridge, 1968.

G.G. Mirchandani, "Towards a Solution of Farakka", *Indian and Foreign Review,* Vol. IV, No. 16, June 1, 1977, p. 12.

Gabriel Almond, "Political Development: Analytical and Normative Perspectives," in *Political Development: Essays in Heuristic Theory,* Boston: Little, Brown and Co., 1970, p. 273.

Girilal Jain, "Relations With Pakistan: Its Security No Concern of Ours", *Times of India,* 11 Febuary 1982.

Gwynne Dyer, "Peanuts for Pakistan", *Sunday Standard,* 16 March 1980.

H.W. Briggs. "The Law of Nations" (1952).

Harold Wilson, 'Machinery for the Modern Commonwealth', *Venture,* London, September 1964, p. 3.

Hiranmay Karlekar, "Tasks for the Janta," *Hindustan Times,* April 1, 1977.

Hiren Mukherjee in Institute of Constitutional and Parliamentary Studies, *Indian Parties and Policies,* New Delhi: Research Publications, 1972.

Horst Hartmann, *Die Struktur des Indischen Parteiensystems* (Koln, 1963) quoted in James Walch, *Faction and Front : Party Systems in South India,* New Delhi: Young Asia, 1976.

Inder Jit, "Making Parliament More Effective," *Economic Times,* December 23, 1973.

Iqbal Narain, "Democratic Politics and Political Development," *Asian Survey* 10 (December 1970): pp. 89-90.

J.A. Naik, "Moscow's hold over Indira," *Far Eastern Economic Review,* May *23,* 1974.

J.G. Tiwari, "The Story of the Soviet Take Over of Afghanistan", *Organiser,* Vol. 30, No. 39, p. 12.

J.P. Jain, *Soviet Policy Towards Pakistan and Bangladesh,* New Delhi, 1974.

J.S. Bains. "The Diversion of International Rivers", *Indian Journal of International Law,* Vol. I, July 1960, p. 39.

J.S. Bains. "The Farakka Barrage: International Law Aspects", *Modem Review,* Vol. CXII, No. 5, November 1962, p. 367.

J.S. Mehta, in the special Political Committee of the General Assembly, quoted in *Indian Journal of International Law,* Vol. XVI. No. 4, 1976.

Joan Edelman Spero, *The Politics of New International Economic Relations,* London, 1977, also see Robin Jenkins, *Exploration: The World Pover Structure and the Inequality of Nations,* London, *1965.*

K. Natwar Singh, 'India and the Commonwealth", in S.C. Parasher. ed. p. 7.

K. Seshadri, *Indian Politics: Then and Now,* Delhi: Pragatee Prakashan, 1976.

K. Subrahmanyam, "Indian Defence Effort in Perspective," *Seminar,* October 1968, pp. 22-23.

K.B. Lall, "India and the New International Economic Order," in Bimal Prasad, ed., *India's Foreign Policy : Studies in Continuity and Change,* New Delhi 1979.

K.M. de Silva, "Sri Lanka's Security and Strategies for Survival," in K.M. de Silva, (ed.), *Sri Lankan Problems of Governance,* Delhi: Konark Publishers, 1993.

Kazi Montu, "Farakka Dispute". *Economic and Political Weekly,* Vol. XV, No. 27, July 5, 1980.

Kenneth Robinson, 'The Inter-governmental Machinery of Consultation and Cooperation', in W.B. Hamilton, Kenneth Robinson, and C.D.W. Goodwin, (eds.), *A Decade of the Commonwealth, 1955-64,* Durham, N.C., 1966, p. 92.

L.N. Sharma, *The Prime Minister: Office and Powers,* Delhi: Macmillan, 1976.

Leslie H. Gelb and Richard H. Ullman, "Keepling Cool At The Khyber Pass", *Foreign Policy,* No. 38, Spring 1980, p 10.

Lloyd Jensen, "Levels of Political Development and Interstate Conflict in South Asia," in *Ibid.,* pp. 191-208.

Lord Home, 'The Scope and Limits of Detente,' *The Year Book of World Affairs 1980,* London, 1980, p. 34.

Lucian Pye, "The Concept of Political Development," *Annals of the American Academy of Political and Social Sciences,* 558, (March 1965): pp. 1-13.

M. Rashiduzzaman, "Bangladesh Today," *Current History,* May, 1982, p. 208.

M. Venkatarangaiya, "The Manifestoes--A critical Analysis," in Pattabhiram, p. 143.

M.B.B. Nair, "India--Image in Bangladesh", *Janata,* Vol. XXX, No. 3, 16 February 1975, p. 8.

M.L. Sondhi. "Wanted: A National Foreign Policy," *Jana-Deep* (BJS 14th Session souvenir, Calicut, December 1967, pp. 47-49).

M.R. Masani, *Congress Misrule and the Swatantra Alternative* (Bombay: The Swatantra Party. 1966) p. 9. See also Howard L. Erdman, *The Swatantra Party and Indian Conservatism* Cambridge, England: Cambridge University Press, 1967.

Mahendra Ved "Fall of Ershad: What next in Bangladesh," *Strategic Analysis;* February 1991, Vol. VIII, No. 11, p. 1266.

Manash Ghosh, "Ershad's Bangladesh-I", *The Statesman,* 11 April, 1985.

Manash Ghosh, "Ershad in Power III; Challenge of Fundamentalism", *The Statesman,* 5 August, 1989.

Max Beloff, *The Future of British Foreign Policy.* London, 1969, p. 79.

Md. Iqbal, "SAARC, the urge for co-operation in South Asia," *Regional Studies* Autumn 1986, p. 50.

Michael P. Todaro, *Economic Development in Third World,* London, 1977, p. 409.

Michael Tanzer, *The Political Economy of International oil and the Underdeveloped Countries,* Boston, 1962.

N.G. Goray, "Indira Government Must Resign," *Janata,* May 30, 1968.

Norman D. Palmer, 'Indian Attitude Towards Colonialism'. *Orbis.* Philadelphia, vol. 1, 1957-58, p. 233.

Patrick Gordon Walker, 'An Evolving Commonwealth', *Dawn,* Karachi, 27 October 1966.

Patrick Seale, "Western Strategists Muddle In West Asia", *The Tribune,* 19 February 1980.

Peter Niesewand, "The Red Army: Preparing For Spring", *Sunday,* Vol. 7, No. 32, 10 February 1980, p. 24.

Peter Worsley, "How Many Worlds", *Third World Quarterly,* Vol. 1, No. 2. April 1979, p. 102.

Pran Chopra, "India's Afghan Dilemma", *Sunday,* Vol. 7, No. 32. 10 February 1980, p. 18.

Pran Chopra, "South Asia, Conflict and covergence" Bhabani

Sengupta (ed), *Regional Co-operation and Development in South Asia,* V-l, p. 64.

R.B. Jain, *The Indian Parliament: Innovations, Reforms and Development* New Delhi : Minerva, 1976, pp. 40-41, 44-46.

R.G. Menzies, *The Changing Commonwealth,* Cambridge, 1960, p. 19.

R.K. Dixit, "Indo-Pakistan Talks on Farakka Barrage and Related Matter," *Indian Journal of International Law,* Vol. IX, 1969, pp. 215-216.

R.M. Burrell, 'The U.S.S.R. and the Indian Ocean', *Soviet Analyst,* London, vol. HI, no. 3, 31 January 1974, p. 6.

Rajni Kothari, *Politics in India* (Boston: Little, Brown, 1970): p. 175 [Indian edn: Orient Longmans, Bombay, 1972],

Rama S. Melkhate (ed) *Regional Organisation, A Third World Perspective,* p. 170; and *Third Concept* V-I, No. 10 December 1987, p.13.

Richard A. Falk, in "Who Pays for Foreign Policy: A Debate on Consensus," *Foreign Policy* 18 (Spring 1975): p. 93.

Robert Jackson, 'Great Powers and the Indian Sub-continent,' *International Affairs,* London, January 1973, p. 41.

Robert L. Heilbrones, "Counterrevolutionary America", in William C. Oslon, et al., *The Theory and Practice of International Relations,* New Delhi, 1977, p. 442.

Roy Lai Shely, "Carter Disappoints the Third World", *The Tribune,* 29 September 1978.

S.D. Muni-Strategic aspects of SAARC; *Strategic Analysis;* Vol. IX, No. 1, April 1984, p. 22.

S.M. Ali, "Arm Race: Dilemma For Asean", *The Tribune,* 14 February 1980.

S.N. Antia, "Afghan Crisis and India's Stakes," *Mainstream,* Vol. 18, No. 24, 9 February 1980, p. 6.

S.S. Bindra, *Indo-Pak Relations: Tashkent to Simla Agreement* (New Delhi, 1981), pp. 98-100.

Seilg Harrison, "Troubled India and Her Neighbours," *Foreign Affairs* 43 (1964-65): pp. 317-18. For Shastri's traditionalism, see Pran Chopra "The Changing Climate of Indian Politics," *Statesman,* August 15, 1964.

Shahram Chubin, *Soviet Policy Towards Iran and the Gulf,* London, 1980, Adelphi Papers No. 157.

Shridath S. Ramphal, *A Testing Time: Introduction to the 1985 Report of the Commonwealth Secretary-General,* London, 1985, pp. 6-9.

Sir Val Duncan, *Report of the Review Committee on Overseas Representation 1968-69;* Cmnd. 4107, 1969, p. 23.

Sunanada Sen, "Indo-Bangladesh Trade Problems and Prospects", *Economic and Political Weekly,* Vol. VII, No. 14, 1 April 1972, p. 765.

Sunil Munshi. "Rivers in Delhi-Dhacca Ties", *Patriot,* October 21, 1982.

Svyatoslav Kozlov, 'The Truth about the Soviet Presence on World Oceans', *Soviet News,* London, 17 April 1973, p. 175.

T.N. Kaul, *Reminiscences: Discreet and Indiscreet,* New Delhi. 1982, pp. 255-6.

T.V. Satyamurthy "Indo--Bangladesh Relations, A Structural Perspective," in K.P. Misra, *Janata's Foreign Policy,* (New Delhi, 1979), p. 227.

Tony Smith, "Changing Configurations of Power in North-South Relations Since 1945", *International Organization,* Vol. 31, No. 1, Winter 1977, p. 409.

V. Gauri Shankar, "The Performance of Transnational Corporations in India", *India Quarterly,* Vol. 33, No. 2, April-June 1977, pp. 181-193.

V.K. Tyagi, "The Farakka Barrage Dispute : A Study in Indo-Bangladesh Relation", *U.S.I. Journal,* Vol. CXXII, No. 469, July-September 1982, pp. 207-208.

Vidya Prakash Dutt, "The Afghan War". *Sunday,* 10 February 1980, p. 15.

W.H. Morris-Jones, "From Monoply to Competition in India's Politics," *Asian Review,* November 1967, pp. 2-3 See also his *Government and Politics of India,* Oxford University Press, 1971.

Index

E

F

G

H

I

J

K

L

T

U

V

W